Race and Homicide
in Nineteenth-Century California

Wilbur S. Shepperson Series
in History and Humanities

CLARE V. MCKANNA, JR.

Race and Homicide in Nineteenth-Century California

University of Nevada Press   Reno & Las Vegas

Wilbur S. Shepperson Series in History and Humanities

Series Editor: Jerome E. Edwards

University of Nevada Press

Reno, Nevada 89557 USA

Copyright © 2002 by University of Nevada Press

All rights reserved

Manufactured in the United States of America

The paper used in this book is made from 50 percent post-consumer waste materials and meets the requirements of American National Standard for Information Sciences—Permanence of Paper for Printed Library Materials, ANSI Z39.48-1984. Binding materials were selected for strength and durability.

University of Nevada Press Paperback Edition, 2007

16   15   14   13   12   11   10   09   08   07   5   4   3   2   1

ISBN-13: 978-0-87417-728-2 (pbk. : alk. paper)

Library of Congress Cataloging-in-Publication Data

McKanna, Clare V. (Clare Vernon), 1935–

Race and homicide in nineteenth-century California / Clare V. McKanna, Jr.

p. cm.—(Wilbur S. Shepperson series in history and humanities) Includes bibliographical references and index.

ISBN 0-87417-515-1 (hardcover : alk. paper)

1. Homicide—California—History—19th century. 2. California—Race relations—History—19th century. 3. California—Social conditions—19th century.

I. Title. II. Series.

HV6533.C2 M246   2002

364.15'2'0979409034—CD21

2002004787

For José Gabriel

and the others who failed to receive a fair trial

Contents

Illustrations

TABLES

Acknowledgments

I especially want to thank Felice Levine, former program director of the Law and Social Sciences Division, National Science Foundation, and seven anonymous reviewers. Felice and the reviewers offered encouragement and provided useful insights that made my final proposal acceptable. The National Science Foundation provided a generous Law and Social Sciences Division Grant (NSF # SES 87-20939, $65,250), 1988–1990. Without this support this project could not have been completed. I will always be grateful.

I owe a great deal to many others who helped make this project a success. Professor Roger Cunniff, Department of History, San Diego State University, a good friend and an honest critic, provided the catalyst that helped me to reformulate my paradigm from one of place to one that focuses on race, which clearly distinguishes this manuscript from my previous work. His insightful reading at a critical stage of manuscript preparation enabled me to refocus on the issues that defined the treatment of defendants in nineteenth-century California. I especially wish to thank Professor Gordon Bakken, California State University at Fullerton; Dr. Martin Ridge, Senior Researcher, Huntington Library, San Marino; and the anonymous reviewers who provided critical analysis that immeasurably improved this book. And a special thanks to Tom Farrington, photography, Instructional Technology Services, San Diego State University. I also wish to thank Sandy Crooms and Chris Campbell, University of Nevada Press, and Jan McInroy, an excellent copyeditor.

I owe a great debt of gratitude to many county records clerks, staff members, archivists, and librarians who helped me during the research process. These include archivists Joseph Samora and Laren Metzer, California State Archives; Richard Crawford, former archivist and director, San Diego Historical Society Research Archives; Julie Rodewald, county clerk-recorder, San Luis Obispo County; Santa Barbara County clerical staff; Nadine Jackson, former county clerk, Calaveras County; Lorrayne Kennedy, archivist, Calaveras Historical Society; Tuolumne County clerical staff; Ralph W. Epperson, county clerk, San Joaquin County; archivist Charlene Gilbert, Sacramento Historical Society Archives; Nancy E. Loe, director, Special Collections and University Archives, California Polytechnic State University, San Luis Obispo; Janene E. Ford, Library/Archives Assistant, Holt-Atherton Department of Special Collections, University of the Pacific; the California State Library; and the San Diego Public Library.

Finally, a special thanks to Leticia McCart and Gene Stein, Grant Information Services, San Diego State University Foundation. Their guidance, encouragement, budget proposal suggestions, and support were instrumental in securing the NSF grant. I will always be grateful.

Prologue

Race and Homicide

The most odious of all oppressions are those which mask as justice.
—Robert H. Jackson, *Krulewitch v. United States*, 336 U.S. 440, 458 (1949)

In the early afternoon of Wednesday, July 24, 1878, José Luís Osuna, a California Indian, rode out to Carl Everhart's ranch in rural San Diego County, where he had been working as a ranch hand. As Osuna approached the ranch he observed John Judkins repairing a pitchfork with a "shotgun laying beside him."[1] After an argument, Osuna pulled his revolver, shot, and killed Judkins. Later, when asked about the crime, Osuna said Judkins "told me that I must not come there any more or he would kill me, so I let him have it."[2] There were no witnesses to verify whether Judkins had indeed threatened Osuna on some other occasion or whether the victim pointed the shotgun at his adversary.

After the shooting, Osuna fled but was apprehended by a sheriff's posse. During the pursuit the posse severely wounded Osuna, and it appeared that he might not survive. Playing on the prisoner's fear of dying, the sheriff informed him that if he confessed, his property would be given to his mother; otherwise it would be confiscated. Osuna gave a full confession to Justice of the Peace Frank Peterson and the sheriff. This confession, taken under duress, ensured his conviction. On November 7, 1878, an all-white jury found Osuna guilty of first-degree murder, and the judge sentenced him to death. With an audience of forty people watching, Sheriff Charles Coyne carried out the execution in the San Diego Courthouse jail yard at 10:20 A.M. on Friday, December 27, 1878. In his last statement, the condemned man claimed "that he was not guilty of murder; that he killed Judkins in self-defense."[3] In a trial that lasted less than two days, an Indian defendant accused of murder had been tried and convicted, and within a little over a month he was executed for killing a white man.

Less than five years later, on March 24, 1883, another homicide provided the scenario for Helen Hunt Jackson's novel *Ramona*. Samuel Temple, a white rancher living in San Jacinto township in northern San Diego County, killed Juan Diego, a California Indian, for allegedly stealing his horse. According to the victim's wife,

1

Temple rode up to Juan Diego's home, called him out, and shot him on the spot. In Temple's version, an Indian came out of the house and advanced "with a knife in his hand."[4] After the shooting, Cahuilla Indian schoolteacher Mary Ticknor examined the body and stated: "It was a sickening sight. He was shot in the forehead, nose, and wrist with a gun, and in the chest with a shot gun. . . . Juan's wife says he had nothing to protect himself with. The murderer says he came at him with a knife. I think the wife tells the truth."[5] Interviewed years later, Temple admitted that he aimed a shotgun "and let fly with both barrels."[6] He also admitted using a revolver to "put three or four shots . . . into him."[7] After hearing testimony in support of the defendant, Justice of the Peace S. V. Tripp discharged Temple "on the grounds of justifiable homicide."[8] The district attorney never seriously considered prosecuting a white man for killing an Indian.[9]

Two remarkable scenarios: an Indian killed a white man who allegedly threatened him, while a white man killed an Indian accused of horse theft. Two killings with very different results, one convicted and executed, the other exonerated and set free. How does one explain this dichotomy? Using a case-study approach, this book will explain the treatment of Indian, Chinese, Hispanic, and white ("white" refers to all Caucasians other than Hispanics) defendants accused of homicide in nineteenth-century California. By examining case files in seven regionally diverse counties (San Diego, Santa Barbara, San Luis Obispo, Sacramento, San Joaquin, Calaveras, and Tuolumne) the reader will be able to gain a good assessment of how the criminal justice systems functioned. I believe that these data are representative of the other counties of the state as well and will provide an important glimpse of the interaction of race, homicide, and justice in nineteenth-century California. The data will show that there were two standards of justice, one for whites and another for minorities.

Previous research has suggested that high homicide rates are best explained by the rapid convergence in the American West of diverse cultures, industrialization, and differing social systems.[10] This study argues that the interaction of race, social status, and marginality in nineteenth-century California greatly affected what happened to defendants within the criminal justice systems, and in fact acted as a stimulus for lethal violence. Given the racial animosity at that time, the results seem predictable. Moreover, social status and marginality add other dimensions that help to explain the treatment of nonwhite defendants. Broad-based studies of more recent legal systems have determined that a person of lower status is more likely to be convicted than one of higher status[11] and that people who are perceived as marginal or outside mainstream society, regardless of race, run a higher risk of being charged with a crime than do well-established citizens within the community.[12] Marginal individuals would be further disadvantaged because many of them would be unable to acquire good legal counsel.

Of the four groups included in this study, California Indians were the least prepared to deal with legal issues in court. They were poor, marginal, and of low status. They could not afford attorneys, and their social support system had been devastated by the Spanish conquest. Many young men drifted back and forth between their own Indian homeland and the white community, looking for work. When they ran afoul of the law and had no money for legal defense, they found themselves at the mercy of the legal system.

Another of the four groups, the Hispanics, had just suffered through the Mexican War and were likewise at a decided disadvantage. Members of a defeated culture, these Hispanic defendants came from two lower-class groups—either poor recent migrants from Mexico and Latin America or poor native-born Hispanics who worked for the elite upper-class Californios, who were the original Spanish colonists of California or their descendants. They were able to hire good legal counsel only if a Californio benefactor offered to provide assistance, which seldom happened. Consequently, they entered a legal system that they did not understand, and they received inadequate legal representation.

The third group of defendants, the Chinese, faced fewer problems. Since they were sponsored by the Chinese Six Companies, they received good legal counsel from the very beginning of the judicial process. Unlike California Indians and Hispanics, the Chinese were part of a cohesive community that seemed to be growing in strength, and their culture had not been proven to be inferior by white conquest.

As for the final group, the whites, coming from the dominant society, were often able to afford attorneys. The data show that they fared well in the courts and that only lower-class whites, some of whom were marginal, were unable to obtain good legal counsel.

Of course, the white society in the California of this time was newly dominant and struggling to define itself while at the same time trying to consolidate its hold on California and control the behavior of marginal residents. The whites had recently defeated Mexican armies and had been aggressively pushing Indians off tribal lands throughout California. Indians, especially, became targets of fear and hatred; they had to be controlled. One way in which the whites attempted to do so is revealed in the high number of death penalties and life sentences meted out to Indians who killed white people. And now the whites were trying to prevent "contamination" from the Chinese immigrants who were arriving at an alarming rate. The factors of race, marginality, and social status combine to provide a useful model to explain the treatment of defendants.

In nineteenth-century California the cultural norms of people from such countries as Chile, China, Mexico, France, Australia, and Peru, those of dozens of California Indian tribal linguistic groups, and those of a white society that controlled the criminal justice system all interacted. A consideration of the significant differences among these norms will help to illuminate the high levels of violence that existed. For example, California Indian societies experienced dramatic cultural disruption in the late nineteenth century (especially during the gold rush), characterized by loss of land, ecological degradation of the regional flora and fauna (which dramatically reduced the food supply, forcing many to steal cattle and horses to survive), limited employment opportunities, and alcohol abuse. Most of the California Indians in this sample were marginal people, largely young males who left their tribal homeland to find work shearing sheep, herding cattle, and working as day laborers. Drifting back and forth between the white and the Indian communities and drinking excessively, this group formed its own third community.

Hispanics in California represented a wide variety of national identities, including Chilean, Peruvian, Mexican, and Californio. Hispanics who arrived during the gold rush failed to develop strong ties to the local Hispanic communities. They also became a third enclave who worked in the gold mines, served as vaqueros on the larger ranches in Santa Barbara and San Luis Obispo, visited cantinas, and drank heavily. Hispanics brought with them a legal tradition developed in thirteenth-century Spain that differed significantly from the English common law system, and their inexperience with the white legal system led some to make self-incriminating statements to police and prosecutors.

The Chinese arrived with a strong cultural tradition, thousands of years old, characterized by a powerful family-clan identity that demanded loyalty, either for the protection of the clan or for the economic interests of the tong or benevolent association. In return for their loyalty the Chinese received housing, employment opportunities, medical benefits, and, most important, legal protection. They also brought with them a legal tradition that was very different from the white criminal justice system. Chinese who emigrated to California had strong group solidarity, originally provided by the Chinese Six Companies and then perpetuated by the tongs that dominated the Chinatowns. Many of the murders within this group involved tong rivalry and were perceived as blood feuds.

Whites brought with them a legal system that had its roots in English common law, modified by the colonial and national experience. They also came with a deeply ingrained racism that allowed them to view Indians, Chinese, and Hispanics as the "Other." When a problem occurred, well-to-do members of the white society received legal counsel at the beginning of criminal proceedings, and with white juries, they tended to fare better in court. Thus whites as a whole were less likely to be convicted, though indigent, marginal whites were at risk.

It is not my intention here to suggest that culture causes high homicide rates; however, the strong group solidarity among Chinese and whites does contrast with the absence of strong cultural norms for Indians and Hispanics to suggest a logical context within which to examine the treatment of all defendants. Cultural values also help to explain attitudes toward homicide. For example, Chinese usually killed other Chinese to protect family-clan economic territory, while Indians killed a significant number of whites because of cultural breakdown and lack of societal controls. Each of these groups is distinctively different, yet the white-dominated society attempted to impose its own cultural and societal values and criminal justice system across the board. In an ideal system justice is blind to color, but in this study the data prove otherwise.

In his historical study of violence in nineteenth-century Philadelphia, Roger Lane suggests that the record of indictment provides the best measure of homicide.[13] However, Lane's approach creates problems for an assessment of violent death in California. Many cases were simply not prosecuted because the population was transient, lawless elements within the society could lynch victims with virtual impunity,[14] or the rough frontier concept of self-defense prevailed.[15] Fortunately coroners' records are available, and they offer data that are useful in explaining violent deaths. Consequently, I used a combination of coroners' inquests and indictments for murder and manslaughter collected from the county registers of criminal actions as the database for this study, thus ensuring a fuller accounting of the actual homicides committed in the seven California counties surveyed.[16]

Coroners' inquests provide an important beginning point; these records offer basic data about the victim and the crime, including race, gender, time, age, occupation, location, relationship, and cause. Victim-oriented, they are the best source for the collection of county-level homicide data and often include extensive testimony by individuals who witnessed the crime.[17] If the perpetrator is known to the coroner's jury, that fact is recorded, but little else about the killer is noted. When linked with court records, prison papers, and newspaper accounts, however, these data form an important statistical base.

District, superior, and county court case files, minute books, and registers of criminal actions provide additional crime details.[18] The registers of criminal actions (perpetrator-oriented) list the defendant's indictment and note the progress and eventual conclusion of the court action, while court minutes provide jury composition and witness lists. Trial transcripts are seldom available unless the case was appealed; therefore preliminary hearings in justice-of-the-peace courts sometimes constitute the only testimony. If the killer received the death penalty, and the case was appealed or a pardon was requested, a transcript will be filed with the governor's office.

The Prison Papers held in the California State Archives in Sacramento offer another rich source of nineteenth-century crime data. San Quentin and Folsom prison registers provide the name, sex, race, nativity, crime, length of sentence, age, occupation, and final disposition.[19] These inmate-related data fill in the gaps that are apparent in coroners' and court records. The Applications for Pardon, Historical Case Files offer an even more rewarding source.[20] This treasure of documentation includes petitions from the inmate's friends, letters from defense attorneys, relatives, district attorneys, and other officials that either call for the prisoner's pardon or pray that he or she will remain incarcerated.[21] The more serious the crime, the heavier the documentation. Since homicide cases often required that information be sent to the governor for commutation of sentence, some files include trial transcripts. When used with California Supreme Court records, case law, newspaper accounts, city directories, census data, and other sources, these records can serve to fill in the gaps and provide a better understanding of homicide in California.

The statistical data collected for this study have been separated into three files, focusing on homicides, indictments, and punishment. These data files, labeled Calhom, Calindic, and Calpris, are available to any researcher for analysis.[22] Each file contains a 100 percent sample and stands alone. The data assembled for Calhom (1,338 cases) focus mainly on coroners' inquest reports from the seven California counties, but also include information gleaned from criminal case files, county histories, and newspaper accounts. The coroner's inquest is the best source for social data about the victim. The use of coroners' reports assures that a high percentage of homicides committed in the seven counties are represented in the data sample. Only Sacramento County's coroner's records were unavailable. This data set has the most "gaps," or missing data, particularly for the accused, who sometimes were not apprehended. Variable information collected included the names of victim and killer, date, time, place, race, gender, weapons, occupation, age, cause, and whether either party had been drinking.

Lynching and police shootings provide some of the most interesting social data. Homicide studies that rely exclusively on indictment data would not record these cases because the killers were seldom prosecuted. Although lynchings make up only a small percentage ($N = 71$, or 5.3 percent) of the total homicides committed, they provide important insights into the attitudes of California society during the nineteenth century. The data on police shooting citizens and the killing of policemen while performing their duties are also revealing. Although the total numbers are small (39 victims of police shootings and 15 policemen killed), they furnish an important look at crime in urban centers such as San Diego and Sacramento. Finally, the interracial component deserves comment. Most recent homicide studies reveal that victims and perpetrators are usually of the same race—but that was not the case in California.

The data from Calindic (789 cases) were collected from indictments filed within the registers of criminal action for the district and superior courts. These data were somewhat uneven, with significant gaps for the period 1850–1854, but

TABLE 0.1

Homicides by Decade, 1850–1900

County	1850s	1860s	1870s	1880s	1890s	Totals
Calaveras	43	56	17	21	21	158
Sacramento	40	82	41	33	71	267
San Diego	16	14	62	70	64	226
San Luis Obispo	19	16	21	23	19	98
San Joaquin	37	33	26	29	35	160
Santa Barbara	27	6	21	19	14	87
Tuolumne	156	96	33	13	23	321
Totals	338	303	221	208	247	1,317

Sources: Coroners' Inquests, Calaveras, Tuolumne, Sacramento, San Joaquin, San Luis Obispo, Santa Barbara, and San Diego Counties, 1850–1900.

thereafter the record was reasonably complete. The variable data included name, ethnicity, crime, court, plea, date, verdict, sentence, and county. With 789 cases it becomes immediately apparent that many defendants escaped prosecution. That explains the reliance on three different information sources for this research project. Data on plea bargaining and verdict when analyzed with race proved to be most illuminating.

The Calpris file (1,901 cases) was developed from the San Quentin and Folsom prison registers. For this file all inmates incarcerated for either murder or manslaughter were selected, yielding a 100 percent sample of all California counties for the period 1850–1900. Variable data collected include name, gender, ethnicity, crime, sentence, age, county, occupation, and disposition. Statistical data proved to be rather complete except for disposition of the prisoner. That column from the prison registers was frequently left blank, even though it was apparent from other data sources that the inmate had been released. Nevertheless, this "disposition of the prisoner" variable proved to be most useful in determining the death rates by race within the prison system. The information provided by these three database files contributes to an understanding of how the California criminal justice systems treated racial groups during the nineteenth century.

With 1,317 homicides[23] recorded within the seven counties, it is easy to see that violent death was common in nineteenth-century California society (Table 0.1). During the 1850s Tuolumne and Calaveras, the gold camp counties, experienced dramatic population growth (critical convergence), with a period of intense violence created by mining claim conflicts, lynchings, robberies ending in death, excessive use of alcohol (which was plentiful in numerous saloons), and the habit of carrying weapons, particularly handguns.[24] The majority of the homicides committed in the gold camp counties occurred within the first two decades. Tuolumne County records revealed 156 and 96 homicides in the first two decades, respectively.[25] A search of Calaveras County records uncovered 43 and 56 homicides during the first two decades. The general downturn in homicides in the third and fourth decades can be attributed to a decrease in population and the development of a more stable society, which accompanied the decline in finding gold in the gold camp counties.

The large number of homicides in Tuolumne (252 cases) during the first two decades is quite striking. The suddenness of the gold rush, with its attractions for all elements of society, particularly rougher types and younger men, helps to explain these dramatic figures. Tuolumne's population reached 8,000 in 1850, doubled to more than 16,000 by 1852, remained at that level through 1860, and then fell by 50 percent by 1870. Sonora, the county seat, acted as the focal point for many Mexicans who flooded into the Sierra foothill mines.

Great Valley counties provide a major contrast. Homicides in Sacramento County doubled in the 1860s, from 40 to 82 cases. The county population almost tripled, from 9,087 to 24,142, which helps to explain the increase. Sacramento County offers a more urban setting than the other counties in the study, and after the 1860s the decline in homicides parallels similar declines in eastern urban centers. Rural San Joaquin County maintained a stable homicide rate from 1850 through 1900 despite a continued increase in population from 3,647 to 35,452. San Joaquin County, with the exception of lynchings in the first decade, exhibited significantly fewer acts of lethal violence as time passed.

Santa Barbara and San Luis Obispo, coastal counties, provide differing patterns but show parallel tendencies. Both experienced gradual increases in population throughout the period under study, while they exhibited a higher number of homicides in the first decade. The increase can be explained by banditry that ended with a large number of lynchings in these counties. By the second decade these pastoral counties settled down, each displaying a stable homicide rate reflecting the general population increase. Santa Barbara County's population increased gradually from 1,185 in 1850 to a high of 18,934 by 1900. San Luis Obispo County experienced a similar increase, from 356 in 1850 to 16,637 by 1900. Both counties remained basically rural.

San Diego experienced moderate growth during the first decade before beginning a dramatic pattern of population increase. Census data indicate that the number of inhabitants jumped from 798 in 1850 to 4,324 a decade later, then doubled during the 1870s before quadrupling in the 1880s. The city of San Diego had gradual growth to 2,637 in 1880 before jumping to 16,159 in 1890, an increase of 512 percent during the 1880s. The white population of San Diego

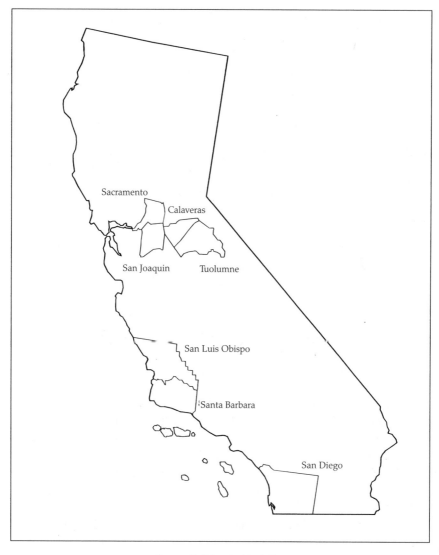

Seven California Counties

County doubled in the 1870s. This effect can be seen in the increase in homicides, from 14 to 62 in that decade. Many of these were white victims killed by young Indian males. In comparison, the increase of homicides in the 1880s was much lower than the population change might suggest, a figure that might be attributed to the influence of urban San Diego, where law enforcement became more professional, or to the decline in lawlessness in the more rural areas.

Males dominated homicidal behavior in nineteenth-century California, both

TABLE 0.2

Victim/Accused Sex by County, 1850–1900

County	Victim		Accused	
	Male %	Female %	Male %	Female %
Calaveras	94.9	5.1	98.9	1.1
Sacramento	87.6	12.4	97.8	2.2
San Diego	90.7	9.3	98.7	1.3
San Joaquin	93.7	6.3	94.4	5.6
San Luis Obispo	95.0	5.0	95.9	4.1
Santa Barbara	93.1	6.9	97.7	2.3
Tuolumne	95.9	4.1	100.0	—

Sources: Coroners' Inquests, Calaveras, Tuolumne, Sacramento, San Joaquin, San Luis Obispo, Santa Barbara, and San Diego Counties, 1850–1900.

as victims and as killers committing 98 percent of the murders (Table 0.2). This is not surprising, since the male-to-female ratio was high in all counties. The 1852 California census reveals that the population in Calaveras and Tuolumne Counties was 92.5 and 91 percent male, respectively. By 1860 these percentages declined to 84 and 78 percent. The other counties display similar patterns. By the end of the nineteenth century, males made up about 60 percent of the population in both Calaveras and Tuolumne Counties. Males dominated in all of the other counties also, but the margin was smaller, especially in San Diego and Santa Barbara Counties, which had around 55 and 59 percent in 1852 and both dropped to 50 by 1900.[26] In California females seldom took the lives of other human beings, but when they did it usually involved domestic disputes.

Thirty percent of the female victims were killed by their husbands, while only one percent of the male victims were killed by their wives. There is a high correlation between the female and male victims knowing the accused. Women victims were more likely to be married (about 30 percent), while only 2.5 percent of the male victims fit that category. Also, females were usually killed by related family members and roommates. Strangers seldom killed females; if they did, the murder had to do primarily with prostitution or robbery. Women were more likely to be victims, and male defendants tried and convicted of killing females often paid a high price for their crime. Thirty percent of these inter-gender convictions ended with death penalties and 26 percent with life sentences. That, however, was not always the case. If a male killed a prostitute, the likelihood of his being convicted dropped dramatically. Social status and race of the victim played an important role in whether county attorneys prosecuted males accused of killing women.

Until recently, virtually no data have been available on weapon use during the commission of homicides in the West. One could only hazard a guess for California cities such as Sacramento, Santa Barbara, San Luis Obispo, Sonora, Angels Camp, Stockton, and San Diego. Data on Eastern cities, however, have been available for some time. In his study of violent death in nineteenth-century Philadelphia, Roger Lane discovered that for the period 1839–1901, 25 percent of the defendants used guns to commit homicides in that city.[27] The same percentage of assailants chose sharp instruments, while 21 percent used their feet, fists, or bodies to kill their victims.[28] Unlike Eastern cities, where murderers seldom used guns, in the cities and counties studied here in California, 60 percent of the perpetrators chose guns.

More significant, most California assailants selected handguns over all other weapons. What was somewhat unexpected, however, was that 54 percent of the Chinese who killed used handguns. This might be a reflection of their tendency to live in urban settings. Certainly cheap handguns would have been more plentiful in Sacramento than in smaller rural communities. Whites employed handguns 51 percent of the time, while Hispanics, African Americans, and Native Americans followed, with 49, 43, and 32 percent, respectively. Previous research revealed that during the period 1880–1920, handgun homicides in Omaha, Nebraska, accounted for 58 percent of the total homicides. Similar patterns have been discovered in Las Animas County, Colorado, and in Gila County, Arizona, where 70 and 61 percent, respectively, chose handguns.[29] Clearly handgun homicides were commonplace in towns throughout the American West.

Historically, handguns have always been perceived as an important part of the West. Viewed by some as an instrument with which to tame the "wild frontier," the handgun became a favorite of the gambler, cowboy, lawman, and miner. Filmmakers and novelists alike have glamorized the handgun as the weapon that "won the West." Unlike shotguns or rifles, commonly used for sporting purposes, the revolver was designed for a singular chore. Bat Masterson said it best: "Always remember that a six-shooter is made to kill the other fellow with and for no other reason on earth."[30]

Men purchased and carried a wide variety of revolvers in California. Some of these early weapons that normally sold for about twenty to thirty dollars brought high prices in the California gold camps, sometimes a hundred dollars or more. The Colt Firearms Company had difficulty filling the numerous orders that poured in after the gold rush began. Although pepperbox revolvers, derringers, and other small pocket pistols proved popular in California during the 1850s, by the 1860s Colt and Smith and Wesson revolvers became the weapons of choice because of their quality and reliability.[31] These weapons maintained a strong following until the early 1880s, when a variety of "suicide specials" were introduced. Patterned on the Webley British Bull Dog double-action, a five-shot revolver developed in 1878, cheap imitations manufactured by Harrington and Richardson, Iver Johnson, Forehand and Wadsworth, and other American companies provided the firepower for numerous homicides throughout California.[32] One could purchase them in hardware stores, general stores, gun shops, and pawnshops, and through mail order outlets. The price averaged between two and three dollars each, while Colts and Smith and Wessons cost twelve dollars or more.[33] At such prices handguns became commonplace. Unfortunately, the presence of handguns ensured that violent physical confrontations would often be lethal.

This study is divided into four case studies, by racial composition of the killer. Chapter 1 examines the California Indian experience, especially in San Diego County, where most of the crimes took place. Here the focus is on the effects of cultural disruption that resulted in limited employment opportunities and alcohol abuse. The Chinese experience is scrutinized in Chapter 2, mainly in Sacramento and Stockton, where sizable Chinatowns provided the backdrop for violent disputes. Strong clan-tong rivalries created high homicide rates, but virtually all were intraracial and within the local Chinese community. Chapter 3 examines the Hispanic experience. With little understanding of the criminal justice system, Hispanics were more likely to make self-incriminating statements to law enforcement officers. Chapter 4, looking at the white experience, reveals that a high level of honor existed, seeming to precipitate many shootings, and shows how white defendants were often able to kill Indians, Chinese, and Hispanics without suffering any penalties. Finally, the epilogue provides a brief discussion of the prison experience, offers an explanation of high homicide rates, and assesses the state of criminal justice in California during the nineteenth century.

Chapter One

Red Man
White Justice

An awful mystery surrounds each of these murders. It is true that in the case
of West, Vanhouse, and Fisk, Indians were supposed to be the murderers,
and three or four who were believed to be the guilty parties
were summarily executed by the people of that section of the county.
—*San Diego Union,* March 27, 1872

This item in a local newspaper partially reveals the dilemma that legal authorities faced in California. How do you provide justice for American Indians when the majority population harbors such hostility? The conventional view sees homicide as a violent act between two people of the same cultural group. Recent historical scholarship has demonstrated that most people—at least in the twentieth century—do indeed kill within their own group.[1] However, exceptions to this general pattern of intraracial homicide in the nineteenth century have been discovered.[2] Interracial killings, a more common occurrence in nineteenth-century California than today, may have increased racial animosity toward American Indians and other minorities. By exploring the treatment of Indian defendants accused of murder in seven California counties, this case study will reveal how the criminal justice systems treated minorities, especially those whose victims were white. The main question to be considered is how the criminal justice systems—especially that of San Diego County, where most of the homicides involving Indians occurred—treated California Indian defendants. Were they accorded the same rights as other groups? Did that treatment differ if the victims were white?

During the nineteenth century California Indian societies were inundated by large numbers of white miners and settlers. This influx of people brought about increased interracial contact and increased the opportunity for violent confrontations between these two groups. The data verify that California Indians had a marked tendency to kill outside their race, more so than any other group. By killing 39 white people (36.9 percent of the total 106) they opened themselves up to a heavier hand of justice by the dominant society (see Table 1.1). A dis-

13

TABLE 1.1

Indian Murderers by Victim's Race, 1850–1900

Race	Number	Percentage
White*	39	36.9
Hispanic	8	7.5
Indian	56	52.8
Asian	3	2.8
Totals	106	100.0

Sources: Coroners' Inquests, Calaveras, Tuolumne, Sacramento, San Joaquin, San Luis Obispo, Santa Barbara, and San Diego Counties, 1850–1900.

*This use of "white" refers to anyone of European origin other than Hispanic.

cussion of a variety of cases involving Indians' killing white victims may provide some insights on interracial homicide.

California Indians were accused of killing 106 victims, and 71 percent of the interracial homicides with California Indian defendants occurred in San Diego County.[3] Indians killed 18 of their 28 white victims (64 percent) during the 1870s. Most of these homicides occurred in isolated areas fairly close to Indian lands, with 7 in San Dieguito Valley, 3 in Jamul Valley, 2 each in Milquaty and Tecate, and 1 each in Julian and Campo. Since the 1870s were an era of economic and social disruption for Indians in San Diego County, it comes as no surprise that many of the whites were killed in this decade.[4]

Frustration and possibly a desire to protest white intrusion and domination may explain why Indian males turned to alcohol and violence in nineteenth-century California. The data suggest that unstable socioeconomic conditions for Indians in San Diego County provided fertile ground for violence, as illustrated by the numerous Indian homicides. These high interracial homicide rates can be explained by the change brought on by rapid and persistent white intrusion into San Diego Indian homeland, which hastened the disruption of the social controls usually exercised by the tribal leadership.[5]

In the historical literature on Native American culture compiled by contemporary authors, the California Indian has been relegated to the lowest echelon of human development and civilization. This perception has become mythologized in the epithet "digger"—a term that has persisted for more than two centuries.[6] The expression "digger" has provided whites "with a handy rubric to suggest all the qualities of extreme primitiveness that European travelers had for decades attributed to California Indians."[7] The Spanish and Mexicans considered themselves cultured, while perceiving the California Indian as an inferior who needed to be awarded the blessings of "civilization."

Religious conversion became the focal point for Franciscan priests, who forwarded glowing reports detailing the baptism of thousands of California Indians. In their summaries to their superiors, some of the Franciscans explained the lifestyle of the California Indians and noted how difficult it was to turn them into Christians. Backsliding was common; they refused to attend church and often ran away from the missions. In 1823 Father Gerónimo Boscana painted a picture that has been hard to change: "The Indians of California may be compared to a species of monkey; for naught do they express interest, except in imitating the actions of others. . . . The Indian in his grave, humble and retired manner conceals a hypocritical and treacherous disposition."[8]

Franciscan priest Fermín Francisco de Lasuén also formed strong negative opinions of California Indians. After serving among them, he claimed: "Here are aborigines whom we are teaching to be men, people of vicious and ferocious habits who know no law but force, no superior but their own free will, and no reason but their own caprice. . . . They are a people without education, without government, religion, or respect for authority, and they shamelessly pursue without restraint whatever their brutal appetites suggest to them."[9] As recently as 1930, Franciscan historian Zephyrin Engelhardt professed: "All accounts agree in representing the natives of California as among the most stupid, brutish, filthy, lazy and improvident of the aborigines of America." He also concluded that "the California savages had no religion whatever."[10] Engelhardt, blinded by his own cultural bias, was wrong.

Whites had a different agenda: they believed that the California Indians were not worth saving. This early image of the "diggers" allowed white settlers to look upon them as passive, worthless, and ready to be pushed aside. White observers, however, were sometimes ambivalent. For example, J. Ross Browne, appointed inspector of Indian affairs, could describe the California Indians as "an ignorant race of Diggers, wholly unacquainted with our enlightened institutions" and later suggest that "a more inoffensive and harmless race of beings does not exist."[11] In 1860, Father Antonio Ubach, who served three decades as the priest for Indians from San Luis Rey southward into Mexico, viewed them as a nonprogressive race and complained that "they take not the slightest pains to improve. In San Diego County the Californians imitate the whites in dress, but in nothing else."[12] Another observer heard complaints from white settlers at San Pasqual and Aguas Caliente who claimed that "they are thieves; they are treacherous; they are vagabonds."[13] In 1866, D. N. Cooley, Indian agent at Tule River Farm, claimed: "A cruel, cowardly vagabond, given to thieving, gambling, drunkenness, and all that is vicious, without one redeeming trait, is a true picture of the California Digger."[14] Not everyone viewed them in these terms, however.

George C. Yount, a trapper turned winemaker, sympathized with the California Indian: "They have been called Diggers. They have been hunted down by the murderous white man. Ardent spirits have been afforded them by the same all exterminating foe [who] have usurped the land, scattered and exterminated their game and fish, corrupted their habits."[15] However, the views of people like George Yount remained the exception.

The California Indian population, which had numbered approximately 300,000 in 1769, by 1848 probably numbered only 150,000. The gold rush decimated them in the Sierras, and the population dipped to 75,000 by 1853 and eventually declined to about 16,000 in 1880.[16] Whites accused California Indians of committing many crimes for which the culprits were of unknown origin. In his journal, William Perkins, a Canadian gold miner who lived in Sonora, California, relates how he and his miner friends treated the Miwoks who inhabited the region from Calaveras south to Mariposa. In February 1850 Perkins complained that a group of Indians entered Sonora at night, killed a Mexican, and ran off with seven mules. An expedition of miners, including Perkins, quickly went in pursuit of the Indians. They soon spied a Miwok *ranchería* and took action. Perkins claimed that "the hill was covered with men, women and children, the latter running like deer, while the men with their bows and arrows stood their ground; but the first volley of rifle bullets was too much for them. The affair did not last more than five minutes. I did not fire my rifle more than three times." After taking the camp, they piled up all of the Indians' food, clothing, and equipment and burned it. Even Perkins had second thoughts: "We had invaded and destroyed the lives and property of these poor, miserable people, to chastise what in their eyes is no crime. . . . I was not entirely satisfied with myself."[17]

One year later, Perkins recorded that along with the Miwoks, deer were fast disappearing from around Sonora, which required white hunters to journey miles up into the mountains to hunt for game. He noted: "The aborigines have received so many severe chastisements, that they are moving farther up into the fastnesses of the Sierra Nevada, and seldom venture down."[18] Most anthropologists believe that there were around 6,000 Miwoks living in the foothills of the Sierras before the white intrusion. The 1850 census taker counted 590 Indians in Tuolumne and 1,982 in Calaveras. The 1860 census lists virtually no Indians, but there must have been some. Although no reliable population data are available for the Miwoks, it is clear that they declined very quickly.[19]

The California government often instituted hard-line measures in dealing with California Indians. For example, on April 22, 1850, the California State Legislature passed the first laws that provided for the binding of California Indians to labor contracts upon approval of the justice of the peace and the flogging of Indians convicted of stealing. The worst laws allowed white men to pay the fines for incarcerated Indians and then use them for forced labor until they had worked off the fine. Some cases are recorded of "vagrant" Indians in San Diego County who were forced to work off fines. If Indians were not employed they could be declared vagrants, arrested, and given to ranchers and contractors for labor. Equally reprehensible, Indian children were kidnapped and sold as servants.[20] Settlers in northern California often took up arms to redress any real or imagined grievances. For example, in 1850 settlers massacred between 100 and 200 California Indians around Clear Lake. A decade later, Major G. J. Raines reported that 188 Native Americans were massacred by settlers near Humboldt Bay; most were women and children.[21] In his 1851 annual message, Governor Peter Burnett stated: "A war of extermination will continue to be waged between the two races until the Indian race becomes extinct."[22] California Indians suffered great damage at the hands of the white-dominated government.

Whites who visited California had a low opinion of Indians and often complained of their drinking habits. In 1852, during a tour of southern California to assess the Indian problem, B. D. Wilson complained that "it is no exaggeration to repeat that the Indians lurking about the Missions, with an occasional exception, are the worst in the country, morally speaking; and the sooner they are removed, the better for all concerned." Wilson criticized the Indian men who left the ranchos and traveled to the cities to indulge themselves in liquor. However, he noted that "in the wilder mountain villages they lead pretty much the same course of life their fathers did eighty years ago."[23] In 1855, traveling through southern California, J. Ross Browne observed Indians "who possessed an extraordinary capacity for drinking ardent spirits . . . who spend their days in idleness and their nights in brawling grog-shops."[24]

Numerous complaints appeared in San Diego newspapers of the time about Indians abusing alcohol. In 1880, for example, a reporter noticed a large number of Indians drinking in front of vacant buildings on K Street. The following year, a reporter counted "no less than thirty Indians" drinking in downtown San Diego. It was reported that Indians under the influence had been in the habit of firing pistols at night, disturbing the neighborhood.[25] Julian residents complained that "Indian [sheep] shearers come in here every few days to get drunk."[26] The implications of the above comments by white observers are that Indians could not "hold" their liquor, an image that persists today despite research to the contrary.[27] If the commentators had studied these revelers, they might have learned something about Indian behavior and protest or "time out" drinking.[28] Furthermore, they might have acknowledged the two or three thousand other San Diego Indians at the *rancherías,* the reservations, and in their homes in the towns throughout the county who were not drinking. But they did not investigate further, and the onerous stereotype of the "drunken Indian" remains.[29]

One of the problems in nineteenth-century California was the absence of

norms for drinking among the Indians. They had only limited previous experience with alcohol, which helps to explain their difficulty in dealing with it. No
doubt some became addicted, but others refused to consume the substance.
George H. Phillips, discussing Los Angeles during the 1850s, notes that "much
of the [Indian] village life was quite normal and routine."[30] Research reveals, however, that many California Indians, mostly young males, who turned to violence
did drink excessively, and being under the influence reduced their inhibitions
and made them more likely to participate in quarrels that could turn lethal.

From the Pacific Coast inland through the desert to the Colorado River, the
Kumeyaay, Luiseño, Cupeño, and Cahuilla had occupied this region for thousands of years. Phillips notes that they "lived as their fathers had before them
for centuries consuming lambs celery, different kinds of rushes, the stalks of sage
and yucca, currants, wild plums, and several varieties of berries."[31] They also
hunted big game, rabbits, squirrels, a wide variety of fowl, fish, and shellfish. It
was a very nutritious diet. A mild climate allowed them to live in houses constructed of bark, brush, and woven mats covering pole frames. During the summer the brush allowed a breeze to flow through the structure much like the
Apache wickiup. During cooler weather, they added more woven mats and bark
around the building to provide warmth.[32]

The Spanish arrival in 1769 changed the lives of most of the Indians living on
the coast and, to a lesser extent, those further inland in the Cuyamaca and Laguna Mountains. Although the Spanish penetrated these mountains, they did
not stay. Spanish influence remained mainly along the coast in the San Luis Rey
and San Diego river valleys, which provided water, arable land, and a significant Indian population that could be exploited. By 1832, the San Luis Rey and
San Diego missions had developed populations that reached 2,788 and 1,455,
respectively.[33] After the Mexican government secularized the missions, the Indian population was generally left to its own devices. Some returned to Indian
rancherías, while others worked for the Californio ranchers or drifted back and
forth between these two cultural poles. After the American conquest of California, however, the status of the San Diego Indians changed rather quickly.

The influx of white settlers during the 1860s and 1870s had a profound impact on the Indians living in the interior, in valleys such as Santa Ysabel, Pauma,
Pala, Ramona, San Pasqual, San Dieguito, Milquaty, and Jamul. The Kumeyaay
and Luiseño were rapidly displaced by a people who had no respect for them
or their rights to the land upon which they and their ancestors had lived for centuries. White ranchers ran their cattle on Indian lands, causing destruction of
crops and native vegetation. During the 1870s a small gold rush occurred in the
hills around Julian in the Laguna and Cuyamaca Mountains, and several thousand miners rushed into the region, quickly depleting the natural food supply

of the Indians.[34] After the gold rush ended, many whites returned to San Diego, but hundreds remained, squatting on Indian land and making life miserable for those who had lived there for generations.

Indians at Pala, Pauma, Mesa Grande, San Pasqual, and other settlements decried the incursions by whites. In 1883, after traveling through southern California to investigate conditions among the "Mission Indians," Helen Hunt Jackson and Abbot Kinney sent a report to the commissioner of Indian affairs that highlighted some of the abuses by white settlers. They found numerous cases of Indians being driven from their land throughout the region. They reported that white men had filed "homestead claims on lands which had been fenced, irrigated, tilled, and lived on by Indians for many generations." In San Pasqual Valley whites had preempted virtually all the land, and Indians were forced into "cañons and nooks in the hills."[35]

Indians who resisted white squatters were sometimes subjected to violence. For example, in the early 1870s, Chatham Helm moved into San Ysidro Cañon a few miles from Warner's Ranch in eastern San Diego County and squatted on Indian land. Jackson reported that in 1877 Helm killed Francisco and "was set free on the usual plea of self-defense."[36] Apparently, about twenty Indians, exasperated by squatters living on their land, had gathered to drive Helm and some of the other white settlers off of their land. They were repulsed by heavily armed settlers, and Helm shot and killed Francisco. Two of Helm's white neighbors, Jim Fane and A. Close, also had made threats against Indians in the same valley. Abbot Kinney found Fane "hard at work, with his belt full of cartridges and pistols. He was a rough fellow, at first disposed to be defiant and blustering."[37] At Mesa Grande they found that several Indians had been forced off of their land by white squatters. Antonio Duro had been evicted from his improved farm, which included a "good wooden house." Numerous threats had been issued by well-organized whites who had squatted on Mesa Grande reservation land. One settler claimed that this group was called "the Protective League of Mesa Grande." However, the Indians knew "that their lives were in danger from it."[38] Some sympathetic whites living in a town nearby agreed that the settlers had organized to threaten Indians off of their land. Jackson and Kinney recommended an investigation into the land dealings at Mesa Grande. There were similar complaints at Saboba, Capitán Grande, Sycuan, Pala, and Pauma reservations.[39]

These land disputes that displaced many San Diego Indians may help to explain the attitude of some of the young Indian men who drifted back and forth between the white and Indian worlds searching for work and economic stability during the 1870s. A majority of the California Indians who appear in this data sample could be labeled marginal people, or individuals who do not identify with any of the major societal groups—a group of people who reflect cultural disintegration. They had left their homeland and worked shearing sheep, herding

cattle, and doing day labor. They were accepted by neither the white community nor the local Indian communities. They drank heavily, got into fights, and
lived at the margins of both cultures. All of the Indian defendants from San Diego
County convicted of murder and sentenced to prison (14 cases) gave their occupation as laborer. Eighty-three percent of all Indian inmates sentenced to San
Quentin Prison for murder (132 cases) also listed their occupation as laborer. An
additional 12 percent were classified as agricultural workers.[40] There is little doubt
that most of these California Indians could be characterized as marginal.

Interracial homicides with Indians killing white victims were common in San
Diego County, especially during the 1870s. For example, in 1874 the brutal mass
murder of the Overend family created fear among white settlers. John Overend
and his family lived on a small farm in an isolated area in San Dieguito Valley,
between San Dieguito and San Bernardo. J. F. Chapin, his nearest neighbor, lived
about two miles distant, and there was no road servicing the Overend farm. One
evening, probably May 14, 1874, two or possibly more assailants allegedly accosted John Overend and beat him to death with a large piece of timber, did
the same to his wife, and then using an ax and clubs they killed four children
aged four months to seven years. The inquest jury included Dr. E. D. French, who
noted that "the blows were evidently all right handed—there was no evidence
of any struggle with the old man and he must have been killed instantly with the
first blow."[41] After holding an inquest, the coroner's jury quickly buried the bloated
and badly decomposed bodies. Several men passed out from the awful task that
confronted them. Exactly who had killed them was not clear, but the inquest testimony suggested that several Indians, who had sheared sheep for the Overend
family about a month previous, were the likely suspects. Since there was no sign
of resistance by John Overend, he must have known his assailants.[42]

The sheriff rounded up several Indians, but eventually released them. The main
suspects were José de Jesús, José del Carme, and Clemente Manteca. In February
1875, by an odd twist of fate, the first two were convicted of killing James Johnson
on a lonely rural road four years previously and sentenced to death.[43] José del
Carme, trying to gain a commutation from a death sentence, claimed that he
knew who had killed the Overends. He stated "that three Indians (himself among
them) committed that awful slaughter. The principal was one 'Manteca,' who beat
out Overend's brains with a big club while he (del Carme) kept watch."[44] Legal
authorities eventually prosecuted Manteca for the Overend murders. The *San
Diego Union* recorded the results: "Yesterday afternoon, a short time before the
hour for the sailing of the steamer *Ancón,* the prisoner, 'Manteca,' was brought
into Court; his plea of 'not guilty' was withdrawn and he plead guilty of *manslaughter!* He was immediately sentenced to *ten years' imprisonment!* handcuffed,
and taken on board the steamer by the Sheriff, who is now on the way to San
Quentin with him."[45] The writer obviously did not consider that justice had been

done in the Overend case. It was indeed an unusual ending to one of the most sensational homicides in San Diego County, and the hysteria surrounding this case may have increased hostility toward Indians.

The typical interracial homicide scenario involved a white male victim being assaulted in an isolated rural area by a young Indian male under the influence of alcohol. For example, on the night of January 9, 1875, Filisario Alipas and Gabriel Cuayos visited a store in the San Luis Rey Valley near Oceanside, purchased a bottle of liquor, and consumed the contents at a friend's house. While discussing the location of a small camp nearby kept by William Rogerson, Cuayos suggested that they visit the "old man" and see if he had any money. Alipas and Cuayos approached Rogerson's camp, talked with him, and finally decided to rob him. They tied him up and took forty-two dollars. Who actually killed Rogerson is not clear, but the testimony indicates that Cuayos suggested to Alipas that the victim knew them and would tell the sheriff. One of them pulled a pistol and shot the bound man twice in the head. Within three weeks the two suspects were apprehended by Constable John Combs and ten members of a posse. Under pressure, both defendants confessed their crime, each blaming the other. A jury convicted them and sentenced them both to death.[46] Each received a sanity hearing, and Cuayos was declared insane and committed to mental institutions.[47] This case provides an example of a common denominator that accompanied many killings committed by Indians in San Diego County. Of the twenty-eight homicides with white victims committed by Indians, nineteen of the perpetrators, or 61 percent, were under the influence. Then—as today—alcohol often played an important role in homicides.[48]

The high number of interracial homicides involving Indians can be explained by several factors. First, the California Indian population was significantly greater in San Diego than in the other six counties.[49] Second, a severe economic recession struck California during the 1870s,[50] causing dislocation of some California Indians employed on the ranches and farms in San Diego County's rural communities near Indian *rancherías*. Third, the formation of reservations created turmoil. In January 1870 President U. S. Grant signed an executive order creating Pala and San Pasqual, the first reservations in this region. Intense criticism from white opponents in San Diego, however, forced the federal government to rescind this order. Mesa Grande, Rincón, Capitán Grande, and Sycuan reservations were not formed until 1875.[51] Fourth, the intense and ongoing internal struggle for control of the Luiseños tribal villages also created discontent. Beginning with Antonio Garra's aborted revolt in 1851 and continuing through the 1870s, a series of California Indian leaders including Tomás, Panto, Manuel Olegario, and Manuelito Cota wrestled for control. Certainly the lack of coherent Indian leadership, coupled with inept policies of the Bureau of Indian Affairs, created instability among the Kumeyaay and Luiseño populations.[52] Fifth, whites began to encroach on Indian lands from Pala south through Pauma Valley, Mesa Grande, Capitán Grande, Laguna, and Manzanita down to the Mexican border.[53] White ranchers gained a foothold in the region and employed Indians to herd their cattle and shear sheep. Squatters, alcohol, tribal disunity, and the slaughtering of cattle for food all created problems for the Luiseño and Kumeyaay in San Diego County.[54] The economic depression that occurred in the 1870s further disrupted San Diego Indian society. Finally, anomie may help to explain what happened. Those suffering from anomie feel estrangement from people around them. They often feel lost, drift within society, lack clearly defined rules, and seem isolated and powerless.[55] The Indian agent at San Pasqual Valley Reservation complained of the demoralized conditions of the Indians in the area. The social disorganization that accompanied the economic depression produced instability and the data suggest that it may have produced a "subculture of violence."[56]

A profile of the San Diego Indian defendants accused of killing white victims is revealing. All were males and, for the most part, young, with an average age of twenty-eight. Robbery appeared to be a factor in at least 62 percent of these cases. All death-penalty cases included robbery as a motive. At least 68 percent of the defendants had been drinking before the commission of their crimes. Since the San Diego Indians as a whole had little previous experience with alcohol, it often had serious consequences when they used it.[57]

In California, homicides committed in isolated rural areas were commonly attributed to American Indians, particularly if there were no witnesses. In some cases that assumption may have been correct, but at least one San Diego newspaper editor became suspicious, suggesting that individuals other than Indians might have committed one or more of the seven reported homicides that had occurred during the early 1870s.[58] With poor police detection methods, sketchy evidence, and cold trails, it was often difficult to locate and identify the real culprits. Several of these San Diego County crimes occurred in isolated areas of the desert, east of the Laguna Mountains, and in one case a posse apprehended and executed three or four Indian "suspects."[59] The use of posses to capture suspected criminals was common throughout the West. Ten other alleged Indian suspects accused of killing whites were never apprehended.[60] The data demonstrate that white authorities in San Diego County vigorously pursued and prosecuted Indians accused of killing white victims.

The highly publicized José Gabriel murder trial best illustrates the attitudes that many whites harbored toward Indian defendants. On December 6, 1892, a *San Diego Union* headline heralded the conclusion of a brief trial that ended with the conviction of José Gabriel.[61] A reading of the newspaper coverage of the trial would lead one to believe that this was an open-and-shut case with little doubt that Gabriel had killed Wilhelmina and John J. Geyser on their small Otay Mesa farm (south of San Diego) on Sunday night, October 16, 1892. Why would a sixty-year-old handyman, who had lived in the San Diego area for twenty-five years and had a record of being a reliable worker, kill two people he had known for more than a year? It is possible that he did not commit the crimes: the evidence was inconclusive.

Within a few hours, eighteen men assembled at the Geyser residence on Otay Mesa, and Constable Thomas Smallcomb took control shortly after midnight. He arrested José Gabriel and began to investigate the scene of the crime.[62] Unfortunately, by the time the constable arrived, many of the farmers had walked around the house, very likely destroying evidence that would have helped to solve the case. Neither the constable nor these farmers understood the concept of a crime scene as it is known today. Smallcomb, although not a professional lawman, did his best to collect the evidence, which included two clubs, three purses, a few coins, a pile of clothes, José Gabriel's shoes, coat, and a demijohn half full of wine. He also noted barefoot prints that came from the barn; however, they did not lead to the kitchen door on the south side of the house.[63] In fact, they led toward the east door. José Gabriel claimed that he had entered the east door. If he had, he would not have seen the bodies.

Everyone at the crime scene believed that José Gabriel had committed the murders. After all, he had been apprehended in the house. No one had sympathy for the alleged killer, who lay bound and bleeding profusely from the severe head wounds suffered during the struggle to arrest him. It was a chilly night, and José asked Smallcomb to cover him with his coat. Some of the farmers expressed hostility toward José and asked the constable not to cover him, stating he should suffer a lot more than a little cold. In court testimony Smallcomb admitted that José "desired to urinate." The constable noted that several farmers made some ridiculous remarks in reply to this request. Defense attorney Melville Rawson asked, "Was his request granted in this respect?" "No sir," Smallcomb replied.[64] The next morning the constable put Gabriel in a wagon and moved him to the county jail in San Diego. Two days later he narrowly escaped an angry mob that gathered at the preliminary hearing in the Otay Justice Court. Some had lynching on their minds, but fast-talking Deputy District Attorney Frank Goodbody calmed the crowd, and quick-thinking Constable Smallcomb retrieved a rope that had been thrown in the street, thus averting mob violence.[65]

What about the evidence against José Gabriel? He had been working for John Geyser only a week or so before, and on Sunday morning John had asked him to come up to his farm either Sunday or Monday and carry away some dirt. Gabriel claimed that he had walked up to the Geyser farm about dark and had seen a light in the house. He entered the east door, found a lamp in the kitchen, picked it up, and walked into the bedroom looking for Geyser.[66] Hearing Fred Piper call out, he turned around. The light went out and he stepped toward the door, where Fred grabbed him.

An inspection of the crime scene offered some clues about the homicide. The barn stood only a few feet from the south rim of Otay Valley. There were also canyons approaching the Geyser farm from the south that ended only a half mile away. The Mexican border was just two miles away, and it was conceivable that on a dark night one or more assailants could have entered the residence, killed the couple, and left without being detected. Many questions about the crime remain unanswered. For example, two clubs were found at the scene, one a greasewood club about three feet in length and the other a long piece of two-by-four. If Gabriel had committed the crime, would he have carried two clubs? That seems unlikely. If he had only one, how and where did he locate the other one in the dark? The closest loose wood was near the barn, sixty feet away. Which victim was killed first? If Gabriel was the lone assailant, why did the bodies end up so close together? Would it have been possible for him to kill both at the same time? If Gabriel killed them, why did he stay around the crime scene so long? Mary and Katie Piper heard Geyser call for help at about 6:00 P.M., just after dark. They immediately rode home to tell their father. It probably took them ten to fifteen minutes to reach the Piper farm, and they took the horse and mule to the barn before going to the house to relate what they had heard. Fred and his son took a few minutes to get coats and hats, then walked across to the Geyser house. During testimony Fred Junior noted that it took him about fifteen minutes to cover that distance; therefore, it must have been at least thirty minutes, possibly more, from the time the girls heard the commotion until Fred Piper arrived at the Geyser house. Would it have taken Gabriel thirty minutes to find the money?[67] Maybe his approach after the murders had scared away the killers?

In his opening statement District Attorney Johnstone Jones suggested that *robbery* was the motive for the crime. About halfway through the trial he changed his idea of the motive to *revenge*. Constable Smallcomb found two purses on the person of José Gabriel and one on the kitchen floor. This evidence certainly suggested that robbery could have been the motive. Yet they contained a total of only $15.28.[68] The constable also found a box containing $170 in the bedroom, but this was not in the possession of the defendant. Gabriel never admitted guilt; he claimed that two other Indians had set him up to be blamed for the crime. At least three men had seen him with Pedro Armento and José Barreras in Otay Valley around 4:00 P.M. on Sunday.[69] José Gabriel claimed he had walked upstream to take a bath and had fallen asleep. He woke up about dusk and clambered up the canyon wall to the Geyser home. It is conceivable that his arrival and hello surprised the assailants, who might have left, heading south to Mexico or west along the road back to Otay Valley.

Gabriel had a fondness for wine. Several witnesses noted that he often drank wine or beer. On the day of the crime, he visited Anton Guatelli's winery, situated about two and a half miles west of the Geyser farm, which had been in business for several years. Around noon José Gabriel had his half-gallon demijohn filled with red wine. He also consumed two glasses of wine at the winery. At the crime scene the constable noted that the demijohn was half full. Since Gabriel was only five feet three inches tall and weighed 140 pounds, if he had indeed consumed half of the bottle, or one quart of red wine, at 12 percent alcohol, along with the two glasses of wine between noon and six in the evening, he would have been under the influence. His blood alcohol level could have been as high as .20, and it is likely that it was at least .12.[70] In that condition, any inhibitions against killing the Geysers might have been suppressed. But then, he had been under the influence many times before and had never been violent. Did he actually kill the Geysers?

The trial and the press coverage offer another chance to evaluate this homicide case. During the preliminary hearing in Otay, Gabriel appeared without legal counsel. The justice of the peace asked him several questions, but he could not respond adequately, since he spoke Spanish and only broken English. Also, the beating he received while being captured had left him suffering a good deal of pain. Apparently he did not comprehend the hearing. His rights were unprotected. At the superior court arraignment he received two court-appointed attorneys, Melville and Frank Rawson.[71] They had one week to prepare their case.

The trial transcript reveals that the prosecution tried to distort the image of José Gabriel by portraying him in negative terms. For example, the only known photograph of the defendant (taken at San Quentin Prison) reveals an image that would make it easy to characterize him as a sinister individual.[72] Gabriel's physical appearance provided an excellent opportunity to increase the power and meaning of the nickname "Indian Joe," which had been adopted by the newspaper reporters and witnesses. Since no summations are available, we do not know how the prosecutor characterized the defendant in his closing statement to the jury. Given the photographic image, however, the judge, the prosecutor, members of the jury, and virtually all court observers (certainly white spectators) would no doubt find it very difficult to identify with or be sympathetic toward José Gabriel. Everything about him (culture, language, physical features, appearance, and personal habits) would be alien to this audience, which presumably perceived him as a dangerous outsider who had invaded their society. Equally significant, his poor command of the English language allowed the prosecutor to further perpetuate this distorted image. Through various witnesses the prosecutor suggested that the defendant was virtually an illiterate. According to prosecution witness Henry Beckley, José Gabriel stated, "I no stealee; I no stealee." Constable Smallcomb noted that Gabriel said, "I no kill them." Frank Sousa indicated that Gabriel said, "I no like him." These are obvious examples of "invented" language. People do not normally speak that way, certainly not in their own language. The prosecutor insinuated that José Gabriel could not put together a well-constructed sentence, at least not in English. On the other hand, the defense called him to the stand, and if the Spanish translator, Reginald Valenzuela, is to be believed, José Gabriel talked intelligently. Rawson asked, "Did you have anything to drink at Anton's that day?" Gabriel: "Yes sir; I drank two glasses there, like they gave there every half hour." When the prosecutor cross-examined him, asking, "Why did you struggle with Fred Piper then when you knew his voice?" Gabriel stated: "They were the ones that grabbed me, or took hold of me; I didn't take hold of them." Testimony reveals that Gabriel could speak proper Spanish, if not good English.[73] The trial transcript verifies that the prosecutor distorted José Gabriel's image. It was a legal tactic that worked.

Considering that José Gabriel had been apprehended on the premises, most court observers believed him to be guilty. However, Gabriel had a legitimate reason to be at the Geyser farm that night. Mr. Geyser had asked him to come up to his farm either Sunday or Monday to haul away dirt. Moreover, while working for Mr. Geyser previously, he had eaten in the house and had slept in the barn.

The trial began on Wednesday, November 30, 1892, and concluded on Sunday, December 4.[74] The final testimony ended at about 3:30 P.M. on Saturday and was followed by arguments, a two-hour recess, more argument at 7:00 P.M., and finally the instruction of the jury near midnight. The jury deliberated for an hour and a half before turning in for the night. In the morning the jury, after several ballots, could not reach a verdict, and so they decided to separate the two issues of the first-degree murder charge and the penalty.[75] After doing so, they brought a verdict of guilty of first-degree murder, but the penalty-phase vote resulted in a deadlock, with six for life imprisonment and six for death.[76] At 10:30 A.M. on Sunday they asked for further instructions. Judge George Puterbaugh asked: "Gentlemen, have you agreed upon a verdict?" Foreman: "No sir. We have not, your honor. Upon the demand of one juror it was agreed to wait for the arrival of the Judge to ask for further instructions as to whether it is optional to the Judge to fix the penalty in case the jury endorses the verdict of guilty in the first degree without stipulation as to the penalty." The judge answered: "In a trial for murder, the jury, if they find the defendant guilty of murder in the first degree, need not declare in their verdict that the punishment shall be death, for if the verdict is silent in respect to the penalty the Court must sentence the defendant to death."[77]

After hearing the instructions of the judge, the jury returned a verdict of guilty on the first-degree murder charge and remained silent on the issue of punishment. When the court clerk polled the jury, one member stated: "Well, I agreed with the rest, but—." He was cut short by the judge, and the verdict stood despite the protests of defense attorney Rawson. At least one member of the jury opposed the death penalty. Had this case been tried thirty years later, changes in case law would have meant that a mistrial would have been declared.[78] Rawson's request for a new trial was denied. On Friday, December 16, 1892, Judge Puterbaugh sentenced José Gabriel to death by hanging, to be carried out on March 3, 1893.[79] The next day the sheriff left on the morning train for San Quentin Prison with José Gabriel in custody. There would be no appeal or commutation of his sentence.[80]

Whether José Gabriel actually killed John and Wilhelmina Geyser remains a mystery. Today modern forensic sciences can solve many cases that would have gone unsolved a century ago. Investigators can tell by the angle and the damage inflicted by the blow what the assailant's approximate height and weight are and whether he is left- or right-handed. Today's crime scene would be roped off and methodically searched by homicide detectives trained in finding and preserving physical evidence.[81] In the nineteenth century an indigent Indian had little chance of obtaining an appeal. Nor could one readily find an accomplished criminal lawyer who would donate his time in filing an appeal for a condemned man. José Gabriel's court-appointed attorney asked to be dismissed from the case more than a month before the execution: he apparently did not care to pursue an attempt at clemency.[82] At his time of crisis José Gabriel stood virtually alone, and he went to his death without complaint.

Whites, of course, were not the only victims of Indians; they also killed twenty other Indians and four Hispanics. San Diego Indians, however, seldom killed females. Only two, or 10 percent, of the victims who were Indians were females. The Manuel Amayo case provides an opportunity to observe the treatment of Indians who killed their spouses. On March 18, 1894, Manuel Amayo assaulted and killed his wife, Luisa Vasilia Escoba, on Pala reservation. After the disappearance of Luisa, a nearby rancher discovered human bones and "shreds of a calico dress and a pair of heavy shoes" near Pala and notified the authorities.[83] Constable Golsch asked Manuel to relate what had happened to his wife. Without understanding the need for legal counsel, Manuel stated that he had come home and begun to quarrel with Luisa. She asked him why he had not brought flour from the store. He replied: "If I had had money I would have been drunk." After he swore and kicked her, Luisa retaliated by hitting Manuel. He picked up a club and struck her on the head, and after she fell, he hit her several more times. He confessed to the constable, "That night, when the moon came up, I took her in my arms and carried her away off in the brush. She was dead. I hid her and came back to the house."[84] Eight days after pleading not guilty, Amayo and his attorney, A. F. Rawson, approached the bench and entered a plea of guilty. Judge W. L. Pierce found him guilty of first-degree murder and sentenced him to life in prison. Manuel Amayo survived less than a month in San Quentin before dying of "consumption."[85]

On December 15, 1879, Juan José Alvarez appeared for a preliminary hearing in the San Diego Township Justice Court. This case is somewhat unusual because during the preliminary hearing Alvarez "cross-examined" those witnesses who had identified him as the person who had attacked and stabbed to death Chican, the victim. The crime, which occurred outside a dance hall in the Stingaree district in downtown San Diego, was one of the few homicides that was committed by Indians in an urban setting. Before the murder both Alvarez and Chican had been drinking whiskey in the dance hall and were probably very drunk. They began to quarrel, and Alvarez grabbed a shawl worn by Guadalupe Domingo. Chican ordered him to give it back. Guadalupe, Chican, and several others chased Alvarez, who turned and stabbed Chican with a knife. During his own testimony and his cross-examination of the witnesses, Alvarez admitted that he had been drinking whiskey and that "we finished the bottle." He also admitted that he stopped at the "Coffee Saloon and purchased half a bottle, of whiskey for 2 bits."[86] Not surprisingly, the testimony suggests that the defendant was not well versed in cross-examination or general court procedures. The defendant was found guilty of first-degree murder and sentenced to life in prison.

Homicides, of course, are not committed within a vacuum. Throughout the nineteenth century, California Indians were forced to "withstand the shock and impact of the Anglo-Saxon invasion."[87] Whites encroaching on and taking over Indian lands caused great ecological damage to the environment. Sherburne F. Cook suggests that the California Indians "were subjected not to invasion but to inundation."[88] While Spanish and Mexican authorities brought Indians into their sociopolitical system, the whites excluded them. It is therefore not surprising that physical violence was the rule rather than the exception in some regions of California.[89] However, while the Maidu, Wintun, Miwok, Yokuts, Yana, and Yahi of northern and central California suffered through blatant wars of extermination, the Luiseño, Kumeyaay, and Cahuilla Indians of San Diego County experienced a different pattern of intrusion. Southern California did not have major gold fields to lure whites; consequently this influx came later and at a much slower rate. Nevertheless, Indians in San Diego County were significantly affected by white population increases.

Using newspapers as his major source, Sherburne Cook discovered 289 homicides with Indian victims in northern California. Cook postulates that "interracial homicide is an outward manifestation and a tangible product of racial conflict and competition. Such a phenomenon could not occur if the two races were separate spatially from each other, nor would it occur if they were living together in a state of unanimity and concord."[90] The increase in racial tension brought a

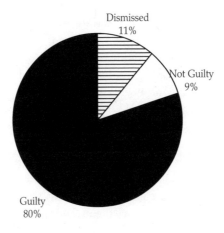

Fig. 1.1. Verdicts: Indian Defendants, Seven California Counties, 1850–1900

concomitant rise in interracial violence. Cook suggests that a rapid influx of whites into Indian territory would result in a significant chance that violence would occur. That theory explains the high number of homicides in northern California in which Indians were the victims of white aggression. However, this study shows that the slower movement of whites into San Diego County meant fewer incidents of homicide.

A brief statistical analysis of the homicide cases involving Indian killers offers a better understanding of the victim/killer relationship. Of the total of 106 cases involving Indians as murderers, 37 percent of the victims were white, 53 percent were Indian, and 7 percent were Hispanic. By killing large numbers of whites (39 of the victims), the Indian defendants increased their chances of being convicted and also received longer sentences. Seventy-five percent of the defendants knew their victims. During the late nineteenth century most Indians who were not living on reservations worked as ranch hands or farm laborers throughout rural San Diego County.[91] Not surprisingly, 83 percent of the crimes were committed in rural areas. A breakdown of weapons shows that Indians used blunt instruments in 26 percent of the murders, handguns in 26 percent, other guns in 12 percent, and knives in 29 percent. The pattern is quite clear: most Indian defendants knew their victims and usually killed them after a quarrel near their home in an isolated rural area.

Although case studies are helpful, a discussion of conviction rates of all Indian defendants provides a more conclusive measurement of how justice was administered. Court records document forty-seven homicide cases that reached the indictment stage. Eighty percent of the Indian defendants were convicted, while 9 and 11 percent, respectively, were found not guilty and dismissed (Fig. 1.1). The data indicate that once a case went to trial, an Indian defendant had virtually no chance of being found not guilty.

Sentencing and plea bargaining offer another check of the criminal justice system and how it treated Indians. Twenty-six percent of the Indian defendants received the death penalty, and an additional 23 percent were sentenced to life in prison. Although Chinese and white defendants seldom plea-bargained during the judicial procedures, 25 percent of the Indian defendants (ten cases) did so. This information indicates that defense counsels, possibly with the encouragement of prosecutors, pressured their Indian clients to cop a plea, with the objective of either escaping the gallows or receiving a lighter sentence. Plea bargaining allowed the judge to sentence the defendant without the long and costly process of a trial. As will be seen, white and Chinese defendants, who had better legal counsel, did not consider this an option. Unfortunately, Indians had little choice, especially with the language barrier and the accompanying inability to comprehend exactly what was taking place in or out of the courtroom. Of greater significance, the criminal justice system required court-appointed attorneys for indigents only at the trial stage. Without legal representation at preliminary hearings, Indian defendants were more likely to be convicted. The wide disparity of court disposition of homicide cases is extraordinary. The legal system found only four Indians not guilty of murder.

This examination of nineteenth-century homicide has revealed examples of racial crossover that created problems for Indian defendants. For example, 37 percent of the victims of the Indian murderers were white. This alone adds an important dimension to understanding what actually happened during the legal process. It is not difficult to imagine what an all-white jury might conclude in a trial involving a white victim and an Indian defendant. In eight cases of Indian defendants sentenced to death, the victims were white, and in one other case the victim was Chinese. Five of eight life sentence cases also involved white victims. Four of the eight plea-bargained cases concerned white victims, with two of the defendants being convicted of first-degree murder. The other case involved Clemente Manteca, accused of killing the Overends. The district attorney apparently believed he had a weak case, therefore he accepted a guilty plea for manslaughter. Clearly Indians who killed white victims received severe punishment. Given the times and the hostility toward Indians, this is not surprising.

While this case study has focused mainly on the treatment of Indian murderers in San Diego County, it should be noted that other regions had similar high conviction rates for Indian defendants during the same era. For example, Sonoma and San Luis Obispo had 100 percent conviction rates (six and two cases, respectively).[92] The reasons for these conviction rates are several. Hostility toward

Indians, of course, was high during this era in California. Particularly with the high incidence of white victims in San Diego County, one can imagine that the criminal justice system might have a tendency to treat Indian murderers with more severity. Newspaper editors often demanded harsher punishment for Indian defendants and complained if the penalty seemed too light.[93] Jurors, as well as most other white citizens, viewed Indian crime, especially homicides with white victims, as more problematic than white crime.

José Gabriel and many other Indian defendants fit the definition of marginal people. For example, Gabriel worked as a common laborer, chopping wood, digging cisterns, and doing other odd jobs. He normally earned from seventy-five cents to a dollar per day for his work. He had been living in San Diego County for twenty-five years and admitted that he drifted around, working for a large number of farmers and ranchers in Poway, Ballena, San Dieguito, Jamul, San Diego, and Otay. During all that time he had lived in the houses and barns of the families who employed him and had never had a real home.[94] Certainly Gabriel lived on the margins of society. Even more troubling was the tendency of the newspapers to label him with the epithet "Indian Joe." It was a way to stereotype him as the "Other"—a menace to society—a marginal person with few, if any, redeeming qualities. Considering the evidence, it seems logical to conclude that the dominant white society and its law really meant red man, white justice.

Chapter Two

Chinese Tongs
Group Solidarity

The great majority of the Chinese in America know nothing about the laws of this country. On the other hand, they know that the Six Companies hire good American lawyers to advise them.
—Walter N. Fong, "The Chinese Six Companies"

In nineteenth-century California Chinese accused of committing crimes were well represented by counsel in the courts. However, an important question needs to be asked: were Chinese who were accused of homicides treated the same way as other defendants were? Recent research has opened a dialogue on the fairness accorded Chinese within criminal justice systems in the American West. John R. Wunder discovered that Chinese "lost seventy percent of their appeals in criminal cases and fifty-nine [percent] of their civil actions" in the Pacific Northwest.[1] While there is extensive scholarship on the physical abuse of Chinese in California, especially during the gold rush,[2] and, to a lesser degree, their experience within the criminal justice system,[3] the treatment of Chinese accused of homicide during the nineteenth century remains largely undocumented.[4] While this case study is supported by statistical data and criminal case files collected from records in seven California counties, it will focus mainly on the experience of Chinese accused of homicide in Sacramento and Stockton.

In California Chinese were less likely to kill outside their own race than any other group (Table 2.1). Clan solidarity and isolation within their Chinatowns help to explain this low interracial homicide rate. Chinese seldom mixed with whites in social situations. They preferred the company of their countrymen in gambling parlors and brothels operated by Chinese businessmen. Of thirty-eight cases involving Chinese as killers in Sacramento County, only one of the victims was not Chinese, and the murderer in that case was never identified.[5] Fifty-eight Chinese were indicted for murder in these thirty-eight cases, but charges against twenty defendants were dismissed. The high number of indictments ending in dismissals reflects the tendency by law enforcement officials to "round up the usual suspects." Indictment information and newspaper accounts suggest that

TABLE 2.1

Chinese Murderers by Victim's Race, 1850–1900

Race	Number	Percentage
White	6	6.5
Hispanic	0	0.0
Indian	0	0.0
Chinese	86	93.5
Black	0	0.0
Totals	92	100.0

Sources: Coroners' Inquests, Calaveras, Tuolumne, Sacramento, San Joaquin, San Luis Obispo, Santa Barbara, and San Diego Counties, 1850–1900.

Sacramento police officers often arrested any "suspicious-looking" Chinese in the vicinity of the crime.[6]

The typical Chinese homicide in Sacramento almost always occurred in Chinatown, tended to be an affair between two males,[7] usually involved rival companies or tongs, and was accomplished with a handgun.[8] For example, about 7:00 P.M. on July 16, 1862, Ah Yuen walked into a gambling parlor on I Street in Chinatown and fired several shots from a revolver into Ah Cow, the business manager for the See Yup Company in Folsom. During the coroner's inquest one witness claimed that a rival group had hired Ah Yuen from San Francisco to assassinate Ah Cow.[9] A similar shooting occurred in the same vicinity a decade later involving Ah Ow. In this case one or more assailants met Ah Ow on I Street between Second and Third and fired several shots. They immediately turned and ran down I Street. Eventually, police arrested Ah Toy, Ah King, Ah Yan, and Ah Lue.[10] Although arrested and detained, none of the alleged assailants was indicted for the killing.

As will be seen, Chinese defendants had a distinctive experience before the bar of justice in California. Because they killed within their own racial group, they faced fewer difficulties than other minorities did. The strong group solidarity and the support of legal representation that they received made their journey through the criminal justice system unique.

Throughout the nineteenth century Chinese immigrants in the United States suffered a great deal of verbal and physical abuse from the white majority. Newspaper editors, city officials, and common citizens used a variety of stereotypes to label them and set them apart from white society. Nevertheless, some white citizens in nineteenth-century California had positive things to say about Chinese immigrants. For example, during an 1886 congressional hearing on Chinese behavior, the chair asked whether the "Chinaman" was equal in his civilization and morals to European immigrants? Solomon Heydenfeldt, former justice of the California Supreme Court, replied, "In every respect." Heydenfeldt suggested that "the Chinese are something better" than many European immigrants. "They are more faithful, more reliable, and more intelligent."[11] Cornelius B. S. Gibbs, an insurance adjuster, believed that many Chinese were good businessmen who were very reputable in their dealings with others. They always paid their bills and treated customers with respect. Another businessman, who operated the Pioneer Woolen Factory in San Francisco, employed mostly Chinese labor and preferred them because they were reliable. "I have found in our factory during the last fifteen years . . . all these Chinese laborers live on the premises . . . and we have not a single case of any kind before the Police Court of murder, or rows among themselves, or theft upon the proprietors. I think that speaks well for them."[12] Another witness, a businessman, stated: "I have dealt a great deal with Chinese merchants in this city. . . . I have always found them truthful, honorable, and perfectly reliable in all their business engagements."[13]

During the gold rush thousands of men from Australia, Mexico, South America, Europe, and the eastern portion of the United States flooded into San Francisco and Sacramento on their way to the gold camps. The Chinese were no exception. They also came in search of riches or, at the very least, a better life. However, the Chinese immigrants encountered special problems since they were easily identifiable because of their dress and hairstyle. An observer might have difficulty visually differentiating between Irish, French, or Australian miners, but there could be no doubt about the Chinese. Their cleanly shaved heads, queues, and blue pantaloons made them easy to identify. Add to this the language barrier, and you had a group that could readily be recognized and isolated.

A legislative committee investigation of the "Chinese problem" in Sacramento completed in 1876 reveals some of the attitudes held by whites about Chinese. The committee chair asked, "What proportion of the Chinese on I Street do you suppose belong to the criminal classes?" Policeman Charles P. O'Neil replied: "On I street there are from one hundred and fifty to two hundred of what we call 'highbinders' living off the houses of prostitution. . . . You might call them hoodlums."[14] Asked whether he would accept a statement from a Chinese witness sworn under oath, O'Neil stated: "As a population the Chinese are largely criminal, when we consider perjury in the list."[15] The chair asked a prosecutor: "Can you rely upon the oaths of Chinamen?" Charles T. Jones, district attorney of Sacramento, testified: "No, sir; not at all . . . they will swear whichever way they may deem most advantageous, irrespective of truth, justice or honesty."[16] Matt Karcher, chief of police, complained of vice problems among the Chinese in Sacramento and also testified that he "wouldn't take their word for anything."[17] When asked about the difficulties in enforcing laws, Jones observed that ignorance of their language created problems, "and unless white witnesses are very familiar with Chinese faces, they have great trouble in identifying them."[18]

The Chinese American experience, especially in California, has been characterized by racial prejudice, discriminatory legislation, and verbal and physical attacks by members of the dominant white population. "American historiography," argues Charles McClain, "bears a large part of the responsibility for this state of affairs. In the first place, most accounts of the great Chinese immigration to the United States in the nineteenth century have concentrated exclusively on the reaction it provoked in the white population; they have tended to ignore the Chinese and their perception of their experience in this country."[19]

Chinese gained passage to California with the aid of one of the Chinese Six Companies that were organized in Canton on the basis of clan affiliations. Originally they were the Ning Yung, Sam Yup, Kong Chow, Yong Wo, Yen Wo, and Hop Wah Societies.[20] These associations provided transportation, employment, housing, health care, recreation, and legal representation. Entering a country dominated by a culture alien to their own, Chinese workers needed the protection provided by a benevolent society operated by others who identified with them. Otis Gibson, an observer fluent in the Chinese language, noted that "it is the universal custom of Chinese when emigrating to any new country, to at once form themselves into a guild."[21] These companies were the linchpin for Chinese immigration throughout the nineteenth century. Virtually every Chinese immigrant belonged to one of the six benevolent societies, and, as McClain observes, the Six Companies were "unquestionably the most important organization in Chinese-American society" during the nineteenth century and had a great influence on the development and control of Chinatowns in Sacramento and Stockton.[22]

Both Sacramento and Stockton had relatively small and compact Chinatowns. In Sacramento, I and J Streets bounded by Second and Third Streets provided the center of it. Within this tiny region were located benevolent association meeting-houses, restaurants, gambling halls, brothels, rooming houses, grocery stores, laundries, and a variety of other shops owned by Chinese merchants. Stockton actually had three small enclaves that could be labeled Chinatowns, but the one located on Washington Street between El Dorado and Sutter Streets proved to be the largest and was the center of Chinese activity. The other two were located on Channel Street between El Dorado and Hunter Streets and at Mormon Slough at Scott's Street bounded by Beaver and Center Streets.

Although little is known about the Chinese enclave in Sacramento, one historian, Sylvia Sun Minnick, has provided a partial reconstruction of Stockton's Chinatown centered on Washington Street. City directories seldom included Chinese businesses, viewing them "as a separate world from their own."[23] In a rare directory listing, however, the Tuck Fong Tai Kee and Company boardinghouse, seven grocery stores, a general merchandise store, two butcher shops, and a drugstore appeared in the 1876 Stockton city directory.[24] Many of the Chinese merchants rented property owned by white landlords. Rooms within apartment buildings or boardinghouses were small, some averaging "only twelve by nine feet." Overcrowding, however, was a way of life in Chinatown. "Bunk beds were stacked to the ceiling; each room was crowded, uncomfortable, unsanitary and hot. But it was a place for the single men to sleep and it was cheap."[25] Gambling proved to be one of the most popular pastimes for the Chinese, and many merchants provided gambling halls. At 104 East Washington Street, the You Lun Company served as a front for the Tai Sang Choy gambling hall. Three other gambling halls, the Ng Woo Tong, Tong King, and Chung Toh, were located at 111, 117, and 121 East Washington Street.[26]

Benevolent associations maintained headquarters on Washington Street to provide their members services that included employment, transportation back to China, medical treatment, and burial benefits. Associations such as Sam Yup, Sze Yup, and Heungshan were soon joined by Suey Sing Tong and Bing Kung Tong, all located on Washington Street. Attempts to control prostitution and gambling often led to feuds between these tongs that sometimes spilled into the streets and included shootings.

During the late nineteenth century the population of Sacramento and San Joaquin Counties included significant numbers of Chinese, while in the other five counties smaller numbers fluctuated with the ebb and flow of the gold mines and other commercial interests that attracted them. Although small during the 1850s and 1860s, the numbers of Chinese in Sacramento increased to 13.4 and 14.2 percent of the total population, respectively, for the decades 1870 and 1880, then declined to 9.7 percent by 1900. San Joaquin County's Chinese population averaged about 5.5 percent.

The Chinese who entered California brought with them a legal tradition that had begun as early as the Ch'in Dynasty (221–207 B.C.). The *Ta Ch'ing Lü Li* is commonly called the Chinese penal code of the Ch'ing (Manchu) Dynasty (1644–1911).[27] Unlike the nineteenth-century California penal code, which breaks homicide into three basic categories, first- and second-degree murder and manslaughter, the *Ta Ch'ing Lü Li* has a wide range of homicide categories that include familial relationships, intentional, mistaken, accidental, and a variety of other forms. It is much more complex than European penal codes, offering a series of punishment gradations based upon familial, class, and social status relationships between victim and killer.

Unlike law enforcement officers in the American legal system, a Chinese magistrate was required to investigate any petition alleging a crime presented by anyone in his local province (*hsien*). Assisted by clerks with legal expertise, the magistrate in effect became the investigator, prosecutor, sheriff, jury, and judge while processing the case. After the investigation into the facts of the case, the magistrate consulted the *Ta Ch'ing Lü Li* to determine what punishment should be meted out to the defendant. In cases involving capital offenses there was an elaborate procedure of automatic appeal to the governor of the province, the board of punishments, the Supreme Court (San Fa Ssu), and finally, the emperor. On important occasions the emperor might declare a general amnesty and release some condemned murderers from their death sentences. It was common to substitute "bambooing or branding" as "a substitute for the prescribed punishment" for death penalty cases.[28]

"An indictment cannot be got up without a lie."[29] This famous Chinese proverb helps to explain Chinese attitudes toward perjury committed during trials. In China the accused often paid witnesses to "testify to their innocence." It was common to avoid involvement in a case as a witness against the accused for fear of reprisals if the defendant was found guilty.[30] In one inter-clan rivalry the two parties chose not to take their complaint to the magistrate. A spokesperson for one of the groups said: "He might do us much greater harm. We prefer to decide the quarrel ourselves."[31] The staff of the magistrates were often rewarded for arresting suspects who were eventually convicted. Consequently, constables were guilty of "loosely arresting the wrong person."[32] In other words, the phrase "round up the usual suspects" has a long tradition, at least in Chinese legal history.

Blood feuds appeared to be common in China, and the "right of revenge" posed a problem for legal authorities. Specific groups, such as tongs, clans, and families, believed they had the right to avenge the death of a member of their group. Blood feuds began early in Chinese history (first century B.C. and A.D.). Huan T'an complained: "Now although those who have committed homicide are punished by the law, yet private hate between two parties still predominates, and revenge is exacted between them for generations."[33] One emperor said: "Life and death depend upon the sentence given. How can a reckless person take revenge at his own volition? Once the law has already meted out justice, the personal enmity is at an end. Killing for revenge cannot be begun."[34] Nevertheless, clan and tong society members believed that they had the right to avenge the killing of a fellow member. And, unfortunately, one killing led to another and another. One Chinese observer of this problem suggested: "To revenge is an expression of the true emotions of a human being. . . . If a wrong is not avenged, the human way would be destroyed and the heavenly way ruined."[35] There was no easy answer to this complex problem and, as will be seen, the homicide sample includes cases that suggest this Chinese tradition continued into nineteenth-century California. It should be noted that blood feuds are common across many cultural groups.[36]

During this time period it was common for California newspapers to label any violent behavior among Chinese as the work of "highbinders."[37] Originally used in the early nineteenth century to describe Irish immigrants accused of criminal activity in New York, the term "highbinder" first appeared as an epithet to characterize Chinese as criminals in the *San Francisco Call.* Newspaper editors used it to attack Chinese "secret societies." For example, a June 1, 1892, *Sacramento Bee* headline blared: A HIGHBINDER WAR. TWO MONGOLIANS LAID OUT IN THE BATTLE. THE CITY PRISON FILLED WITH MURDEROUS MONGOLS.[38] Such headlines attacking Chinese partially reveal the racial prejudice against them harbored by newspaper editors, reporters, and the general public. Numerous racially charged headlines helped create a myth of the Chinese as a criminal class.[39] Pejorative phrases such as "highbinder," "Mongolian Mafia," "Celestial," and "murderous Mongols" turned the Chinese into caricatures, removed their humanity, developed the image of a society to be feared, and made them objects to be controlled. To white observers, the benevolent societies automatically became "secret societies" that symbolized vice, corruption, and violent behavior.

The story that appeared in the June 1, 1892, *Sacramento Bee* suggested that the Chinese involved in a homicide that occurred on Third Street between I and J Streets in Sacramento were members of a secret society employed to kill two Chinese businessmen. Homicide seemed to be a common occurrence, and, in this case, a fight between two rival Chinese groups ended with Yee Kie and Lee Gong lying dead on a Sacramento street. This type of "secret society" killing, typical in both Sacramento and Stockton during the nineteenth century, illustrated that the societies were committed to protecting the economic turf of the company, clan affiliation, or tong involved.[40]

On October 10, 1881, a group of Chinese met at a house on Third Street, between I and J, to celebrate. During the party Yee Ah Gee pulled a knife and threatened Yee Ah Pong. Confronted with an armed adversary, Yee Ah Pong took out a revolver and killed him. During the trial, the issue of whether Yee Ah Pong acted from fear for his life or acted rashly in shooting became paramount. With a large number of witnesses present, the prosecutor was able to make a strong case that ended in the conviction of Yee Ah Pong.[41] In another incident, which occurred at Third and I Streets on August 8, 1889, Ah Heong and another unnamed assailant allegedly accosted Suey Kay. When police arrived, Suey Kay claimed that he had been robbed and that Ah Heong had pulled a revolver and shot him twice. With witnesses and the dying declaration by the victim, the prosecutors were able to gain a conviction and life sentence for Ah Heong for killing Suey Kay.

However, the governor and the pardons board apparently were not impressed with the evidence. With the aid of attorneys supplied by one of the Chinese companies, Ah Heong was pardoned after serving only one year in San Quentin.[42]

Cases that ended with a conviction for Chinese defendants in Sacramento were the exception. In most of the homicides involving Chinese killers and victims the prosecutors were unable to make their case. Police and prosecutors often encountered great difficulty in investigating Chinese homicide cases because of the language barrier and the tendency for Chinese to deal internally with their own problems. Possibly fearing reprisals, and preferring to follow their own legal tradition, many Chinese refused to testify against other Chinese accused of homicide. In other cases, Chinese victims were listed as killed by "persons unknown," a common euphemism used by the coroner when he was unable to locate eyewitnesses. Since most of these homicides at the hands of unknown assailants occurred within the Sacramento Chinatown section, it is probable that the "unknown" killers were also Chinese.[43]

With a significantly smaller Chinese population, San Joaquin County had fewer Chinese homicides—only thirteen cases involving Chinese murderers. The most celebrated among the cases involved Ah Mow, Ah Chung, and Ah Cheen, who were accused of killing Sam Gee, Ah Yup, and Ah Bow on September 10, 1876. The killings occurred in Stockton's Chinatown, in a gambling room on Washington Street between Hunter and Eldorado Streets. The prosecutor charged that Ah Mow and his accomplices had attacked and killed the three victims during a dispute between two Chinese companies. Apparently a fight broke out while they were gambling, and several parties drew pistols and began to shoot. Only Chinese witnesses from the See Yup Company were used during the prosecution of the defendants, who were members of the Yong Wo Company. One witness claimed that a dispute over a bet occurred between Ah Yup, the dealer, and several men seated at the gambling table. Ah Chung drew a revolver and said, "God damn you I will kill you."[44] The pace of the battle soon quickened and spilled out onto Washington Street. A white witness, H. L. Farrington, recalled that a little past noon people were coming from church when he saw a Chinese male start firing into a store. He believed that four or five shots were fired in quick succession. He could not identify the shooter. Two victims, Ah Yup and Ah Bow, died from gunfire, but Sam Gee expired from wounds inflicted by a sharp object.[45]

Juries found Ah Mow, Ah Chung, and Ah Cheen guilty of murder and sentenced them to life in prison. However, nine years later all three were pardoned and released from prison because of perjured testimony by several Chinese witnesses. William Gibson, a lawyer who had assisted the district attorney, claimed that after the trial he traveled to San Francisco to visit the See Yup Company. There he had a discussion with Ah Sing, one of the main witnesses in the case against the defendants, and asked him what really happened in Stockton. In a moment of candor, Ah Sing related to Gibson "that when one Chinaman did another an injury or wrong, that if the friends of the one who had been injured or wronged could not get hold of the wrong-doer, that they sought out the nearest relatives of the wrong-doer and tried to punish him."[46] Since the alleged killers had escaped arrest, Ah Sing testified against the defendants, who were also members of the Yong Wo Company. After hearing these comments, Gibson notified J. A. Hosmer, the San Joaquin County district attorney, and contacted the Yong Wo Company. Because the newly revealed evidence indicated perjury, Ah Cheen received a pardon. This particular case reveals that Chinese defendants who were represented by lawyers provided by their company could eventually obtain some measure of justice.

Secret societies have a long historical tradition in China, probably originating during the Han Dynasty (206 B.C.–A.D. 220). One of the most famous groups, the Triads, is usually traced from the seventeenth century and is based upon the Hung.[47] Originally involved in attempts to overthrow the Manchu Dynasty, Triads eventually established operations in the United States that included prostitution, opium smuggling, and gambling parlors. More important, they opened lodges and offered protection for their members "against outsiders, companionship in a hostile environment, and a sense of community,"[48] and developed elaborate ritualistic ceremonies to initiate members. Most secret societies in California cities based upon the Triads were called tongs.[49]

Although "tong" refers to a hall or meeting place, Ko-lin Chin defines tongs as "fraternal associations" that were developed among Chinese immigrants in Chinatowns "as self-help groups."[50] Tongs appeared in Sacramento and Stockton within the first decade of Chinese immigration. Unlike the companies, which often restricted membership to specific clan affiliation, tongs accepted any Chinese who wished to join. Lacking such clan restrictions, tongs grew rapidly, became numerous, and had larger membership than the Six Companies. Tongs behaved similar to the companies, and in exchange for a membership fee they provided clients with housing, employment, medical care, and legal aid. Tongs quickly moved into such economic endeavors as gambling, opium dens, and prostitution.[51] These enterprises became lucrative because of the large numbers of Chinese males seeking recreational outlets during leisure hours. The high demand for such pleasure-related businesses heightened the rivalry among tongs, companies, and other benevolent associations. To increase their economic power, tongs forced Chinese businessmen to join their association for protection. To protect their economic interests tongs resorted to gunmen, called "hatchet men" by the local press. Enforcers who were caught committing crimes received full legal protection from the tong, which often included perjured testimony.[52]

In discussing Chinese rivalry, one historian, Stanford M. Lyman, observes:

"These wars did generate a widespread stereotype of Chinatown that included lurid stories about opium dens, sing-song girls, hatchet men, and tong wars. The real Chinese society was difficult to discern behind this kind of romantic illusion." Lyman suggests that "violent conflicts" occurred mainly because of attempts to control "illegal commerce in drugs, gambling, and prostitution."[53] Tongs tried to resolve their disputes by arbitration whenever possible, but sometimes they turned to gunmen to pressure the rival tong into a settlement. Virtually all disputes between these secret societies occurred in the local Chinatown, and outsiders such as police or city officials had little impact on them. One exception would be the bribing of police officers to gain an advantage over a rival tong.[54] This, however, had little long-term impact on tong rivalries. Throughout the nineteenth century, these benevolent associations controlled the destiny of Chinatowns in Sacramento and Stockton.

Tongs were usually perceived by Americans as organizations "associated with underworld criminal activity."[55] Speaking of Chinese rivalry in San Francisco's Chinatown, Stanford Lyman suggests that it was "remarkable for its fierce internal conflicts, its lack of solidarity, and its intensive disharmony."[56] He discovered rivalry between the Chinese Six Companies and newer groups, which developed secret societies or tongs to compete for "control of vice" and attempt to gain political power at the expense of the clans and companies.[57] This helps to explain the numerous shootings.

The Chinese competition for gambling, prostitution, and other economic enterprises occurred irregularly within the Chinatowns. Violent conflicts developed there periodically because of aspirations by rival groups to control commerce in gambling and prostitution. Most of the killings that occurred in Sacramento's Chinatown involved tong-controlled gambling and women. Many homicide cases did indeed indicate Chinese rivalry among the various benevolent organizations. For example, around 1:00 P.M. on March 1, 1873, Ah Fat and Ah Wee met Ah Quong on the southwest corner of I and Third Streets. After a brief argument, Ah Fat struck Ah Quong from behind with a hatchet, and Ah Wee pulled a revolver and fired several quick shots at Ah Quong, who died within minutes. Police quickly apprehended Ah Fat and Ah Wee, seized their weapons, and jailed them. With the aid of eyewitnesses, a jury found Ah Fat and Ah Wee guilty and sentenced them to life in prison.[58]

On the surface this case appeared to be a typical quarrel between Chinese males, but underlying the newspaper reporter's description of the crime were other indications of a rivalry between two business groups. During the trial the prosecution explained that there had been three men involved in the killing—Ah Fat, Ah Wee, and Ah May. An embarrassed prosecutor admitted that Ah May had been inadvertently released from jail and had fled their jurisdiction. Members of the company to which the victim Ah Quong had belonged contributed a considerable effort to assure the conviction of Ah Fat.[59] The court documents reveal that Ah Quong had been an important member of a Chinese company and had frequently volunteered as an interpreter in numerous court cases involving Chinese defendants. Just before the shooting, Ah Quong had been acting as an interpreter in the alleged kidnapping of a Chinese woman by two Chinese men. The police court had a packed house of Chinese men apparently divided between two factions and very excited about the trial. One side wanted the defendants convicted, while the other opposed the proceedings and made threats against Ah Quong, who was apparently in favor of conviction. After the court adjourned around noon, the Chinese observers moved into the street, "greatly excited and talking loudly."[60] Ah Quong stepped into the street and walked away from the courthouse. At the corner of I and Third Streets, less than two blocks away, he was accosted and allegedly killed by Ah Fat, Ah Wee, and Ah May.

A decade later, a reporter for the *Sacramento Bee*, covering a homicide story involving Chinese rivalry, commented that "armed gangs of Chinese highbinders parade" through the streets of Chinatown and they "all carry pistols." The reporter noted that recently "the celestial arrested by officer Ash" was arraigned and the judge "fined him $30 for carrying a pistol."[61] However, in the reporter's view, this was an exceptional case; they seldom were charged with carrying concealed weapons. The data indicate that many Chinese kept handguns on their person. Constable George Rider arrested Mock Soon and found "a revolver, a hatchet and a pair of derringers." At the coroner's inquest it was revealed that two men, Sing Due and Lung Yek, came to their deaths on Sunday, November 11, 1883, "at the hands of parties unknown."[62] The prosecutors had difficulty finding those responsible for the crimes; however, they were able to find members of the rival group who would cooperate even if it meant perjury. R. T. Devlin, an attorney for Mock Soon, admitted that when his client was arrested, he "was armed with a pistol" and "was ready to fight but was not actually engaged in battle."[63]

During the trial several witnesses claimed that there was a riot in Chinatown at the corner of I and Third Streets on the day of the crime. Such chaotic conditions made it difficult to identify the killers. The witnesses for the prosecution also proved to be vexing. In a petition supporting the pardon of Mock Soon, R. M. Clarken claimed that "the case was bitterly prosecuted by the company opposed to the defendant." All of the evidence against Mock Soon was "given entirely by Chinamen belonging to the rival faction." Clarken also asserted that of all those charged, only Mock Soon was prosecuted for the murders. This was especially troubling, since "dozens of pistol shots were fired" and there was no proof that Mock Soon had even fired his revolver. Finally, Clarken concluded that "the animus exhibited on both sides showed a feverish anxiety to secure a victim on one side or the other and Mock Soon was selected."[64]

On May 31, 1892, a rivalry between the Bing Kong Tong and the Chee Kong

Tong ended with a gun battle on Third Street between I and J Streets in Sacramento's Chinatown. Lee Gong and Yee Kie were killed in the shootout. The local newspapers ran banner headlines claiming that a "Highbinder War" had ended with two dead and the city jail was full of "Murderous Mongols."[65] Police arrested and the prosecutor indicted Chin Hane and Hoey Yen Sing for the murder of Lee Gong. The prosecution based its case on the testimony of Lee Gong's widow, Ah Wah, and Yee Chim. The prosecutor claimed that Chin Hane had entered Lee Gong's store, pulled out a pistol, and killed Lee Gong. Both defendants were members of the Bing Kong Tong, and the witnesses against them belonged to the Chee Kong Tong. During cross-examination, one witness admitted that he worked for the Chee Kong Tong in dealing with criminal cases. A. L. Hart, attorney for the defendants, based his argument primarily on what occurred outside Lee Gong's store. Hart informed the jury: "We will show you that a great number of shots—nearly all of them were directed from the outside toward Lee Gong's store." The evidence collected included "bullet holes in the posts on the outside from Lee Gong's."[66] A streetcar conductor testified that a "great many shots were fired," around seventy to eighty. Two other observers stated that "the firing was coming up Third Street and was followed down towards the Bing Kong Tong." The defense attorney argued that the "fight did not commence in Lee Gong's" but instead began on the street outside. Hart further claimed that the fight was started by members of the Chee Kong Tong, who chased Bing Kong Tong members back to their hall.[67] The jury chose to believe the prosecution and found both defendants guilty of first-degree murder. They sentenced Chin Hane to death. Attorneys appealed to the California Supreme Court, but the justices affirmed the lower court's decision. The defendant was executed in Folsom Prison on December 13, 1895.[68]

Other cases exhibited similar circumstances. For example, in 1897, Sacramento district attorney F. D. Ryan, in a motion to dismiss a charge of murder against Ling Ying Toy, admitted that the jury was hopelessly deadlocked seven to five for acquittal. He commented: "This case is what is known as a Chinese case. They are the most difficult to try, because they involve a character of witnesses that . . . makes it almost impossible to get a fair understanding of the testimony, because it necessarily has to come through an interpreter; and it has been my experience in Chinese murder cases, that, usually, it is one society or organization against another." Ryan suggested that it would be impossible to gain conviction in this case. "My experience has taught me that, in dealing with this class of people, the crime of murder is committed as a matter of revenge . . . and that the killing of one Chinaman usually results in the killing of another."[69] Further, Ryan candidly admitted that although he believed that the defendants knew something about the circumstances of the killing, he was not convinced of the guilt of either defendant.

After hearing the motion by the prosecutor, Judge E. C. Hart commented: "We also know from common experience . . . that where a member of one of the 'tongs' has been killed, as a usual thing—and it is so generally—they are not satisfied until some member of the 'tong' to which the murderer belonged is punished for it."[70] After years of experience in the police court and on the superior court bench, Judge Hart further observed: "In other words, it is a fight between the 'tongs,' and it matters little to them, as a rule, which one of the members is prosecuted and punished for it." Finally, he concluded, "I know that I would not . . . want to take any human being's life, whether he be a heathen, or a civilized person, or a savage, upon testimony which is so conflicting, and particularly, coming from the source from which the testimony in this record came."[71] He dismissed charges against the defendants. Other cases reveal similar complaints by the prosecution.[72]

The data reveal that most of the Chinese-committed homicides in Sacramento occurred in a very small, highly concentrated area centered on the corner of I Street and Third Street. This corner was the site of thirteen killings, and four more were recorded less than a block away, on I Street between Third and Fourth Streets. All but two of the other Chinese homicides occurred within a two-block radius. This region, of course, was the main cultural center of Sacramento's Chinatown. Both the Bing Kong Tong and the Chee Kong Tong were located within the block bounded by I, J, Second, and Third Streets. Chinese societies, hotels, restaurants, laundries, and other businesses completely filled the block, and because of disputes involving economic territorial rivalries among Chinese societies, it became the homicide hot spot in Sacramento.

In California Chinese rarely killed outside their racial group, but on the night of May 5, 1878, Henry Connoly became involved in a dispute with three or four Chinese about paying a toll to cross Connoly's bridge over the Calaveras River near San Andreas. After some heated discussion, pushing, and shoving, apparently one of the Chinese involved in the dispute pulled a knife and stabbed Connoly in the abdomen. He died the next day. Three suspects—Ah Ton, Ah Song, and Ah Kum—were charged with murder. Defense counsel entered a plea of guilty of second-degree murder for Ah Song and Ah Kum, and they were sentenced to life in prison. Ah Ton, who went to trial in January 1879, was convicted of murder in the first degree and sentenced to death.[73]

This case is intriguing because it involved a Chinese man killing a white male in a region with a long history of prejudice and abuse against Chinese. On the surface this case would seem simple: identify the suspect, make the arrest, prosecute him, and justice would be served. But that is not what happened. The only eyewitness, Toby Flam, proved to be untrustworthy, and the victim was so much under the influence of alcohol that his "identification" of the killer was unreliable. That is precisely why this case is important. Moreover, the final outcome proves that a Chinese defendant could gain redress if he had good legal counsel.

The circumstances of the trial illuminate the problems that Chinese defendants encountered in California, where many white citizens harbored deepseated anti-Chinese feelings. The facts of the crime seem fairly simple. Henry Connoly operated a toll bridge over the Calaveras River and charged fees to anyone who wanted to cross. Connoly, who lived in a small house beside the bridge, had a reputation for being a heavy drinker and a history of abusing Chinese. Toby Flam claimed that he saw the altercation between Connoly and the Chinese. Flam said that one assailant drew a pistol, but Connoly knocked it out of his hand. Another grabbed Connoly, and yet another attacker stabbed him with a knife. Flam stated: "I do not know the name of the Chinaman that stabbed him, but this is the man here." Toby Flam pointed to Ah Ton, the defendant, as the man who did the cutting. Flam also testified: "I went [to] Connoly's about 2 o'clock. He was sober and continued sober. He did not have any liquor."[74] Testimony by various witnesses make it clear that Flam was certainly lying about Connoly's drinking and most probably about the identity of the killers.

In a petition supporting a pardon for Ah Ton, several prominent citizens noted: "[W]e know from the general reputation of the deceased Henry Connoly, that he was a man of extremely intemperate habits and for years scarcely a day passed over his head that he was not intoxicated."[75] J. Salcido stated: "I saw Connoly on an average of 3 times a week and 9 times in 10 he was drunk." He also had a reputation for tormenting and physically attacking Chinese who sometimes refused to pay his toll and walked under the bridge. Salcido claimed that Connoly often threw rocks at Chinese who walked across "the creek instead of passing over on the bridge." While trying to caution against such behavior "he became intensely abusive and declared his intense hostility to Chinamen."[76] William Lewis, a local attorney, claimed that "Connoly had for years kept up a steady persecution of Chinamen. He drank . . . and when drunk quarreled with them."[77] Toby Flam also disliked the Chinese. He testified: "I hate all Chinamen and have tried to kill two or three—tried to kill them with little rocks—rather see a Chinaman hang than not. If I had a good gun would try to kill them."[78]

After the trial, defense counsel hired private detective James Galbraith to investigate the circumstances of the case in order to gain information to submit to the governor to secure a pardon for Ah Ton. During his questioning of J. B. Machavilli, a storekeeper in San Andreas, the detective learned a great deal about the drinking habits of Connoly. Just before the commission of the homicide, the victim had been drinking for several hours at Machavilli's store and had begun to abuse Ah Ton. This occurred on the morning of May 5, 1878, the day of the crime. Machavilli gave Connoly a full bottle of whiskey and helped him home to the bridge. "When he arrived at the bridge . . . between 11 and 12 o'clock, he was in fact drunk."[79]

The issue of identifying the killers suggests that those convicted were not the guilty parties. For example, Sheriff B. F. Haines testified that both Toby and Connoly recognized Ah Ton as the assailant.[80] Dr. E. B. Robertson, the physician who attended the victim, claimed that when the suspects "were brought before him [Connoly] for the purpose of Connoly's identifying these Chinamen, that he was too intoxicated to identify the Chinamen or tell one from another." The case hinged on only one eyewitness, and a bad one at that. J. B. Reddick, the lawyer hired to defend Ah Ton on appeal, claimed Flam was "less than *half witted*" and lying.[81] When asked about a document shown to him, Toby Flam admitted during testimony: "I can not read, do not know one paper from another."[82] His father, August Flam, stated that "Toby is not of sound mind and judgment . . . he is not [to] be believed in his statements."[83] Nevertheless, a jury convicted Ah Ton.

Unlike most Chinese defendants, Ah Ton did not receive good legal counsel. One trial observer, J. F. Washburn, stated that Ah Ton's "attorney was entirely incompetent; being too intoxicated to try any case whatever, much less a trial for life." He also indicated that "there were men on the jury who were known to have prejudices against the Chinese; and, after rendering their verdict, they went about the street boasting of what they had done."[84]

After reviewing the case, E. C. Marshals, the attorney general of California, informed Governor George Stoneman: "I am satisfied that a full and unconditional pardon should be granted to each of the parties [Ah Ton, Ah Song, and Ah Kum]. Only two witnesses testified to the fact of the killing . . . one Toby Flam was a boy of 14 years old weak minded . . . the other witness was the man Connoly who was killed. His dying declaration was taken and on its face is inadmissible under the ruling of Supreme Court." The victim "was very drunk at the time his declaration was taken, and both the identification of the accused and the details of the fight are contradictory and improbable."[85] Marshals strongly recommended them for pardon.

Three members of the California Supreme Court informed the governor that "the [court] record itself contains the suggestion that in some instances the defendant's rights may have been inadvertently stipulated away." The justices stated that on the basis of the briefs submitted by counsel, they could not reverse the judgment of the court. Nevertheless, they made it clear that if the defense counsel had provided the "statement of one Ah Yong which . . . testified to and believed by the jury would have gone far to acquit the prisoner at a second trial." The justices also complained: "[W]e feel that the case taken altogether presents such doubts as to make it our duty as it is our pleasure, to call it to the attention of Your Excellency. . . . We think the circumstances could well be considered by Your Excellency in exercising the attributes of clemency."[86]

Surprisingly, defense counsel prevented Ah Song and Ah Kum from entering pleas of not guilty. William Lewis, lawyer for the defendants, admitted this but claimed, "I made them [Ah Song and Ah Kum] plead guilty to save their necks.

I know they would hang the whole three of them if I went to trial."[87] "If you ask me why, I answer, owing to the prejudice existing at the time against the Chinese, it has grown into a common saying that when a Chinaman is to be prosecuted, 'it is an easy thing.'"[88] Chung Fun, the interpreter, noted that Lewis tried to get them to plead guilty to a reduced charge of second-degree murder. However, both defendants refused, insisting that they were not guilty. At that point their attorney asked the sheriff to remove them from the courtroom. Despite this maneuver, when Chung Fun was asked by the court clerk to translate their pleas, he repeated their statements: "You may hang me if you please, but I am not guilty." Chung Fun stated emphatically: "Ah Kum and Ah Song did not plead guilty when called upon by the court to answer to the charge of the murder of Connoly."[89] The attorney general concurred and informed the governor that "two of the parties [Ah Song and Ah Kum] were sentenced on a plea of guilty which it is clearly established, they never consented to."[90]

Further investigation suggested that if the defense counsel had been competent, the defendants might have been acquitted. For example, in a deposition made later, Henry Bright claimed that the "next morning after Connoly was stabbed two chinamen left Benson's [boardinghouse] and went west." Constable Driscoll talked to one of them, who cried that "another Chinaman Ah Hing cut the bridge man," not Ah Ton.[91] William O. Swenson, editor of the *Calaveras Advertiser*, called the trial a "farce." He said that if his son, Alfred Swenson, "had been properly examined [he] would have gone far to clear all the Chinamen as he met three Chinamen near the bridge coming from San Andreas" the next day. The manager of Benson's boardinghouse at San Andreas claimed that "Ah Hing and Lee Ah Hung, the two chinamen who fled," committed the crime. They had been living in his boardinghouse and left quickly the morning after the crime.[92]

This case reveals that it was possible for unjustly accused Chinese in California to gain justice. By receiving the support of the Chinese legal community in San Francisco, as well as prominent citizens in San Andreas, the defendants were eventually able to gain redress of this miscarriage of justice. Ah Ton escaped execution, and after languishing in San Quentin for three years he received a full pardon from the governor. Ah Song and Ah Kum served six years each before receiving pardons.

Some homicide cases provide important insights on rules of evidence and procedure practiced by attorneys and judges and also illuminate the appeals process that was available to Chinese defendants. For example, on August 22, 1875, a little after 8:00 P.M., an argument involving several Chinese males in San Luis Obispo ended with the shooting death of Captain Jack.[93] A. A. Oglesby, the district attorney, filed murder charges against Ah Sing, Ah Him, Ah You, Ah Loy, Ah On, Ah Charley, Ah Look, and Ah Jim. Five days after the crime, a San Luis Obispo grand jury indicted all eight "suspects," and they were held for trial. After the jury heard the evidence, Judge Eugene Fawcett advised the jury to ignore charges against Ah Loy, Ah On, Ah Look, and Ah You because the evidence was insufficient "to warrant a conviction."[94]

Lawyers for the defendants appealed to the California Supreme Court. Defense counsel focused on Judge Fawcett's instructions to the jury, noting that three instructions requested by defense counsel were refused. Testimony revealed that Captain Jack, the victim, tended to be "a quarrelsome person and a boisterous fighting man." Further, defense counsel claimed that the defendants "never instigated" the fight and "were acting in self defense."[95] The judge refused to admit this testimony and also refused to instruct the jury as to these facts. However, the jury instructions on reasonable doubt proved to be the most damaging issue to the prosecution and the court in this case on appeal. The California Supreme Court decision written by Chief Justice William T. Wallace noted the failure to admit testimony by defense witnesses, but then turned to the more significant issue of reasonable doubt. In his instructions Judge Fawcett informed the jury: "*If the evidence is such that a man of prudence would act upon it in his own affairs of the greatest importance, then there cannot remain a reasonable doubt within the meaning of the law.*"[96] The justice noted: "It is certainly a mistake to say that there cannot remain a reasonable doubt when even the evidence is such 'that a man of prudence would act upon it in his own affairs of the greatest importance.'"[97] The judgment was reversed, and the case was sent back for a new trial. After reviewing the evidence, the district attorney dismissed charges against the defendants.[98]

About 11:00 P.M., on a Saturday night in June 1860, Lum Sow, a twenty-year-old man, was assaulted by six Chinese males and stabbed to death outside a house of prostitution in Chinatown at Big Oak Flat, Tuolumne County. The dispute involved a women who had left Le Chou, one of the defendants, and gone off with Lum Sow, the victim. The four defendants, Chung Litt, Ah Hung, Ah Cum, and Le Chou, arrived in Big Oak Flat and, according to several witnesses, threatened to kill Lum Sow. John LaCosta, a baker, heard loud noises being made by Chinese, so he stepped into the street to see what was going on. He observed Lum Sow standing at the door of a house and "another man trying to push him out." Then suddenly "a man stabbed him and he fell dead."[99] E. M. Archer, deputy constable, happened to be coming down the street when the homicide took place. He said the victim "ran out of the alley and met me, and said Chinaman had killed him, he came with open hands. I caught hold of him, thought he was drunk. I then saw blood on him, laid him down and as I done so a knife dropped from his arm or side."[100] True to form, Constable Thomas Corcoran "rounded up the usual suspects." Under cross-examination about the actual number of suspects arrested, Corcoran replied, "I first arrested, 8, 10, or 12. They were discharged that night after my return from Humbug."[101]

Chu Sow, who was asked to identify the assailants, had known the defendants

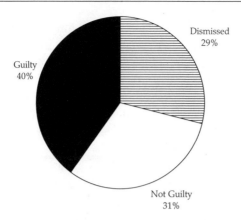

Fig. 2.1. Verdicts: Chinese Defendants, Seven California Counties, 1850–1900

for a long time. He said that all of them "wanted to kill the boy." Chu Sow witnessed the killing and testified: "I stood 3 feet from the killing, so close that blood squirted on me. The killing lasted 1 or 2 minutes."[102] Constables Archer and Corcoran, accompanied by Chu Sow, went to Little Humbug, about five miles away, where they identified and apprehended the suspects in a small cabin. Corcoran "picked a knife off of the head of Chung Litt's bed." After taking the knife out of the sheaf and examining it, they noted that it was bloody. They arrested the four suspects at about 1:00 A.M. Chu Sow, who accompanied the constables to identify the suspects, said Corcoran discovered the knife in Chung Litt's bed. His codefendants protested, "[W]hy did you not throw the knife away? What did you bring it back for?"[103]

With such damaging evidence and open statements made by the defendants, it is not surprising that the jury found them guilty. They were convicted of murder in the first degree and sentenced to death. The California Supreme Court denied the defendants' appeals and let the sentence stand.[104] All four were hanged in Sonora on Friday, March 22, 1861. A newspaper account noted that "three of them protested their innocence of the crime of which they were convicted." Only Chung Litt "died stoically"; the others "made great lamentations."[105] For Chinese who were executed, the seven-county survey data showed only these four and one other defendant.

California authorities indicted a total of 103 Chinese males for murder or manslaughter in the seven counties. No women were indicted for murder. This, of course, reflects the overwhelming gender imbalance of the virtually all-male immigration movement. Conviction rates for Chinese defendants averaged 40 percent for the seven counties, while 31 and 29 percent, respectively, were found not guilty or dismissed (Fig. 2.1).

Although Sacramento prosecutors indicted fifty-eight Chinese defendants in thirty-eight homicide cases, they convicted only fourteen, or 24 percent, of those indicted. Thirty-eight percent of the Sacramento County defendants were found not guilty, and an additional 38 percent were dismissed.[106] Equally interesting, of all defendants indicted in Sacramento and San Joaquin Counties, Chinese defendants had the highest dismissal rates, 35 and 30 percent, respectively. In other words, of the Chinese indicted in Sacramento and San Joaquin Counties, 76 and 50 percent, respectively, were released from custody by the criminal justice system. Calaveras indicted twenty-two Chinese defendants for eleven homicides, while Tuolumne County authorities indicted only ten defendants for twenty-five homicides. Law enforcement officials were unable to identify suspects in six and five cases, respectively, for Tuolumne and Sacramento Counties. Since few officers understood the languages spoken by the Chinese, the police in Sacramento and Stockton, as well as law enforcement officers in the gold camps, often arrested everyone near the scene of the crime. Before the trial, when it became clear to the prosecutors that they could not make a case against some of the Chinese defendants who had been indicted for murder, they released those suspects. Plea bargaining was minimal, with only four cases, two each in Sacramento and Calaveras Counties.[107] The data also confirm that Chinese tended to kill almost exclusively within their own group; virtually all of their victims (98 percent) were Chinese also.

What can we conclude from this discussion of the treatment of Chinese defendants in California during the last half of the nineteenth century? First, since the Chinese entered California with the solid support of clans and the Chinese Six Companies, they maintained a strong group solidarity that permeated their Chinatown communities. No matter what city these immigrants moved to, they could always find a Chinatown with Chinese organizations that would provide housing, food, employment, medical treatment, and legal defense. Second, because of protection provided by the Chinese Six Companies, tongs, and other benevolent societies, most Chinese defendants were well represented by legal counsel in court. Thus they enjoyed a decided advantage because they received crucial legal advice before and during the preliminary hearings when defendants were "fair game" for aggressive sheriffs, police, and prosecutors anxious to gain a conviction. Third, although the intermixing of racial groups created tensions that were reflected by interracial killings, Chinese killed only within their own group and therefore were less likely to receive the death penalty for their crimes. Fourth, the failure of some Chinese witnesses to testify against other Chinese was an important factor in explaining the low conviction rates for Chinese defendants. This refusal to testify, of course, was deeply ingrained in the Chinese legal tradition. On the other hand, sometimes witnesses would commit perjury with the objective of convicting a member of another tong, a practice that created a problem for prosecutors and judges trying to sort out the facts of these cases. Consequently, a significant number of cases were overturned when reviewed by the California Supreme Court. Finally, the Chinese legal tradition created significant difficulties for the California criminal justice systems. Since many prosecutors did not understand Chinese customs and legal traditions, they were unable to effectively prosecute Chinese defendants, and on occasion they convicted the wrong person.

But what accounts for the 60 percent release (not guilty, hung jury, and dismissed) rate of Chinese defendants from the seven-county criminal justice systems? One explanation would be that the defendants had access to the legal representation provided for by one of the Chinese Six Companies or by the tongs.[108] If a Chinese member of a benevolent association became involved in legal difficulties, he could rest assured that the society would protect his rights. Unlike other minorities, such as Indians and Hispanics, who had difficulty obtaining counsel, the Chinese had immediate access to legal representation, which meant that they were protected during the early stages of questioning and preliminary hearings before justices of the peace.[109] The language barrier also worked in favor of Chinese defendants in that it presented great difficulties for constables, sheriffs, and prosecutors who were trying to sort out the facts of the homicide cases. Sometimes a long delay allowed the guilty parties to escape, and on occasion the guilty were released and fled the legal jurisdiction of the local authorities. The data verify that despite verbal and physical maltreatment by the white majority, the legal representation provided by the companies, associations, and tongs did assure that at least some of the Chinese defendants could gain a reasonable form of justice within the criminal justice systems of these seven California counties.

Chapter Three

Hispanics

Justice in a Conquered Land

*[I was] advised by the officer and a lawyer . . . to "plead guilty and git [sic] a
light sentence," and in my ignorance and bewilderment I did so, but in the light
of later years I see the error of such a plea.*
—Augustin Castro to Governor Henry T. Gage, January 18, 1899

Indigents charged with murder, most of whom knew virtually nothing about law,
faced the paralyzing dilemma of whether to plead guilty, in the hope that by
thus speeding up the criminal justice process and saving taxpayers' money they
would be given a light sentence, or to insist on their innocence, with the strong
chance that they would ultimately suffer the maximum punishment for the alleged crime. One such impoverished defendant, Augustin Castro, illustrates this
dilemma. After all, he had only himself to blame for the predicament in which
he found himself. Unfortunately, his trusting acceptance of the advice of the legal system resulted in many years in prison rather than the lighter sentence he
may have expected. In a drunken stupor Castro allegedly killed Matthew
Alderson, the owner of the Challenge Saloon in San Diego. Although this case
study chronicles only the legal struggles of Hispanic defendants, what happened
to Castro in the summer of 1872 was repeated over and over again among defendants throughout California, regardless of racial background.

During the period 1850–1900, the coastal counties of Santa Clara, Monterey,
San Luis Obispo, Santa Barbara, Los Angeles, and San Diego provided the cultural setting for a major confrontation between Hispanic society and white society. Although a significant body of scholarship has analyzed racial clashes on the
mining frontier,[1] the struggle for land in coastal California,[2] the marginalization
of Hispanics, and the development of ghettos in Los Angeles, Santa Barbara, and
San Jose,[3] criminal behavior—especially homicide—during this era remains relatively unexplored. By examining the treatment of Hispanic defendants in diverse
California counties, this study will provide a better understanding of how these
two cultural groups struggled to gain political and social power and the impact
of that struggle on the administration of justice during the nineteenth century.

TABLE 3.1

Hispanic Murderers by Victim's Race, 1850–1900

Race	Number	Percentage
White	48	27.5
Hispanic	103	58.9
Indian	17	9.7
Chinese	5	2.8
Black	2	1.1
Totals	175	100.0

Sources: Coroners' Inquests, Calaveras, Tuolumne, Sacramento, San Joaquin, San Luis Obispo, Santa Barbara, and San Diego Counties, 1850–1900.

Hispanics had the second-highest (behind Indians) interracial homicide rate, with 40 percent of their victims being non-Hispanic. The social mixing of Hispanics and whites, and to a lesser extent Indians, in saloons and brothels helps to explain the high rate. Such interaction created opportunities for petty squabbles, lubricated by alcohol, to turn violent. Hispanics killed forty-eight white people from 1850 to 1900 (Table 3.1). For example, on April 30, 1855, José Sabada and José M. Escobar quarreled with J. Sheldon outside a saloon on Washington Street in Sonora, Tuolumne County. The two Hispanics pulled knives and stabbed Sheldon to death. This killing especially aroused citizens of Sonora because the victim was a deaf mute. A jury found both men guilty of first-degree murder, and the judge sentenced them to death by hanging. On August 3, 1855, a crowd of "three to four thousand people—men, women and children" gathered to witness the execution.[4]

Hispanics also killed seventeen California Indians (Table 3.1) and were indicted in five of those cases (31 percent). Probably the most unusual case involved a Hispanic rancher in San Diego County. Because of the intrusion by Hispanic and white ranchers on their tribal land, California Indians had difficulty finding sufficient food to survive, and it was common practice to occasionally kill and butcher a steer. Sometime in late December 1850 or early January 1851, María Antonio Ortega discovered two California Indians butchering a steer on his Santa Ysabel Ranch. The justice of the peace described what happened: "I asked him [María Antonio Ortega] how he got those Indians, and he told me that he surprised them when they [were] skinning a beef cattle near St. Margarita, he took them prisoners, escorted them to his rancho tied, and shot them both."[5] With their hands tied behind them, Ortega shot each of them in the forehead with a pistol. Although legal authorities investigated these killings, they refused to prosecute.[6]

Hispanic legal heritage can be traced to Roman law and Las Siete Partidas, a code of law developed by Alfonso X in the thirteenth century that provides the strongest imprint on the Spanish judicial character.[7] Under Alfonso's guidance a group of scholars created this landmark document, which became the legal code, both civil and criminal, for Spain and her colonies. The legal jurists completed the final document in 1263, but Siete Partidas was not adopted until 1348. During the colonial era this code provided the basis for the practice of Spanish law in the colonies. Much of it was still being used during the nineteenth century.[8] This discussion will be limited to the application of the criminal section of Las Siete Partidas, especially homicide, in Mexico, California, New Mexico, and Texas during the eighteenth and nineteenth centuries.

On the eighteenth-century Spanish frontier the alcalde served a role similar to our justice of the peace.[9] If someone reported a crime, the alcalde would begin the legal process by holding a *sumaria* (similar to an indictment hearing) to determine the facts of the case, and then he would usually follow through by handling the legal proceedings from the *sumaria* to the completion of the process with the sentencing. His first duty was to arrest and imprison the accused to prevent flight from prosecution. During the *sumaria* the alcalde assumed that the accused had indeed committed the crime. Similar to the Chinese legal system, the alcalde received assistance in the investigation of the crime. He questioned witnesses to determine the name of the victim, the location, the type of weapon used, and other facts that might help in prosecuting the case. The *sumaria* would hopefully reveal the "truth" about the crime.[10] After determining the facts, the alcalde would confront the accused and request an *auto de confesión*. Usually the defendant would deny the crime and offer his own version of what happened. This "confession" ended the *sumaria* phase of the proceedings.[11]

During the second stage of the judicial proceedings, the *juicio plenario,* the prosecution and defense tried to prove their respective positions by producing witnesses to testify. The defendant usually asked someone to act as a *defensor* during the *plenario.* If he could find no one to defend him, the court provided legal counsel. It should be noted that there were virtually no trained lawyers on the northern frontier of New Spain and Mexico during the eighteenth and nineteenth centuries. Consequently, many defendants requested the services of well-established members of the community, such as wealthy landowners, businessmen, or tradesmen, as their *defensors*. If the alcalde failed to uncover all the facts in the case during the *plenario* he might call for a "face-to-face confrontation between the parties" to finally discover the truth.[12]

After the facts of the case had been determined to the satisfaction of the alcalde, he would proceed to the *sentencia,* the final phase of the judicial proceedings. In this stage of the legal hearing, the alcalde decided if there should be punishment and, if so, what type. Historian Charles R. Cutter notes that the judge had a variety of options and "might absolve the defendant, impose punishment, or strike something of a compromise between parties." Hispanic punishment proved to be much less severe than white-dominated discipline applied in nineteenth-century California. The alcalde wished to "repair the damage" and "to correct the defect of the guilty party" and hoped that the punishment would "serve as a deterrent to others."[13] After determining the form of punishment, he issued a "public proclamation" so that the entire community would know the final outcome of the judicial proceedings.

In most criminal cases the punishment took the form of a fine or a period of confinement. Spanish and Mexican authorities rarely executed defendants convicted of murder. In his study of homicide in colonial Mexico, William B. Taylor discovered 152 and 56 homicide cases in the provinces of Central Mexico and Mixtec Alta that ended with 4 (2.6 percent) and 10 (17.9 percent) executions, respectively.[14] Charles Cutter, in his study of crime in colonial New Mexico, noted that the Audiencia (judicial body) of Guadalajara handled 265 criminal cases and sent 7 "to the gallows in absentia," but "did not issue a single death sentence" in 1798.[15] David J. Langum discovered four executions in his study of Mexican California.[16] Similarly, historian Jill Mocho failed to uncover a single death sentence carried out in New Mexico during the period 1821–1846.[17] Richard L. Carrico also found that executions were rare in trials involving Indian defendants in Spanish California. Spanish authorities sentenced four Indian defendants to death but commuted the sentences to corporal punishment.[18]

Two main features reveal the disparity between Hispanic and white legal traditions. First, the Hispanic judicial process operated without trial by jury. Whites who became involved in the Mexican legal system in California complained bitterly about this. In civil cases it deprived them of trial by jury. Second, the Hispanic system failed to provide "a separation of judicial and executive functions."[19] Whites felt that allowing the alcalde to handle virtually the entire process—the *sumaria, plenario,* and *sentencia*—was unfair. In other words there was no separation of powers; the alcalde acted not only as the executive official but also as the magistrate or justice of the peace. The whites resented this judicial procedure that seemed so alien from their understanding of English common law. Equally problematic was the absence of lawyers on the Mexican frontier, which made it more difficult for white defendants, who would not trust a *defensor* of Hispanic heritage. Despite these complaints, Langum concluded that "there is no evidence that suggests they were treated more harshly than Californios were for equivalent activities."[20] Whites also complained about the prosecution of criminal cases; however, Langum determined that "for serious crimes there was generally vigorous investigation and prosecution."[21] Nevertheless, it was the "alien" process that most rankled the whites in Mexican California.

The Hispanic machismo code of honor preceded the white concept of the "Code of the West" by several centuries.[22] Though what will be described here is based upon recent research, it is believed that a machismo connection existed between the nineteenth century and today. The concept of machismo has a long history that originated in Spain and was introduced into Mexico and South America. It still exists today throughout Latin America and also is prevalent in other Mediterranean countries besides Spain. *Macho* means "power" and is associated with men. It implies someone who is strong and virile: to be macho is to be a good fighter, lover, horseman, to be fearless and to accept any challenge to your masculinity. There is a cult in Latin America surrounding the *hombre macho.* To be *muy macho* is to have power, and the *hombre macho* usually wields it without any thought of consequences. In the Hispanic culture a man has only two choices; he can be a *chingón* or he can be a *chingada.*[23] The *chingón,* of course, is the *hombre macho* who inflicts pain upon the *chingada,* a person who is passive or lacks significant power. In the context of machismo you either inflict pain or you receive it. To be a *chingada* implies that you are a failure and lack the male qualities of machismo. If you fail to accept the challenge of a *chingón* you lose face in front of all of your friends who may be watching. To be a *chingada* not only implies failure but also suggests that you are homosexual—a great insult in Hispanic culture.[24] To be called a *chingada* is the worst insult in the Hispanic world and often leads to violence.

One who lives in a society dominated by machismo must be strong, aggressive, and able to assert his masculinity. Machismo is a socially constructed, learned, and reinforced set of behaviors that constitutes the content of male gender roles in Hispanic society. This behavior is considered a public and not a household role. One often hears the expression "the woman is of the house, and man is of the street."[25] Away from home the male is free to pursue sexual liaisons with other women.[26] Hispanic wives tolerate their husbands' absence so long as support continues, and even express relief to be freed of their beatings and excessive drinking. Some suggest that machismo is used by males to "repress feelings of femininity." In other words, the *macho* uses the role of the virile he-man and the man of action to counteract this ambivalence. Consequently, the issue of bisexuality, or flight from femininity, is at the heart of Hispanic machismo.

The modern macho, who has to prove himself, is the insecure product of this "metaphysical bisexuality." Haunted by femininity, he tries to compensate by assuming the hypermasculine Hispanic role, which disdains and fears women and everything feminine. From early childhood the boy must struggle with the dichotomy of the machismo-versus-*mariansimo* polarity—maleness versus femininity. At an early age the young macho develops an ambivalence toward women, who are clearly less valued in Hispanic society. In later years he pours out his resentment by devaluing, depreciating, and humiliating his wife or mistress. The ambivalence that he experiences is extended toward two types of women: good women (meaning his mother, sisters, wife, daughters) and bad women (meaning those who are less respectable and who can be taken as mistresses). During childhood the sign of virility for the Mexican male is courage to the point of recklessness, aggressiveness, and unwillingness to run away from a fight. In rich language and with great attention, the macho woos his future mate. But after marriage she is expected to become her husband's "slave" and satisfy his every desire.

Hispanic men gathered in *pulquerías,* or saloons, to pass time by drinking and gambling.[27] In this setting patrons expected alcohol to be a source of *alegría,* or happiness. However, the release of emotions and the hurling of insults could be dangerous. If the victim of such abusive language failed to challenge his tormentors, he would be labeled a *chingada.* Verbal and physical aggression were a common outcome of drunkenness, and *pulquerías* became centers of violent confrontation. Violence between Hispanic males often began with "fighting words" or insults such as *puta* ("whore"), *cabrón* ("he-goat" or "cuckold"), *alcahuete* ("pimp"), *borracho* ("drunkard"), and *perro* ("dog"). Such epithets could quickly start a fight that might turn lethal. An especially offensive phrase in Mexico was *hijo de la chingada,*[28] which basically means "son of a violated woman." This expression proved to be the most dangerous of all the fighting words. In his study of homicide in colonial Mexico, historian William Taylor identified a great variety of fighting words that carried a strong macho tone.[29] Taylor concluded that in many homicides that took place in *pulquerías* the killing occurred mainly in response to verbal challenges.

In a study on homicide in frontier New Mexico, Jill Mocho discovered several murders that were the "result of a spontaneous outbreak of violence between friends or acquaintances, provoked by humiliation or injured pride."[30] Mocho found that when a man caught a friend or acquaintance *in flagrante delicto* with his wife the outcome was usually death—and most Hispanic courts did not convict the husband under such circumstances. Hispanic homicides in California reflect this strong emphasis on macho; a male must either answer the challenge or lose face. To allow someone to take advantage of his woman was the most deadly challenge to a man's masculinity.

Perhaps the Joseph Hurtado murder case provides the best example of the dangers and legal implications of machismo, the Hispanic code of honor. Joseph Hurtado worked as a boat pilot on the Sacramento River, a job that kept him away from home a good deal of the time. Eventually he became suspicious of his wife's behavior, and after finding evidence sufficient to satisfy his own mind, Hurtado "suddenly charged his wife with having been unfaithful."[31] After first denying it, she finally admitted having sexual intercourse with José Estuardo on a number of occasions. Suffering great anguish that night, Hurtado got up and went to see A. W. Morrison, the bookkeeper for the Western Hotel, confided in him about the seduction of his wife, and "expressed an intention of going and killing Estuardo on sight."[32] Morrison cautioned him not to take such action for the sake of the child, and instead suggested that Estuardo might be encouraged to leave town in order to resolve the marital issue. Morrison convinced Hurtado that he must control himself, and he took Hurtado's gun for safekeeping. The next morning Hurtado confronted Estuardo, who begged, "[D]o with me as you please but for god's sake don't kill me."[33] Hurtado returned home and after a long argument his wife agreed to a separation; she would go to San Jose and live with her family for a while. After several weeks she returned to Sacramento and agreed never to see Estuardo again. The first day in their new house, Hurtado, returning from work, saw Estuardo emerging from the building. Walking on down the street, Estuardo said, "Hello, José, I see your wife has got back."[34] Infuriated by this comment, Hurtado went to his apartment, picked up his handgun, marched back down the street, and smacked Estuardo in the face with the gun. Two days later, Estuardo swore out a warrant against Hurtado for assault with a deadly weapon. After being arrested, Hurtado posted bail and appeared at the police court to ask for a continuance, which was granted. Estuardo, attending the proceedings, stood up in the courtroom and demanded in a loud voice, "Judge I want that man held on a more serious charge, that of assault to murder. He is a dangerous man to be at large."[35] An angry Hurtado left and went to a saloon across the street, where he began to drink with three friends. After a few minutes one of his friends, who was looking out the door, said, "[H]ere comes Estuardo." Hurtado "immediately rushed out of the saloon in an uncontrollable passion and shot him dead."[36] In March 1882 authorities in Sacramento arrested and indicted Joseph Hurtado for murder. He was tried, convicted of first-degree murder, and sentenced to death.[37]

Superior Court judge John Aunstory, who fixed the time of the execution but did not actually try the case, suggested that the death sentence was too harsh a punishment for the crime. He recommended that "justice will be accomplished by commuting his sentence to imprisonment for life."[38] The *Vidette,* a local newspaper, editorialized that the alleged crime was, at the worst, "justifiable homicide." The editor suggested that Estuardo was a brute who "not only seduced his [Hurtado's] weak-minded wife, but boasted of what he had accomplished. Hurtado killed him, we think he did right."[39] In a petition for clemency, a group of citizens complained that Hurtado "was denied the privilege of proving to the jury, in defense of said homicide, the *fact* of such seduction" of his wife that led to the shooting.[40] R. F. Del Valle, an attorney from Los Angeles, complained that "a man has been convicted of one of the highest crimes known to the law, and to suffer its extreme penalty for defending his manhood, home and family [is unfair]."[41] Del Valle clearly understood the importance that Hispanic honor played in this crime.

During an appeal to the California Supreme Court, an appellant brief revealed that Hurtado's counsel tried to introduce testimony to prove that the deceased had committed adultery with the defendant's wife. Prosecution objected to the testimony and was sustained by the court. During the appeal, defense claimed that "under our statute manslaughter is the unlawful killing of a human being upon a sudden quarrel or *heat of passion.*"[42] Defense counsel argued that the knowledge that adultery had taken place would be "a provocation recognized by the law as being sufficient to arouse the passion, and thus to reduce the crime to manslaughter, and therefore that fact is admissible in evidence for that purpose."[43] Further, "the killing of the deceased by the defendant was a conceded fact; the only question in issue was as to the condition of the defendant's mind, and proof of communicated statements made by the wife prior to the homicide, must have tended to illustrate the question."[44] During the trial, defense counsel requested that the court instruct the jury: "It is proper for the jury to take into consideration the statements made to him of the seduction of his wife by the deceased, as proper for you to consider in arriving at a conclusion as to whether he understood and was legally responsible for the killing; also, to aid in arriving at the conclusion as to whether the act was premeditated, or done with malice."[45] The judge refused and instructed the jury that "neither the seduction of the defendant's wife by the deceased, nor an adulterous intercourse between her and the deceased, will constitute an excuse or justification for his killing."[46] Defense counsel argued that this last instruction, "when stated without qualification," would mislead the jury.

After hearing arguments in this case, California Supreme Court justice E. W. McKinstry wrote the opinion. The court ruled that "the law . . . makes the offense manslaughter when it is committed under the influence of passion caused by an insult or provocation sufficient to excite an irresistible passion in a reasonable person."[47] During the trial, testimony by saloon keeper Thomas Waters revealed that Hurtado had visited his saloon on the day of the crime. Waters noticed that after buying drinks for himself and three companions, Hurtado got up and went to the door to look out toward the police court twice before leaving. Waters stated: "[I]t was less than a minute from the time he went out before I heard the first shot."[48] The court concluded that this evidence suggested that the defendant "lay in wait" for the deceased. Further, it concluded that "it was for the jury to determine from the evidence whether defendant was justified in arming himself and in using his arms."[49] The court could find no error that "demands a reversal of the judgment or a new trial." Judgment of the court was affirmed.[50]

If Hurtado had been tried by an alcalde in the Mexican judicial system or by a jury of Hispanic "peers" in Sacramento County, he would most likely have been found not guilty.[51] However, the prosecutor, judge, and jury came from a different cultural background. Still, if Hurtado had caught Estuardo *in flagrante delicto* with his wife, the jury might have been sympathetic. The verdict suggests that the prosecutor painted a convincing picture to the jury of the "evil" Hurtado "lying in wait" for his victim. Considering the circumstances, the portrayal seems a little thin, but the jury accepted the prosecutor's version of the killing. From a Hispanic perspective the concept of machismo required action from Hurtado; otherwise he would lose face in front of his drinking pals in the saloon. The Hispanic honor code thus claimed another victim by violence, and Hurtado had to pay the price for that moment when he became the *chingón* and killed Estuardo, the *chingada*. As is often the case in Hispanic society, the machismo honor code proved to be costly. Many other similar cases involving love triangles also illuminate the *macho* cult and its dangers.[52]

Some homicide cases more than others provide illumination of the criminal justice process and the treatment of indigent Hispanic defendants. On Friday night, April 5, 1872, a group of people gathered in Matthew Alderson's Challenge Saloon at Fifth and Columbia Streets in San Diego to drink and listen to music being played by the proprietor and two other men. It was about 9:00 P.M. when W. B. Carleton stated that he noticed a "Spaniard or Sonoran" who appeared to be under the influence enter the saloon. The Mexican began drinking at the bar, talked loudly, and called for more wine. The bartender refused.[53] Finally, one of the bartenders put him out of the bar, but he came back in. He began to display a knife with the tip of the blade broken off, and Alderson asked him to put it down and leave. After walking out the door, the Mexican asked for his knife, and Alderson picked it up off the table and stepped out the door. A few moments later, Carleton heard a shot and rushed out the door, but he could not see anyone because it was so dark and there were no streetlights.[54] He began to grope about on the porch and found Alderson lying in a pool of blood, shot one time in the head at very close range. Dr. R. J. Gregg, the examining surgeon, found one wound, with the bullet lodged in the base of the brain. "The appearance of wound, close shot, powder marks" indicated that the assailant was very close to the victim.[55] Although Carleton did not see the shooting, he stated: "I think that Mexican did it." J. Mathias, the bartender, identified the man that he put out the door as the defendant, Augustin Castro.[56]

Ben Mannasse had been in the saloon for a while that evening and then returned to his home, just across the street. He heard Alderson and Castro talking outside, and when he looked out of the window, he saw them both in front of the saloon. A few moments later Mannasse heard a shot fired and saw a flash from the gun.[57] He then heard someone running toward the Government Corral, but he did not see who it was because there were no streetlights and it was a very dark night. H. Baslow testified that he was standing in front of a market across from the saloon when he saw two men come out. A shot was fired, and a man ran across the street. Another witness heard the man running say, "God damn you, I've shot you."[58] Constable A. M. Young was the first law enforcement officer to reach the crime scene. After hearing what had happened, he borrowed a pistol from one of the patrons and then with their help began to search for the assailant. Constable Young walked over to the corral, followed the fence, and about two hundred feet from the crime scene he discovered Castro. Young testified that Castro "was preparing to shoot me when I rushed upon him."[59]

On the surface of it, this appears to be an open-and-shut case. At the trial, Sheriff S. W. Craigue testified that although Young found Castro first, "I went up to him; he was laying alongside of the fence in what I considered at the time, and do now, a drunken stupor; stupidly drunk." He did not have a gun in his hand, and he was not about to "shoot or rush" Constable Young. Sheriff Craigue continued: "[W]hat convinces me that he was unconscious is that it was an hour after the occurrence, [of the shooting] and it being a very dark night he would have escaped, I think, if he had been in his senses." When Castro woke up the next morning in his cell, the jailer informed the sheriff that the defendant had no idea where he was or why he was there. The sheriff concluded, "I consider from what I saw and learned that night was a blank to him."[60]

On April 25, when the defendant was taken before Justice Skinner, he waived examination, and the justice ordered him held in jail to await grand jury action.[61] On July 11, Castro, with attorney Chalmers Scott, appeared before District Court judge H. C. Rolfe. Castro, on the advice of defense counsel, pled guilty to murder.[62] The judge then ordered the defendant sworn and examined. Castro, a twenty-three-year-old Hispanic, testified that he had been born in San Francisco and had lived most of his life in Santa Cruz. He had arrived in San Diego County about a month before the killing and had been employed herding and shearing sheep and had come to town on the day of the crime. Castro admitted drinking wine most of the afternoon and said: "I don't know where I went to this day, until I was locked up in jail." The defendant also claimed he neither knew Alderson nor saw him the day of the killing. Castro stated: "I don't remember of being in the saloon that night."[63] He admitted that he seldom drank wine until that Friday. After hearing the testimony of Castro and Sheriff Craigue, Judge Rolfe found the defendant guilty of second-degree murder and sentenced him to life in prison.

Even though no one actually saw him shoot the victim, the evidence that Castro committed the killing is convincing. Machismo may have been an important factor that helps to explain this murder. It is possible that Castro viewed being put out of the bar as a challenge to his manhood. And since he was already heavily under the influence of liquor, his judgment might have been impaired, but probably not his feeling that a "gringo" had challenged him in front of many people. Also, some of the facts cloud the verdict. For example, Constable Young testified that he found a Colt revolver in the possession of the defendant with "two chambers empty."[64] But why did the constable and the sheriff fail to examine the gun to determine whether it had been recently fired? And does "two chambers empty" mean that two shots had been fired? All witnesses testified that they heard only one shot. Maybe the constable meant that one chamber had been fired and another chamber had no cartridge in it. With single-action Colt revolvers, it was common to leave empty the chamber over which the hammer rests in order to prevent an accidental misfire. However, there is no indication that that was what the constable meant when he testified about the crime; he was suggesting that the gun had been fired twice.

Another mystery is the lack of any legal defense by counsel for the defendant. Typically during this era, indigent defendants received court-appointed counsel—in this case Chalmers Scott.[65] Considering that most of the evidence was circumstantial, defense counsel might have gone to trial and fought for a reduced charge of manslaughter. Three things might explain why the defense attorney did not take this approach in defense of the client. First, Alderson had become an influential member of the community and, immediately after the crime had occurred, some local citizens threatened to take the prisoner by force. Fearing mob action, Sheriff Craigue rushed down the street with his prisoner.[66] The sheriff reached the jail safely and quickly locked Castro in a cell for safekeeping. Under these circumstances, it is possible that defense counsel felt that he would be unable to find a sympathetic jury for his client.

Two other explanations for the lack of defense seem more plausible. Chalmers Scott had recently arrived in San Diego and had very little experience in the practice of law. In fact, he had spent much of his life working as a surveyor. With limited criminal law experience, Scott may have felt that his defense efforts would fail. A third explanation also presents itself, however. Scott and the district attorney, W. T. McNealy, had worked together on the prosecution of the highly publicized Fenwick homicide case, in which Scott had made the opening argument for the prosecution.[67] It is significant that the Fenwick case finished in the courts just a few weeks before the Castro case came to trial. Scott, acting as Castro's defense counsel, apparently recommended to his client that he plead guilty, probably with the stipulation by the prosecution that they not seek conviction for first-degree murder.

While in San Quentin, Castro had virtually no one to intercede on his behalf, but he learned by experience that if the prosecutor and judge who presided over your trial could be induced to write letters, it was possible to gain executive clemency. After spending eighteen years in San Quentin, Castro began to write letters to McNealy and Rolfe, the two men most responsible for sending him to prison. By this time both men were convinced that he had served enough time for his crime. McNealy wrote to Rolfe:"I agree with you, that this man [Castro] has been sufficiently punished."[68] In a letter providing facts about the Castro trial and asking for executive clemency, Rolfe wrote:"At the time I had doubts whether he was not more unfortunate than criminal."[69] Prison authorities paroled Castro on June 19, 1901, and the governor granted him a full pardon in January 1903. Castro had entered San Quentin a young man of twenty-three; at age fifty-two he left the prison walls to start a new life.

The 1860s were the major historical watershed for changing political fortunes in Santa Barbara County. During that decade the influx of white immigrants overwhelmed the Hispanic majority. While Hispanics dominated Santa Barbara with "70 percent of the total population" in 1860, a decade later whites, with 54 percent of the population, had gained control of Santa Barbara society and politics.[70] Within that decade of dramatic population and political change, one homicide case, the killing of the Frenchman Domingo Abadie by Francisco Javier Bonilla, best illustrates the transformation that occurred between Hispanic and white society. The Bonilla case is especially significant for several reasons: it reveals the methods that the district attorney used to impanel a jury; it illuminates the emotional and racial divisions within the community; and it provides an opportunity to examine the criminal justice system in Santa Barbara County.

Abadie, a Frenchman married to Refugio, Isabel Yorba's daughter, lived in Santa Barbara. Isabel Yorba, owner of Rancho Laguna southeast of Santa Barbara near Point Mugu (now Ventura County), had hired Patricio Bonilla as *mayordomo* to manage livestock on her property. Apparently, Abadie quarreled with Patricio over the movement of some horses on Rancho Laguna. During the argument, Abadie grabbed Patricio by the beard, shook and pushed him, forcing Francisco to intercede; the scuffle ended with harsh words from both men. The next day Patricio sent Francisco into town with a message for Isabel Yorba requesting instructions on the management of the ranch.[71] Abadie, an influential man in Santa Barbara, had Francisco arrested and held in jail for three days. On July 24, 1868, Abadie returned to Rancho Laguna armed with two shotguns and a pistol.[72] Apparently, after arriving at the ranch Domingo Abadie began to argue with Teodosio Bonilla, claiming that his father was no longer the *mayordomo* and therefore he and Francisco had no right to put horses into the corral. According to one witness, when Francisco encountered Abadie, Domingo talked loudly and attempted to draw his pistol. Francisco immediately drew his pistol, fired four shots, and killed Domingo Abadie.[73] After the shooting, Juan Abadie claimed that his brother Domingo had been unarmed. Juan Abadie admitted in court that although he did not see them, he heard the argument from the kitchen and quickly came to the aid of his brother. When Juan attempted to shoot Francisco, his gun misfired. Moments later Juan fired at Teodosio Bonilla, Francisco's younger brother, who returned the fire. Neither was injured, and Francisco quickly fled Rancho Laguna on horseback. Francisco remained in hiding for a month before finally being brought in to the home of José Antonio de la Guerra y Noriega by his father and turned over to the sheriff.[74]

Bonilla's trial opened in Santa Barbara in the First District Court, with Judge Pablo de la Guerra presiding. The impaneling of the jury proved to be a decisive victory for the prosecution. The district attorney hired A. Packard, a well-known and persuasive lawyer, to assist him in his prosecution of the Bonilla case. The district attorney and defense counsels Charles E. Huse and William D. Chillson had a jury pool of seventy-nine men, including eighteen Hispanics (22 percent), from which to select. Eight of the first twelve jurors drawn for impaneling were Hispanic, but not a single one was accepted as a juror. The final jury consisted of eleven whites and one "Spaniard," Ysidro Obiols, who was selected in the final voir dire.[75] Defense attorney Huse failed to put a single Californio on the jury. Later, in a commutation appeal sent to the governor to save Bonilla from the death penalty, Huse complained: "[T]he jury, as the record of their names shows, were all Americans, or Europeans from the North of Europe, who had no sympathies in common with the race to which the prisoner belongs, except one juryman who was a Spaniard, from old Spain." The Spaniard proved to be a problem for the defense, and Huse protested: "[I]t is well known that there exists a hereditary hatred between natives of old Spain and the mixed races of Mexico, to which the prisoner belongs."[76]

Huse and Chillson had been hired to defend Bonilla against the charge of murder. Huse seemed an odd choice for defense counsel, for he had a long record of hostility toward Californios. In 1852, after spending two years in San Francisco, he had moved south and settled in Santa Barbara. He soon became a strong force in local politics. Huse had claimed that the Californios in "Santa Barbara were the scum of the earth."[77] During his short career as reporter and editor for the *Santa Barbara Gazette*, he used it as a forum to attack Californios.

This trial is unique among the hundreds of homicide cases examined because testimony was given in both Spanish and English. Huse complained that the "Spaniard was the only man in the jury who understood the Spanish language in which all the material testimony was given."[78] The questions were put to Hispanic witnesses in Spanish, or occasionally in English. The answers from Hispanic witnesses, however, were always given in Spanish. The intriguing question is this: did the white jurors understand all of the testimony? The court transcript offers nothing to verify or refute Huse's statement to the governor about the prejudiced jury. Huse, who spoke Spanish, Italian, German, and English, had "made his early living as a lawyer and an interpreter for Judge Joaquin Carrillo," so his judgment on the language problem would seem to be accurate.[79] In 1860,

Judge Pablo de la Guerra explained to a friend the difficulty that often occurred in dealing with language issues in court. Discussing the questioning of witnesses, the judge lamented:

> He is asked questions of which the witness does not understand the largest part thoroughly because the interpreter does not know how to speak to him in his own language and the witness responds to it in a language that the interpreter does not understand well and this makes translations full of errors at least so disfiguring that the witness speaks of a shearing and the interpreter speaks of a full and robust body. . . . I have seen much, very much, of which the principal culprit [is] the poor translator who ought not to know Castilian but the language of the ranchers, he who surely does not know it of the interpreter.[80]

The case for the charge of first-degree murder against Bonilla was not strong. The testimony of prosecution witnesses on whether Domingo Abadie was unarmed was inconsistent. José Dolores Chapman testified that Domingo "usually carried a six shooter with him." Juan Antonio Rodriguez said Juan Abadie had a pistol in his hand, but failed to mention whether Domingo Abadie had one. Teodosio stated that Domingo "spoke loud" in addressing him and appeared to be somewhat excited.[81] It seems doubtful that Abadie was unarmed. Years later, one newspaper reporter suggested that after the argument between Abadie and Patricio Bonilla, "Abadie returned to the ranch armed to the teeth, had two or three double-barreled shotguns in his buggy when he passed through San Buenaventura."[82] Horace Bell claimed that Abadie "deserved killing" and that Bonilla was justified. Bell said that "it was absolute self defense."[83] Of course the victim also had supporters; the editor of the *Ventura Free Press* complained that "Abadie spoke roughly to Benilla [sic] who retired, armed himself, returned immediately and shot his employer dead." District Attorney J. H. Kinkaid informed the governor that "the killing was an unprovoked cold blooded malicious murder."[84]

There is no way of knowing whether Domingo Abadie was armed that day, but considering the strong gun culture of the era, one would expect that he probably was carrying a handgun. A more serious issue is why Bonilla fired four shots from his revolver and whether they were rapid-fire or spaced out. If he had fired only one or two shots, he might have been able to claim self-defense, but four shots suggests malice aforethought—thus first-degree murder. The jury apparently believed the prosecution's interpretation of the facts as given by their witnesses. Whether the jury allowed their own prejudices to enter the deliberations is unknown. One writer suggests that "a jury verdict is a quotient of the prejudices of twelve people."[85] Oliver Wendell Holmes may have provided the most astute observation on juries when he said: "[O]ne of the gravest defects from the point of view of their theoretical function [is] that they will introduce into their verdict a certain amount—a very large amount, so far as I have observed—of popular prejudice, and thus keep the administration of the law in accord with the wishes and feelings of the community."[86] Our system of justice is predicated on finding twelve jurors who can set aside their biases and prejudices while accepting testimony and judicial instructions. That may have been impossible in Santa Barbara in 1868.

The composition of the jury in this case merits further analysis. The white-dominated system of jurisprudence assumes that defendants are tried by impartial juries and that prospective jurors "appear in court with a blank slate, neutral and untainted by life experiences or pretrial publicity."[87] That, of course, just does not happen. Another assumption is that through the voir dire process the lawyers and the judge will eliminate those prospective jurors who are "irrevocably prejudiced" against the defendant. Anyone who has watched *Twelve Angry Men* must have been bewildered by the flagrant display of racism and bigotry by some of the jurors and the unlikely premise that this bias could be overcome by discussion and result in a verdict of not guilty. How did these bigoted jurors survive the voir dire process? The rational answer is that in many cases lawyers do not probe the jurors deeply enough to reveal bias or prejudice. In the Bonilla case the prosecutor challenged all prospective Hispanic jurors, with the exception of the "peninsular Spaniard," who may have harbored prejudicial feelings toward the mestizo defendant. Unfortunately no impaneling testimony that would enable us to assess the voir dire proceedings is available. Did defense attorney Huse make a critical error by not requesting an additional voir dire with more Hispanics to choose from? Did the prosecutor indeed "outfox" the defense? The conviction of Bonilla supports this view.

By 1868, whites dominated the jury pool in Santa Barbara County. White merchants, farmers, and ranchers certainly did not share a common heritage with the defendant, and most probably viewed Bonilla as an outsider. The distinct cultural differences in values, speech, dress, and behavior between the jurors, prosecutor, and defense counsel on one side and the defendant on the other would not easily be bridged during the trial process.[88] In other words, the defendant had a great deal of cultural baggage that proved to be a liability. Even the Hispanic judge came from a very different tradition, especially in terms of social status and economic wealth. The Spanish language provided the only cultural bond between them, and that, too, would be disparate. The jurors, many of whom had recently arrived from Eastern states, were unable to relate to Bonilla's culture, and perceived it to be inferior to their own.[89]

In the final instructions to the jury, the judge stated that if they believed that Patricio Bonilla had been *mayordomo* in charge of Rancho Laguna and that Domingo Abadie had interfered with the management of the ranch and was killed during the quarrel, they could not find the defendant guilty of first-degree murder. Further, if they found that the defendant "killed the deceased without malice, either expressed or implied, but in the heat of passion . . . the killing was not murder . . . but only manslaughter."[90] After deliberating for less than four hours the jury found Bonilla guilty of first-degree murder. Judge Pablo de la Guerra sentenced Bonilla to death by hanging, to be carried out on November 28, 1868.

Sometimes murder cases like this one take interesting twists. Charles Huse, with the aid of the Coffroth and Spaulding law firm, immediately filed an appeal with the California Supreme Court. Huse argued that the indictment against Bonilla stipulated that the homicide was committed "with *premeditation* and with malice aforethought," and during the trial the judge refused to give the following instructions: "In order to convict the defendant of murder in the first degree, under an indictment which alleges a *premeditated design* to effect the death of the person killed, the premeditated design or express malice must be proved." Appellant also claimed that the death warrant "order of the 8th of January, 1869, was irregular and void."[91] Justice Silas W. Sanderson delivered the opinion that the court of origin "properly refused" to give the instructions. "Malice is of two kinds—express[ed] and implied—and either equally supports a verdict of guilty in the first degree."[92] On the second issue the court ruled that the execution warrant was technically improper because "the day should be designated in the warrant, and not in the judgment." That error, however, did not invalidate the death penalty sentence. To correct the problem, the court simply needed to bring the defendant back into court, date and issue a new warrant, and remand the defendant into the custody of the sheriff for execution of sentence.[93]

After failing to win at the supreme court level, defense counsel turned quickly to seek a commutation of the death sentence to life in prison. Huse, Judge Pablo de la Guerra, and many other supporters inundated Governor H. H. Haight with petitions and letters in an attempt to save Bonilla's life. In his letter pleading for clemency, José A. Godoy, the Mexican consul, stated that he understood the governor's position that "all the circumstances of this case had been taken into consideration" when he refused to commute the sentence. But, pleading that Bonilla was just eighteen years of age, Godoy asked: "Would you, Ex[cellency], send a mere boy to the scaffold?"[94] Judge Pablo de la Guerra argued that Bonilla's father, Patricio, "himself delivered his son" to the sheriff, knowing that the law had to be upheld but "earnestly believing at heart that the blood of his own son would not be shed by hands of the law." De la Guerra concluded: "This I think is one of those cases for which the power of pardoning or commuting a sentence has been put in your hands."[95] A petition signed by 221 Santa Barbara citizens was forwarded to the governor, requesting that he commute the death sentence to life imprisonment.[96] With so many pleas, the governor changed his mind and, just eight days before the execution date, he commuted Bonilla's sentence to a term of thirty-five years in prison.[97]

Robberies committed in the gold camp counties sometimes escalated into homicides. Shipments of gold from the mines were always an enticement for men who wanted to get rich quick. On Saturday, September 30, 1868, four men lay in wait for Elkanah Said and two mine employees, who were transporting a shipment of gold from the Petticoat Mine, located near Railroad Flat a few miles from Mokelumne Hill in Calaveras County. About three miles from the mine the four men ambushed the gold carriers, but instead of using a barricade to stop the buggy and its occupants, the robbers posted two men to step in front and two men to come in behind the buggy after it passed, hoping to prevent anyone from escaping. Upon seeing the buggy approaching, Paul Tibeaux stepped out in front of it, shouted stop, and fired two blasts from a shotgun, killing Said, the driver, instantly. E. E. Meeks, one of the men in the buggy, jumped out the back and ran toward the bushes but was stopped by José Coyado and Baptiste Denny. The latter robbed him of his money (sixty-three dollars in cash) and let him go. In the meantime, the quick-thinking Daniel Keese, who was riding in the front of the buggy with Said, grabbed the reins, whipped the horses, and escaped with the victim's body and the gold shipment, galloping all the way to Mokelumne Hill.[98] By failing to block the road, the robbers missed the large gold shipment and had only sixty-three dollars to show for their trouble. Worse, they were now wanted for murder. Molina, Tibeaux, and Denny split the money three ways and headed south to Mariposa. Coyado, who had only recently met his accomplices, turned and followed the road north to Fiddletown in Amador County.

   After arriving in Mokelumne Hill with Said's body, Keese told the sheriff what had happened. At the coroner's inquest Dr. A. H. Hoerehner examined the body of the deceased and discovered three large shotgun pellets. One had hit the victim in the face, "tearing away a portion of the lower jaw, one in the right side of the neck, and the other passing through the upper portion of his heart."[99] G. W. Hopkins, owner of the Petticoat Mine, offered a two thousand–dollar reward for the apprehension of the robbers. Sheriff R. K. Thorn traced the three who were traveling south until the trail turned cold, and after leaving information on the suspects with the sheriff of Mariposa, he returned to San Andreas, Calaveras County. On January 14, 1869, Mariposa authorities located and arrested Molina and turned him over to the Calaveras County sheriff. About three months later, Sheriff Thorn arrested Coyado near Fiddletown (Amador County) and put him in the Calaveras County Jail.[100]

   Just four days after his arrest, Coyado talked to the sheriff without advice of counsel. Sheriff Thorn recalled that Coyado asked to talk to him on April 18. Coyado provided the sheriff with detailed information about the botched robbery, the names of the other three men, numerous details of how they met, where they went to get supplies, what time they had arrived in the vicinity of the mine, and how they had planned to rob the gold shipment. Coyado explained that Tibeaux and Molina were to stop the buggy, but Tibeaux "shot the same time [he shouted stop] and fired again immediately." Under cross-examination by defense counsel, Sheriff Thorn admitted that the first time he talked to Coyado they spoke in Spanish: "I can't talk Spanish grammatically. Don't understand thoroughly. I believe that I did understand every word used by prisoner in the first conversation."[101] When Coyado was arraigned (April 19, 1869), he began to talk again, so the sheriff took him aside in an office with two other witnesses to take a complete written statement. Walter L. Hopkins, the court-appointed attorney for the defendant, complained, and the sheriff returned the prisoner to the courtroom.[102]

During the impaneling of the jury, the judge had to ask Sheriff Thorn to return with a special venire to complete the selection. Defense counsel objected that Sheriff Thorn, in front of prospective jurors, had expressed his "beliefs that the defendant was guilty of the offence charged."[103] The motion to quash the panel was denied. After the prosecution presented its evidence, Hopkins, the defense counsel, "moved the Court, for the discharge of the defendant on the grounds that there is a substantial variance between the evidence adduced herein and the crime charged in the indictment."[104] After that motion was denied, the defense counsel refused to present any evidence on behalf of the defendant. Final arguments were made, the judge instructed the jury, and they retired to deliberate. The trial ended with a guilty verdict, murder in the first degree. Defense counsel filed an arrest of judgment and called for a new trial, both of which were denied. On November 2, 1870, Judge A. C. Adams sentenced Coyado to "be hanged by the neck until you are dead."[105]

Defense counsel quickly filed an appeal to the California Supreme Court. In his brief Hopkins claimed that the court had committed an error by overruling the defendant's challenge to the panel and list of jurors appearing in the special venire needed to complete the impaneling. Hopkins also claimed that the indictment alleged that "*Paul Tibeaux* did kill and murder one Elkanah Said" and that two others, along with José B. Coyado, aided Tibeaux in committing the murder. The evidence submitted proved only that a Frenchman named "Paula" had actually "fired the fatal shot," not Paul Tibeaux. Further, defense counsel contended that "there was no evidence tending to prove that the defendant José B. Coyado, was in any manner concerned or implicated in the killing of Mr. Said, except as an accessory before the fact."[106]

California attorney general Jo Hamilton, for the respondent, argued that "the challenge referred to in Section 337, relied on by appellant's attorney, relates only to special jurors, but does not refer to trial jurors at all, but applies alone to grand jurors." Further, Hamilton claimed that "if, on the trial under the second count in the indictment, any of the defendants did the killing, and the defendant aided and abetted or assisted," they were equally guilty of murder.[107]

Justice Jackson Temple delivered the opinion, with which three other justices concurred. Turning to the complaint by defense counsel that Sheriff Thorn had prejudiced the special venire by suggesting that the defendant was guilty, the court ruled that "Section 337, of the Criminal Practice Act, provides that a challenge may be made to the panel on account of any bias of the officer summoning them, which would be good ground of challenge to a juror; and we think the ruling of the Court in denying the challenge clearly erroneous."[108] Turning to the indictment, Temple argued that "the evidence was that the fatal shot was fired by a Frenchman by the name of Paul, and there was no evidence to show that Paul Tibeaux had anything to do with the homicide." This may have been an oversight by the prosecution, "but the total absence of proof upon that point is fatal to the verdict. It would be contrary to the instruction of the Court, and therefore, erroneous."[109] The California Supreme Court reversed the judgment and ordered a new trial.

In April 1872 the second trial reached a similar conclusion, the defendant was convicted of murder in the first degree and sentenced to death by hanging to take place on Friday, June 21, 1872. Despite an attempt to gain clemency, the governor refused to intercede.[110] Coyado seemed "unconcerned about his fate" until the day of the execution; however, when he became aware that the execution would not be stopped, he began to show signs "of the keenest anguish." He refused to eat supper the night before the appointed date of the hanging, but on the morning of June 21, Friday, he had ham and eggs. "Early in the forenoon a dispatch was received from the Governor . . . stating that he had examined the facts in the case and saw no sufficient reason for preventing the law from taking its course."[111] This news devastated Coyado. After the condemned man was given the last rites, Sheriff Thorn led him to the gallows, where he was asked if he had any last words. Coyado replied through an interpreter "that he was being unjustly hung . . . because he was poor and ignorant."[112] A newspaper reporter described the execution:

> His arms and legs were pinioned, the noose adjusted and a black cap drawn over his face shutting out the world from his view forever. There was a moment of almost unbearable suspense, even to the spectators. Sheriff Thorn placed his hand upon the lever that supported the trap, the door flew violently open with a muffled thud, and at precisely 22 minutes past 12 o'clock José B. Coyado expiated his crimes with his life.[113]

In retrospect, it becomes clear that Coyado made a fatal mistake when he talked about the crime with the sheriff without an attorney present. Even though he had killed no one, he paid with his life for his error.

*   *   *

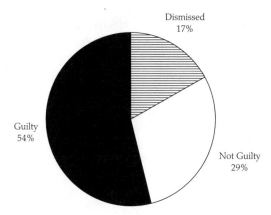

Fig. 3.1. Verdicts: Hispanic Defendants, Seven California Counties, 1850–1900

In the seven-county area under consideration here, authorities indicted 119 of 175 accused Hispanics for manslaughter or murder. Calaveras and Tuolumne Counties had the highest numbers of indictments—22 and 21, respectively— while San Joaquin County had 10. Conviction rates for Hispanics averaged 54 percent (Fig. 3.1). Hispanic defendants in Santa Barbara were more likely to be found guilty (78 percent were convicted), while in San Luis Obispo, the conviction rate was 31 percent, the lowest of the seven counties. An average of 29 percent of the Hispanic defendants were found not guilty and another 17 percent had their cases dismissed.

When Hispanics killed white people their conviction rates increased significantly, to 65 percent, and the not guilty and dismissal rates dropped to 15 and 20 percent, respectively. The data suggest that murder of a white person was considered more important than murder of a Hispanic, Indian, or Chinese person. These figures parallel those for Indian defendants accused of killing white victims. Sentencing data show that 25 percent of the Hispanics convicted received the death penalty, while 14 percent were sentenced to life in prison. Fifty percent of the death penalty cases (eight defendants) involved white victims, and 50 percent involved Hispanic victims.

After researching Hispanic-white rivalry in southern California, historian Richard Griswold del Castillo stated: "[D]uring the period 1887–1900, out of 194 men admitted to the bar in California, only 3 were Spanish-surnamed." He further observed that by 1873 "only 2 percent" of those serving on juries were Hispanic, and he suggested that the absence of Hispanics serving as jurors, lawyers, and judges explained the large number of convictions.[114] The Francisco Bonilla case in Santa Barbara, among others, confirms the absence of Hispanics on juries, but the reasons relate more to legal strategy during impaneling than to Hispanics not being available for jury duty. In fact, Hispanics accounted for 36 percent of the pool of jurors for the Bonilla case.[115] However, the prosecutor challenged some Hispanic jurors for "bias" because they knew the defendant, and others were eliminated with peremptory challenges. In other words, in cases dealing with Hispanic defendants, a prosecutor could challenge and prevent a good number (if not all) of the prospective Hispanic jurors from serving on the jury. It was an effective strategy that increased the prosecution's chances of gaining a conviction. Defense counsel, many of whom were court-appointed, failed to deal with this issue properly. In other instances defense counsel would sometimes enter a guilty plea in collusion with the prosecutor or in order to avoid a case that, because of the indigent status of the defendant, would provide no significant financial reward.

Many of the Hispanics in this sample would be considered marginal people. They worked mainly as vaqueros, sheep shearers, and day laborers. They drifted back and forth between established Hispanic communities and the white world, ignored by both groups. Since neither group readily accepted them, these Third World people were at risk in California. Californios and white citizens probably viewed them as misfits, loners, deviants, outcasts, or drifters—in short, as a threat to established society. Marginal Hispanics tended to move from job to job, seldom lived in one place very long, drank heavily in local saloons, and sometimes got into trouble in established communities. Ninety-three percent of the Hispanic males sentenced to prison for murder or manslaughter claimed that they were either common laborers or vaqueros.[116] They tended to be underemployed because there was not enough work to keep them fully engaged throughout the year. It was a vicious cycle that often led to violence and occasionally to death.[117] Any offense they committed against substantial citizens of the community would be considered serious.

Augustin Castro and José Coyado fit this image of the marginal man. In Coyado's case, unfamiliarity with the rules of criminal procedures proved to be disastrous. He made the fatal mistake of talking to the sheriff about his role in the crime without the benefit of an attorney to provide legal advice. Castro also made a miscalculation by agreeing to accept a plea bargain of guilty to a lesser charge. His attorney appeared to be working in tandem with the prosecution on this case and certainly provided poor legal counsel. The result was that Castro languished in prison for more than two decades before being released. On the other side of the ledger, some Hispanic defendants, such as Francisco Bonilla and Joseph Hurtado, received aid from other Hispanics and were able to hire adequate legal representation. Consequently, Hispanic conviction rates were significantly lower than those of Indian defendants.

San Diego County Courthouse, built in 1892. José Gabriel ("Indian Joe") was tried in this new courthouse in 1893. Courtesy of San Diego Historical Society

San Joaquin County Jail in Stockton, built on Market Street between San Joaquin and Hunter in 1853. Courtesy of Holt-Atherton Department of Special Collections, University of Pacific Libraries

José Gabriel, San Quentin No. 15173, sentenced from San Diego County for murder, first degree, death. First inmate executed in San Quentin. Courtesy of San Quentin Prison

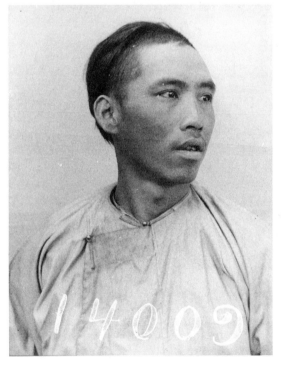

Ah Keong, San Quentin No. 14009, sentenced from Sacramento County for murder, first degree, life. Courtesy of California State Archives

A Castro Murder

Augustin Castro, San Quentin No. 5335, sentenced from San Diego County for murder, first degree, life. Courtesy of California State Archives

William McLaughlin, San Quentin No. 14045, sentenced from Calaveras County, for murder, first degree, life. Only white defendant convicted of killing an Indian. Courtesy of California State Archives

Prisoners congregating, San Quentin, Stones. Courtesy of California State Archives

Iron door on Stones cell, San Quentin Prison. José Gabriel occupied one of these cells before his execution. Courtesy of California History Section, California State Library

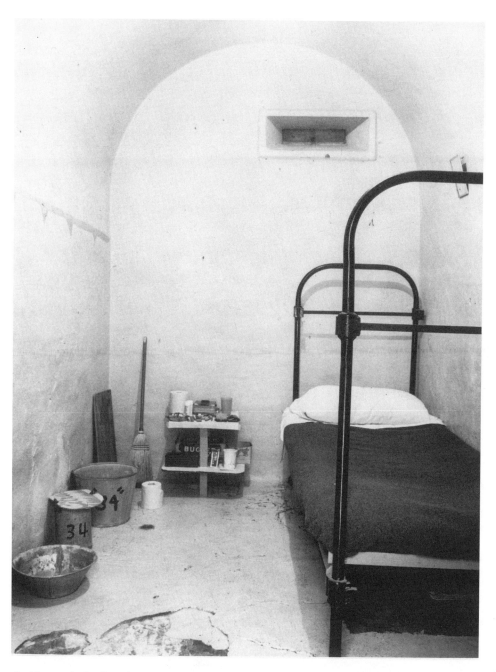

Inside a typical cell in the Stones cellblock, built in 1853, San Quentin Prison. Note the absence of windows. José Gabriel was housed in one of these cells on the newly established "Murder's Row" in 1893. Courtesy of California History Section, California State Library

David S. Terry, former California Supreme Court justice, killed in Lathrop, San Joaquin County, California. Courtesy of Holt-Atherton Department of Special Collections, University of Pacific Libraries

Lathrop train station, where David S. Terry was shot and killed by U.S. Marshal David Neagle, bodyguard to Supreme Court justice Stephen J. Field. Courtesy of Holt-Atherton Department of Special Collections, University of Pacific Libraries

Sheriff Thomas Cunningham, San Joaquin County, fourth person from the left, ca. 1880. He served as sheriff from 1871 to 1899 and participated in the capture of Black Bart. Courtesy of Holt-Atherton Department of Special Collections, University of Pacific Libraries

*Judge Pablo de la Guerra,
First District Court, Santa
Barbara. Courtesy of
California State Library*

*Judge W. T. McNealy,
District Court, San Diego
County. He relocated from
the South and supported the
"Code of the West." Courtesy
of San Diego Historical
Society*

Chapter Four

White Man
White Justice

In the tradition of the Old West . . . they walked toward each other in the area
of the Plaza. Couts was carrying a shawl. He dropped it, to reveal a shotgun.
Mendoza . . . turned to flee and was struck with a blast from both barrels.
He staggered . . . and fell dead.
—Richard F. Pourade, *The Silver Dons*

This dramatic image of a shoot-out that occurred in 1865 on the streets of Old Town San Diego follows the famous cinema tradition.[1] In the film epic *High Noon* the gunfight was supposed to take place at "high noon" with a marshal facing three men just released from prison in the streets of a dusty little town. It indeed was a myth. In the San Diego "gun battle," Cave Johnson Couts, an influen-tial local citizen, allegedly faced Juan Mendoza, a former employee who had made threats. Not surprisingly, this romanticized account leaves out much of the real story. Couts did not meet Mendoza face-to-face but instead stepped into the street behind him with a double-barreled shotgun, hollered at him, and fired. Although he apparently missed with the first shot, Couts fired the second round into his victim. A grand jury indicted Couts for murder, and he was tried and found not guilty.[2] Although this story may be somewhat troubling to the reader, it was not uncommon to find defendants not guilty under such circumstances. Using a series of homicide case files, this chapter will evaluate the treatment of white defendants accused of murder.

Whites had a significantly lower interracial homicide rate, at 21 percent, than any of the minorities except the Chinese. Nevertheless, the 164 interracial cases do suggest that interracial mixing created ample opportunity for lethal violence. With white killers, however, power (legal and extralegal) is an important factor. A significant number of the nonwhite victims (36 cases) were killed by mob or vigi-lante actions involving alleged crimes of homicide and property theft. A typical example occurred in January 1871, when a "posse" of white citizens approached an Indian *rancheria* in southern San Diego County and seized two Indians accused of killing whites. Big Foot and an unnamed Indian were quickly bound and shot

TABLE 4.1
Murder Victims by Race, 1850–1900

Race	Number	Percentage
White	627	79.3
Hispanic	101	12.8
Indian	35	4.4
Chinese	24	3.0
Black	4	.5
Totals	791	100.0

Sources: Coroners' Inquests, Calaveras, Tuolumne, Sacramento, San Joaquin, San Luis Obispo, Santa Barbara, and San Diego Counties, 1850–1900.

by their white captors.[3] Most of the murders of San Diego Indians by whites occurred during the last two decades of the century.

Whites killed 791 people during the five-decade period reviewed here (see Table 4.1). More of the victims were Hispanic (101) than any other racial group. Many of the murders involved alcohol and petty squabbles. For example, around midnight on March 11, 1878, a fight occurred at Clements' Saloon in San Luis Obispo. Fred Scheifferley and Corobel Villa, both under the influence of alcohol, argued over a poker game. Scheifferley accused Villa of taking twenty-five cents that did not belong to him. They began to argue loudly and walked out of the saloon to settle their differences in the street. Scheifferley "drew out a pocket knife and struck him in the left side, immediately under the heart." The victim died almost instantly.[4] The killer claimed self-defense, and, as was typical in such cases, the coroner's jury agreed and no charges were filed. Whites accused of killing Hispanics were seldom indicted (28 of 101 cases), and conviction rates were significantly lower for those white defendants who were indicted.

Twenty-four cases involved Chinese victims. Although thirteen white defendants were charged with murder, five were found not guilty and the other eight had charges against them dismissed. Ten of these cases occurred in Sacramento County and the other three in San Joaquin County. The killing of Chinese by whites took a variety of forms, including lynching. Some authors have treated lynching as an acceptable means of "controlling lawlessness" on the frontier.[5] There is no doubt that lynchings were homicides, yet all of the killers avoided criminal prosecution. White citizens viewed this kind of punishment as a reasonable response to any serious crime committed by others, especially minorities. For example, on November 12, 1861, white miners lynched a Chinese victim in the vicinity of Prairie City, several miles east of Sacramento. In this and two other Chinese lynchings, on October 18, 1858, and September 7, 1864, law enforcement officers made no attempt to apprehend or prosecute the identified killers.[6]

The data show that whites seldom killed minorities; instead, they usually murdered other whites. A strong spirit of personal honor was behind many of these homicides. In nineteenth-century California, the combination of young men, alcohol, petty squabbles over property, the pervasive gun culture, and devotion to honor often proved to be lethal.

During this time, cattlemen in the American West were believed to have developed a code of behavior to settle disputes, commonly called the "Code of the West."[7] Although it became legend, it was especially associated with cattlemen in Texas, New Mexico, and Colorado. Though no definitive statement of the code exists, a variety of sources suggest that it included four basic tenets: (1) never shoot an unarmed man, (2) never shoot a man in the back, (3) never accept an insult without a fight, and (4) never retreat from a fight.[8] Many historians believe that the Code of the West actually existed, but there is some difference of opinion as to what it really meant, whether it was accepted, and, if so, by whom. It is very possible that the code was used only in the cattle country and never reached California, except when Texas cattlemen resettled along the Pacific Coast. Lewis Atherton suggests that "the fighting code of the West consisted primarily of the rule that one must not shoot an unarmed man."[9] In his opus *The Cattle Kings* Atherton notes that most cattlemen "urged their foremen to discourage cowboys from carrying firearms," and some, like Charles Goodnight, even threatened to hang any cowboy "guilty of committing a murder" on the trail.[10] Exactly why the code was developed is unclear, but C. L. Sonnichsen states that the "lack of written law" forced cattlemen to frame their own, which was "merely a gentleman's agreement" on trail conduct that was respected by most on the range.[11] Robert Utley notes that "the code demanded personal courage and pride, reckless disregard of life, and instant redress of insult, real or fancied."[12] According to Joseph G. Rosa, "Both antagonists were expected to be armed and facing each other when they were provoked into an exchange of shots."[13] In California, however, this was the exception, and back shooting seemed to be a common practice, as it probably was in other parts of the American West.

Another concept that seems to be part of the code is the "no duty to retreat" doctrine, which suggests that you do not have to back away from a fight. English common law demanded that a person confronted with a fight had to retreat until his back was against a wall. If no wall existed, one was to continue retreating. Killing the assailant should be the last resort. During the early national period in the United States, however, that concept was modified until, by the late 1870s, "no duty to retreat" became generally accepted. It basically meant that you had the right to stand your ground and kill your adversary if that was necessary to preserve your own life. Historian Richard Brown suggests that we can trace high homicide rates to this concept because it encouraged men to use violence to settle disputes that might have been defused if one of the combatants had "retreated."[14] Many Californians violated the Code of the West and used the "no duty to retreat" doctrine to its fullest extent, especially when honor was an important factor.

One of the most famous nineteenth-century California homicides in this category occurred on the morning of August 14, 1889, in the San Joaquin County town of Lathrop, a few miles south of Stockton. It involved a dispute between Stephen J. Field, associate justice of the U.S. Supreme Court, and David S. Terry, a transplanted Southerner from Texas. Terry had gained notoriety in 1856 by drawing a bowie knife and severely stabbing S. A. Hopkins, a member of the San Francisco Vigilance Committee. Fortunately for Terry, who at the time was the chief justice of the California Supreme Court, his victim recovered. Like many other Texans, Terry believed in the Code of the West, meaning that you stood your ground and anyone who besmirched your reputation had to be challenged. In San Francisco, Terry made a speech in 1859 attacking Democrats who supported U.S. senator David C. Broderick. The next day Broderick commented on the speech in a San Francisco hotel: "I once considered him [Terry] the only honest man on the Supreme bench but I take it all back."[15] Terry, of course, took exception to this statement, so after resigning his judgeship, he met Broderick in a duel in San Mateo County. The first attempt was thwarted by legal officials, but the two men met again, and Terry shot and killed Senator Broderick. Despite legislation that prohibited dueling, the San Mateo County prosecutor refused to press charges.[16] Terry returned to Texas to fight in the Civil War, and later he resettled in Stockton, where he operated a ranch and practiced law.[17] He was a very aggressive person, and since he usually carried a bowie knife, any threat that he made had to be considered a serious one.

Exactly when the feud between Terry and Field started is unclear, but some believe the squabble began with the killing of Broderick, since Field and Broderick had been friends since 1851. Field was serving on the California Supreme Court with Terry when the latter resigned to fight the duel with Broderick. Others think that the impetus was the civil litigation by Terry and his wife, Sarah Althea Hill Terry, that took place in Field's court that set him off.[18] During a court hearing on September 3, 1888, after a violent outburst from Sarah Terry, U.S. Supreme Court justice Field "directed the removal of Mrs. Terry from the court." David Terry, reacting violently to the judge's actions, "drew a murderous knife and attempted to use it on the court's officers."[19] Field ordered him arrested and jailed for six months. After the incident, threats were made against Field's life, and Terry "told many people that Justice Field would not dare come out to the Pacific Coast."[20]

A little after 7:00 A.M. on August 14, 1889, a train en route to San Francisco stopped at Lathrop, and Justice Field stepped out of the railroad car to have breakfast. He was accompanied by U.S. marshal David Neagle, who, because of threats on the judge's life, had been assigned as his bodyguard while he was traveling in California. As chance would have it, David Terry and his wife were on the same train. Field and Neagle entered the hotel, sat down at a long table, and ordered their meals. A minute or two later Terry and his wife entered the dining room. Apparently Sarah immediately spotted Field and wheeled around, heading back to the train to retrieve a bag containing a loaded handgun. T. W. Stackpole, proprietor of the hotel, saw her leave, so he quickly approached David Terry and asked him, "Your wife would not be so indiscreet as to go to the car to get a pistol to make trouble in the dining room, would she?" Terry asked, "Why? Who is here?" After Stackpole explained that Judge Field was in the dining room, Terry uttered, "Don't let her come in; watch her."[21] Apparently Terry looked around, spotted Justice Field, and walked up behind him. Exactly what happened next is unclear. Several witnesses claimed that Terry hit Justice Field either on the back of the head or on the side of the face twice and was about to hit him again when Neagle shouted: "Stop! Stop! I am an officer!" The marshal pulled his revolver and fired two shots in quick succession. Terry fell mortally wounded. All witnesses testified that Terry came up behind Field, but there is conflicting testimony as to whether he hit the judge or just gave him "a tap" to get his attention. When questioned about the attack, Justice Field admitted, "[O]f course I was for a moment dazed by the blows."[22] Although he did not witness the shooting, Stackpole said he turned and "Judge Field was just tottering from his chair and seemed to be very pale, and I thought he was the party that was shot."[23] As Terry's wife rushed back into the dining room, Stackpole grabbed the bag containing the revolver. She struggled to keep the bag and screamed, "Let me get at it, I will fix him."[24] She then began to console her dying husband. After the shooting, Justice Field and U.S. marshal Neagle returned to their railroad car and went on to San Francisco. A constable from Lathrop boarded the train and stopped it at Tracey, where he placed Neagle under arrest, removed him from the train, and transported him to the county jail in Stockton. Another U.S. marshal met Field at San Francisco to provide protection, but attempts to arrest and charge Justice Field with murder were unsuccessful.

Later, Justice Field testified: "I did not see him, and he struck me a violent blow in the face, followed instantaneously by another blow. Coming so immediately together, the two blows seemed like one assault." After the assault Neagle claimed that Terry moved "his right hand at once to his breast, evidently to seize the knife which he had told the Alameda County jailer he 'always carried.'"[25] Given Terry's reputation for carrying and using a bowie knife, Neagle at that point feared a knife attack on the judge, drew his Colt revolver, and fired. Several minutes after the shooting, deputy coroner John Barrett searched the body of David Terry and found papers, some cash, and "a small pocket knife."[26] Some have theorized that when Sarah began to grieve she collapsed on top of Terry and took the bowie knife when she got up. The train conductor said that he saw Mrs. Terry lying over her husband's body, and that when she finally got up she unbuttoned his vest and said, "You may search him; he has got no weapon on him."[27] With Terry's past history of using a bowie knife and his reputation of refusing to "retreat," others were also unconvinced that he had been unarmed. A Sacramento reporter claimed that it was well known "that Terry always went armed," and a San Francisco newspaper story reported that Terry "invariably carried arms and that he boasted of his ability to use them."[28]

A U.S. attorney filed a writ of habeas corpus demanding the release of U.S. marshal Neagle. The circuit court in northern California heard the case and ordered Neagle released from custody.[29] California attorney general G. A. Johnson appealed to the U.S. Supreme Court, but the order of the lower court was affirmed. Before reaching its decision, the court examined more than five hundred pages of documentation, a process that has provided some insights into the Terry-Field squabble. For example, the court noted that when Justice Field ordered Sarah Althea Hill Terry removed from his courtroom, David Terry "succeeded in drawing a bowie-knife, when his arms were seized by a deputy-marshal and others . . . they were able to wrench it from him only after a severe struggle. The most prominent person engaged in wresting the knife from Terry was Neagle, the prisoner now in court."[30] The court also noted that Terry's wife, Sarah, had tried to bring a satchel into Justice Field's courtroom, but marshals confiscated it and found a loaded revolver inside. Both Terry and his wife had made threats against Field's life. For example, Mrs. Terry "repeated a number of times that she would kill both Judge Field and Judge Sawyer." The court concluded "that both Terry and wife contemplated some attack upon Judge Field during his official visit to California in the summer of 1889, which they intended should result in his death."[31]

Turning to the protection of Justice Field, the court noted that correspondence between the offices of the U.S. attorney general and the U.S. marshal indicated that they quietly took steps to protect the justice from an attack. The U.S. marshal's office received permission to hire at least two marshals to protect the judge in the courtroom, with one being assigned as a bodyguard to accompany the judge at all times. When Judge Field and Marshal Neagle were on the train, the marshal was alerted that Terry and his wife had boarded the train in Fresno. Neagle, fearing trouble, went to the conductor and asked him "to telegraph to the proper officers of that place [Lathrop] to have a constable or some peace-officer on the ground when the train should arrive."[32] Upon their arrival at Lathrop no constable or other officer could be located, so Marshal Neagle suggested that Field take his breakfast on the train. He refused and, of course, the attack and homicide occurred within minutes. The court ruled six to two (with Justice Field abstaining) that Neagle had killed Terry in the performance of his duty. The decision noted "that in taking the life of Terry, under the circumstances, he [Neagle] was acting under the authority of the law of the United States, and was justified in so doing; and that he is not liable to answer in the courts of California."[33] The court affirmed the circuit court's ruling.

In retrospect, this homicide seems almost inevitable. David S. Terry had a long history of violent behavior that included stabbing a vigilance committeeman with a bowie knife, the killing of Broderick in a duel, and the issuance of many threats against Judge Field. If the judge had been without a bodyguard, it is very likely that he would have been killed, if not by Terry, then by his wife. This feud, played out in a small town in the Great Valley, illustrates the violent nature of many men who brought their code of honor with them to California. Terry was willing to attack a U.S. Supreme Court justice, and possibly kill him, to gain satisfaction for a real or imagined grievance against himself and his wife. Probably, only the quick action of U.S. marshal Neagle prevented the death of Justice Field. And tragically, other honor-bound men were also willing to kill, regardless of the consequences of their actions.

Occasionally, well-established members of local communities virtually got away with murder. Two cases in San Diego County during the 1860s provide insight into this phenomenon. During the winter of 1862–1863 a smallpox epidemic scared many of the local citizens. In January, district court judge Benjamin Hayes drafted an order to deal with smallpox in southern California by limiting visits of Indians from the *rancherías* to the city of San Diego and requiring that they "immediately report" to local physicians for vaccination.[34] Cave Johnson Couts, the owner of Rancho Guajome near San Luis Rey in northern San Diego County, expressed concern, writing, "[W]e are all badly scared by the smallpox" and noting that he kept a vaquero posted as a sentinel to warn against the approach of strangers.[35] Fearing the further spread of smallpox, Couts sent his younger brother, William Blunt Couts, to the San Luis Rey Mission cemetery to stop the burial of Ysidro María Alvarado, owner of Rancho Monserrate, who had recently died from the disease. By 1863, both Cave J. Couts and his brother William (usually called Blunt) had become a major force in local politics. Blunt had held a variety of government positions such as clerk of the Court of Sessions, San Diego County clerk from 1854 to 1857, auditor, and clerk of the district court.[36] The brothers were clearly prominent citizens in northern San Diego County, with a great deal of influence.

On January 13, 1863, Tomás Alvarado and five other men had finished lowering the coffin of Ysidro María Alvarado into a grave that had been dug in the small cemetery next to the mission. Tomás Alvarado, son of the deceased, testified that "we were about throwing the first earth over the coffin, when Blunt Couts arrived, suddenly."[37] Couts, accompanied by his brother's servant, Miguel, and Ramón Sepúlveda, drove up in a carriage. Both Blunt and Miguel, armed with double-barreled shotguns, walked quickly to the cemetery, while Sepúlveda, also armed with a shotgun, remained with the carriage. Witnesses claimed that Couts said in a loud voice: "Como diputado del sherif del condado, no es permitido que este señor se entierra aquí." Translated literally: "As deputy sheriff of the county, I advise you that you are not permitted to bury this man here."[38] Apparently Couts's sudden appearance and declaration infuriated León Vásquez, a member of the burial party, who advanced toward Couts with a spade in his hand. Blunt fired one shot at him but missed. As Vásquez jumped up on the wall surrounding the cemetery, Blunt fired a second shotgun blast that caught him full in the face, killing him instantly. When several other members of the burial party began to advance toward Couts, Miguel, Cave Couts's servant, quickly fired two blasts from his shotgun, hitting Ramón Castro in the arm and wounding Syriaco Estrada in the face. Blunt and Miguel ran to the waiting carriage, jumped in, and sped off to Rancho Guajome. Tomás Alvarado suggested that "the whole affair was the act of a moment, Blunt's arrival, our seeing him, his arming, Vásquez's movement toward the wall, the shots and death—all was 'muy pronto.'" José Alvarado agreed that the "whole affair happened almost instantaneously."[39]

After the shooting Tomás Alvarado ordered the other members of the funeral party to "leave the corpse as it is, to represent the facts to the authorities."[40] Tomás immediately sent a letter to district court judge Benjamin Hayes explaining what happened and asking for permission to bury his father. Judge Hayes soon replied, directing him "to proceed to complete the funeral." Cave Couts also sent a letter to Judge Hayes to explain what had taken place at the cemetery. Cave wrote that he had sent orders "for no one to be buried at San Luis Rey who had died of small-pox, stating that it was by your [Judge Hayes's] order." In an attempt to put the shooting incident in a more favorable light for Blunt, Cave noted that Vásquez, the man shot, "is known as a bad character." He further suggested that the men with him were a bunch of "roughs from Pala" and that "the fellow killed is really not worth noticing."[41] After Blunt's indictment for murder in the county court by a grand jury, Benjamin Hayes, no longer a district court judge, appeared for the defendant and tried to have the indictment set aside because it was "irregularly formed" and therefore void.[42]

No documents within the court records indicate either a jury venire or a trial for Couts. The charges were dismissed. This may have occurred because the facts concerning the homicide were contested. All those who testified at the preliminary hearing in the San Diego County Court were members of Ysidro María

Alvarado's funeral party. They basically told the same story. One historian, taking Couts's side, claims that he "was attacked by a Sonoran with a knife" and killed his assailant in self-defense.[43] That Vásquez would be advancing with both a spade and a knife in his hands is unlikely. There is no indication that any of the members of the funeral party were carrying either pistols or knives, and there are no records suggesting that Blunt Couts had legal authority as a deputy sheriff.[44] Being an influential member of the local community, he may have felt that he had such police power, but there is no proof that he had any right to prevent burial within the mission cemetery. Judge Hayes's smallpox order of January 1863 did not forbid burials.[45] Nevertheless, considering the attitudes of the dominant society, it is not surprising that a white man could get away with killing a Hispanic under such circumstances. If it had gone to trial, Couts could have invoked the time-honored "no duty to retreat" doctrine. What is interesting is that both Couts and Miguel, after emptying their shotguns, beat a hasty retreat to the safety of their carriage and hurried back to the ranch. Couts may have suddenly realized the gravity of his rash actions. There is no doubt that the Couts brothers feared the spread of smallpox, but preventing the burial at the local cemetery did not seem to be a logical way to resolve this issue.

Two years later, Cave Couts committed a similar homicide. Cave had even greater influence within the community, as well as notoriety at that time. A West Point graduate from Tennessee, he arrived in San Diego a lieutenant of the First Dragoons in 1848. He married Ysidora, the daughter of wealthy landowner Juan Bandini, in April 1851 and soon resigned his army commission. As a wedding present Ysidora received Rancho Guajome from Abel Stearns, her brother-in-law. Living on his rancho, Cave also held political positions within the community. For example, he was appointed Indian subagent for San Diego County in 1852; two years later local voters elected him justice of the peace and school commissioner of San Luis Rey Township; and he also served briefly as county court judge. Cave became deeply involved in the Democratic Party in San Diego County, serving as a vice president of the county Democratic convention and entertaining William H. Seward at Rancho Guajome in 1869.[46] Couts was certainly a substantial and active citizen of San Luis Rey and San Diego County. There was, however, a troubling side to this complicated man.

In 1855 a grand jury indicted him for severely beating two Indians with a knotted rope. He was acquitted of a charge of assault in one case; nevertheless, a grand jury allegedly indicted him for manslaughter on another count—the second victim had died. Eventually the charges were dropped in that case as well.[47] In May 1870 he inflicted "dangerous wounds" upon Waldemar Muller, a teacher whom Couts had hired to tutor his children at Rancho Guajome. After Muller had allegedly assaulted one of his daughters, Couts "nominated himself as a one-man prosecutor, jury, and executioner" and "unloaded two charges of bird shot" into Muller. The teacher survived and may have been paid "a large sum of money" with the stipulation that he quickly leave the community. One historian suggested that "Couts's actions were sometimes the result of haste, anger, and expressions of his own fallible observations." In other words Couts had a tendency to "shoot first and examine the target afterwards."[48] Another writer stated that "Couts had an unfortunate propensity to commit acts of violence" and suggested that "this undesirable behavior may have been caused by excessive drinking, a problem that afflicted him most of his life."[49] Couts often acted quickly and rashly when confronted with some real or imagined grievance.

On February 6, 1865, Cave Couts was conducting business in Old Town San Diego. Looking out the door of a butcher shop, he saw Juan Mendoza, a former employee who had threatened him, walking down the street. Couts picked up a double-barreled shotgun, stepped into the street, and shouted at Mendoza, who turned and ran. Couts fired a shot, which missed, then fired the second barrel and killed Mendoza instantly. The killing of an unarmed man with a shotgun is an ugly sight, and it is not unusual to see such events described and embellished in rather captivating phrases to make them more fascinating to the reading public. For example, as noted earlier, in Richard Pourade's narrative Couts and Mendoza "walked toward each other in the area of the Plaza. Couts was carrying a shawl. He dropped it, to reveal a shotgun. Mendoza, according to witnesses, turned to flee and was struck with a blast from both barrels."[50] This dramatic account, probably taken from Rufus K. Porter's letters to the *San Francisco Bulletin,* is basically fiction.

Both Pourade and Lyle C. Annable have painted a portrait of Mendoza as a sinister individual who probably deserved killing. Pourade notes that Mendoza had developed "a reputed career as a badman in Sonora" and that "armed with a six-shooter and a knife" he visited saloons in Old Town making threats and "sending challenges to Couts."[51] Annable sees Mendoza as a "Mexican renegade" who had "become involved in the power struggle for control of Baja California." He suggests that Couts employed "the bandit" as *mayordomo* "but later had cause to dismiss him." Annable's version of the story also has Couts living in fear of an ambush, and then finally "Couts came face-to-face with Mendoza, and the latter was shot and killed."[52] Both of these accounts have their facts confused.[53] What really happened that day in Old Town plaza?

About 7:30 A.M., on February 6, 1865, Cave Couts was talking with George P. Tebbetts, owner of a butcher shop in Old Town San Diego. Just then Juan Mendoza walked by on the street, and Couts, observing him only after he had passed, asked, "Who was that?" Tebbetts replied, "That was Juan Mendoza." A few minutes later, as Mendoza passed by again, Couts retorted, "[T]hat man threatened my life on sight," picked up his shotgun, and stepped into the street behind

Mendoza. Suddenly realizing what Couts was about to do, Tebbetts exclaimed, "Don't shoot him!" The butcher also heard Mendoza exclaim, "Wait a moment," followed by Couts's first shot. Tebbetts turned around and saw "Mendoza step 15 or 20 steps when he fell, this was after the second shot."[54] Louis Rose also witnessed the shooting. He observed Cave Couts in the street aiming a shotgun. "When Mendoza was about 20 or 25 yards from Couts the first shot was fired. I heard Mendoza uttering some words . . . when about 5 or 6 yards farther, I heard the second shot fired, but did not see him fall."[55] Rose testified that he saw Mendoza running across the plaza and around Lyon's corner when Couts fired.

These two accounts suggest that Couts caught Mendoza by surprise, probably unarmed, and gave him little chance to escape before blasting him with both barrels of a shotgun. In violation of the second Code of the West dictum, never shoot a man in the back, Couts took his revenge—probably with a great deal of satisfaction. Rufus K. Porter admitted that Cave J. Couts had shot "an unarmed man while walking in broad daylight across the Plaza."[56] It is doubtful that Mendoza knew that Couts was in town, and at such an early hour he probably did not consider wearing a sidearm. Couts, on the other hand, was well armed, indicating that he had been thinking about the alleged threats by Mendoza. This scenario would also suggest premeditation and malice aforethought, the basic legal definition of murder in the first degree. The evidence presented at the coroner's inquest proved sufficient, and a grand jury indicted Cave Couts for murder.

What about Mendoza's threats? Were they real or contrived by Couts? The only evidence of threats comes from Couts himself, a rather unreliable source, and from the deposition of Eugenio Morillo taken October 11, 1866, just before the trial. Morillo testified that Mendoza had lived in his house for eighteen months and that he had known him for many years. When asked about Mendoza's character, Morillo stated: "[H]e was a violent man in Lower California, he killed Andres Manríquez there, shooting him from behind." When cross-examined by the prosecutor, Morillo admitted that he was not present at the Manríquez shooting, but had heard about it secondhand. Morillo was asked, "[H]ow do you know that he was an assassin, of your own knowledge?" Morillo replied, "I never saw him kill any one."[57] More important, Morillo provided no information to suggest that Mendoza had actually threatened Couts.

There are no court transcripts or minutes, but Rufus Porter, the jury foreman for Couts's trial, offered his "official" version of the court proceedings for the *San Francisco Bulletin*. Porter's account should be read with caution since his prejudice in favor of Couts is well displayed in his letters to the *San Francisco Bulletin*. Benjamin Hayes and Volney E. Howard, a Los Angeles attorney, defended Couts before Judge Pablo de la Guerra's First District Court in San Diego. Porter suggested that testimony by the defense revealed that Cave Couts did not visit San Diego for about "six or eight months" because of "fear of being ambushed and murdered" by Mendoza. In his account of the trial Porter refers to Mendoza in negative terms, suggesting that "Mendoza and his devils" had murdered "nearly a dozen people in cold blood" in Baja California before crossing the border into San Diego County. Porter stated that "it was proved, and the witness was the reliable Don Juan Forster, that Mendoza constantly went around with a six-shooter and a knife."[58]

Testifying on his own behalf, Couts related that he "constantly received threatening messages from him [Mendoza] which he believed would be carried out if opportunity offered." After several months Couts had to drive to San Diego to conduct business. Porter's version of the killing asserted that Mendoza walked toward the defendant and then Couts fired at Mendoza when he turned and ran. Couts called for him to stop and then fired two shots. One might ask the question, Whom do you believe, Couts's version or that of the two eyewitnesses, Rose and Tebbetts? The jury may have accepted Couts's version, even if it was not plausible, because they agreed with him. Mendoza had threatened him, therefore Couts did not have to retreat—even though he was actually behind his victim with a shotgun. As Porter notes, the discharge of Couts from legal custody "was received with much applause, and the verdict of 'not guilty' pronounced righteous."[59] So far as the citizens of San Diego were concerned, Cave J. Couts, an influential member of the community, had been vindicated.

One of the interesting facets of this case is the absence of documentation to "prove" the bad character of Mendoza. For example, Couts claimed that Mendoza had sent "threatening messages" but produced no documents as proof. The attempts to paint Mendoza as "reputed bad man" and a "Mexican renegade" also lack veracity. Indeed, Mendoza may have been a tough character, but there was no evidence to verify this. Even Morillo, who had known him for many years, had no proof that Mendoza actually had committed homicides. Baja California had been in turmoil during this period, and "revolution" or political intrigue was not uncommon. Mexico had been suffering political chaos since 1821, and politics in Baja California, a province so far from Mexico City, were probably even more turbulent. But all this talk of Mendoza being dangerous seems to be a straw man. It is doubtful that a jury of white males would have convicted Couts even if all of these alleged character traits were false. Mendoza, whatever his reputation, probably made threats, and one was enough to allow Couts the "right" to kill his adversary, whether he was unarmed or not. It was common practice that if a man threatens you, shoot first and ask questions later.

The evidence shows that in these two cases the Code of the West was ignored. Both brothers clearly violated one of the major tenets of the code—never shoot an unarmed man. Of course, Blunt could claim that Vásquez had a spade and therefore was "armed." Blunt also declared that he had been deputized as a sheriff by his brother, consequently his actions were in the performance of his duties as a law enforcement officer. Cave Couts violated at least two tenets of the code—never shoot a man in the back and never kill an unarmed man. Cave might have argued that he had been threatened and therefore had to take action to avoid being killed. That might seem a bit thin today, but it would have been accepted by most white males in San Diego during the nineteenth century, as the jury's verdict suggests. Many would argue, Why wait until someone tries to shoot you from ambush? It made sense to take action, and in this case Couts caught Mendoza completely by surprise and gave him both barrels.

Other shoot-outs in California also suggest that guns were an invitation to violence. In the true tradition of the American West, gunfights did occur in California, especially in San Luis Obispo County. These incidents reveal both the presence of a code of honor among men who participated in them and the danger of carrying firearms with the intention of using them to resolve disputes. Although the historical gunfights were not as spectacular as the Hollywood versions, California shoot-outs were frequently deadly. For example, about 6:00 P.M. on Sunday, March 1, 1884, Benjamin F. Morris, a rancher originally from Texas, rode into San Luis Obispo. After dismounting from his horse Morris spied George W. Walker on Higuera Street in front of the Central Hotel and shouted, "Look out!" Both men drew pistols and began to fire. Morris fired once, while Walker rapidly fired five or six shots. After Morris fell mortally wounded, an angry Walker walked up and struck him on the head with his pistol. Morris was dead, and Walker had received a severe gunshot wound. The shoot-out lasted "less than fifteen seconds."[60] The cause of the "duel" was unclear. Some thought that the men, formerly friends, had become enemies because of a horse race gone sour. Others gossiped that Walker's wife had left him and Morris had become friendly to her. This gunfight had all the markings of a Code of the West duel. As noted previously, a man always accepted a challenge and never backed down. He faced his enemy—both of them, of course, armed with handguns. Any disparaging remarks or comments, especially about a woman, could explode into a dangerous confrontation. Morris had recently resettled in San Luis Obispo from Texas, where the "chivalry" code was highly accentuated and often led to feuds that continued for years.[61] A reporter suggested that Morris "was more demonstrative, always carrying a pistol and on many occasions he has threatened to use it." Walker was not indicted after the shooting. Although it was ruled self-defense, the shooting revealed a common problem in San Luis Obispo. A newspaper reporter noted: "This fatal tragedy will be long remembered, and it is to be hoped it will be the last to mar the fair record of this city. It was the result of the pernicious custom of carrying deadly weapons."[62]

A little over a year later an "OK Corral"–style gunfight involving two groups of young men who called themselves the Vigilantes and the Hoodlums occurred in Estrella, about twenty-five miles northeast of San Luis Obispo. This particular gunfight also resulted from an issue of "honor." Joe Sanders, the schoolteacher in Estrella, approached a group of farmhands working nearby and complained about an insult made by the crew. Sanders accused the men of "hallowing" at him during school and said, "[Y]ou was calling me a son-of-a-bitch."[63] They denied it. The next day, Tuesday, July 7, 1885, about 9:00 A.M., Sanders, Edward Stowell, Francis Rhyne, Dewitt Clinton Brooks, James Booker, Byron Fortney, and the Ballard boys left the school armed with Winchester rifles and pistols.[64] Henry Huston, George Huston, John McKenna, Melvin Congdon, and Martin Heenan, the crew of the header, were also armed, with shotguns and pitchforks. As they approached, Sanders once again complained about the insults shouted the day before. Huston replied that his "boys had been hollowing at dogs chasing rabbits." Obviously perturbed, Sanders shouted, "That's too damn thin they were hallowing at me and I know it."[65]

Neither side admitted firing first, but according to participants, within a few seconds thirty or forty shots were fired by the two groups. Edward Stowell and Dewitt Clinton Brooks were killed, and four others suffered wounds ranging from severe to minor. Later the members of the Vigilantes who had killed the two Hoodlums surrendered to the sheriff. A jury found Melvin Congdon guilty of second-degree murder and Sanders guilty of assault with a deadly weapon, and acquitted Huston. Congdon and Huston had been armed with shotguns, while Sanders had a Winchester rifle. Sanders received a pardon from the governor. These two cases reveal that the carrying of handguns, shotguns, and rifles was commonplace in California and that the results could be deadly. The newspaper editor wrote: "The habit of going armed in a farming region anywhere in California seems an insult to law and order. . . . The presence of arms engenders strife."[66]

Six years later, John Kelshaw, justice of the peace, became involved in a fight with A. M. Sherwood on the streets of Paso Robles, a small town twenty miles north of San Luis Obispo. A few weeks before the fight Justice Kelshaw had fined Sherwood fifteen dollars for battery on a young boy. During the court proceedings Sherwood became so abusive that Kelshaw fined him for contempt. Sherwood refused to pay, and Kelshaw had him placed in custody until he paid his fines, whereupon Sherwood, a man with a violent temper, made threats against the justice. On November 12, 1891, about 2:00 P.M., Sherwood, "of large and powerful build, irascible in disposition, and determined and dangerous when aroused," attacked Kelshaw in the street and began to beat and stab him with a sharp screwdriver. Knocked to the ground, Kelshaw drew his pistol and fired three times in quick succession. Sherwood jumped on Kelshaw and continued his attack. Eventually, Kelshaw broke loose, got up, and began hitting Sherwood with his pistol. Judge Fletcher came to Kelshaw's aid and parted the two men.

"Sherwood fell exhausted" to the ground and soon died. Although Kelshaw was placed under arrest, the coroner's jury ruled that he had acted in self-defense. The San Luis Obispo County data indicate that the carrying of weapons, concealed or openly, increased the danger that minor quarrels would turn lethal.[67] Equally important, it also reveals the presence of the Code of the West that forced men to escalate a fight into a killing because it would be unmanly to back down.

On the other hand, some homicide cases demonstrate noncompliance with the Code of the West. On May 11, 1875, Royal Barton and John Tannahill became involved in a violent confrontation over a property line between their farms in Valle de las Viejas in rural San Diego County. Apparently, four years earlier, Barton's brother Guy claimed some land, decided to leave, and sold the land to his mother. The land remained vacant, and Tannahill soon arrived and filed a claim to the property. After hearing that Tannahill was moving a house onto the land, Royal Barton "proceeded to the spot with a double-barreled shotgun to warn Tannahill to desist."[68] Barton fired two shots, but somehow missed. Tannahill drew his pistol and shot Barton in the leg, where the bullet just missed the femoral artery. No doubt Tannahill could have killed Barton; however, he chose not to do so. Barton's younger brother arrived and helped him back to their farm, where a local doctor removed the bullet and dressed the wound. The issue over land ownership was not resolved but continued to divide the farm community of Valle de las Viejas for several years.

Less than two years later, on June 23, 1877, Tannahill and some farmworkers were cutting hay when they saw Barton loading hay that had been cut on the disputed land. Tannahill and A. P. Tyler, his hired hand, started moving their wagon across the field toward Barton to pick up the hay. According to Tyler's testimony, "When we got within about 20 steps of Barton he raised his gun without speaking and fired at us." Tannahill immediately jumped out of the wagon and began to chase Barton, who had turned and run toward his farmhouse. After chasing him for about 150 feet, Tannahill began to catch up with Barton, who turned around and aimed his rifle on Tannahill, apparently to fire a second shot. When he was about six feet away from Barton, Tannahill, who was running over uneven ground, stumbled and fell. Barton moved forward and, using his rifle barrel as a club, bashed his fallen adversary on the back of the head at least three times. Barton then turned and ran for his house while Tyler, carrying a pitchfork to defend himself, quickly arrived to find that Tannahill was already dead. Another farmer, C. B. Robinson, also saw the attack. Robinson stated: "I saw the smoke and heard the report of a rifle."[69] He jumped from his wagon and began to run toward the two men, but before he arrived on the scene Barton had clubbed Tannahill with the rifle barrel and run off. Robinson testified: "I examined Tannahill's body and found his skull mashed in on the back part of his head and bleeding profusely."[70] He further observed that Tannahill "had no pistol about his person." Robert Hill and J. H. Tyler also witnessed the attack on Tannahill. Barton proceeded to town and gave himself up to the sheriff.[71] Sheriff James McCoy and Coroner T. C. Stockton immediately went to examine the body.

During the trial the facts regarding how the confrontation took place were disputed. Defense counsel claimed that José Delores, a laborer employed by Barton, saw the chase and said that Barton "turned and struck him with the gun, only saw him strike him once."[72] Another Barton employee provided a similar contradictory story about the killing, claiming that Tannahill "did not fall until he was struck." In other words, defense counsel was suggesting that Barton had turned and struck Tannahill with the rifle in an attempt to defend himself. But the autopsy revealed that the wounds occurred only on the back of the head, clearly indicating that the victim had fallen facedown and was then attacked by Barton. Barton was indicted for murder. The first trial ended with a hung jury, but the second concluded with a conviction of murder in the second degree and a sentence of ten years in state prison.

At the sentencing, Judge W. T. McNealy asked the defendant if he had any last words before sentence was passed. Barton had prepared a statement, which he read to the court. It began: "I think I can show to you . . . that on the morning of the 23rd of last June I was pursued by a man—a man who had not only threatened my life and threatened it repeatedly—but a man who had attempted to take my life on a former occasion . . . and that when I gave the blow or the blows which caused his death, that I did as any other man would do." Barton claimed that Tannahill had been chasing him for about a hundred yards when he turned and struck him. He suggested that the guilty verdict against him was based "upon the hypothesis that my action was wrong."[73]

This case provides an opportunity to further examine how juries, judges, and governors interpreted the "no duty to retreat" doctrine and self-defense. Barton waged a three-year battle to gain release from prison and a full pardon. He was successful. In a letter to his sister, he suggested that the judge and the district attorney had "said in substance that I am not guilty."[74] During the pardon process, Barton's friends obtained the signatures of a large number of citizens living in the San Diego area, but they were unable to obtain the signature of Judge W. T. McNealy, who had presided over the trial. Governor William Irwin sent a letter to the judge asking for information on the crime to enable him to make a decision on the pardon request. McNealy admitted that he had refused to sign Royal Barton's pardon petition and explained why in great detail in a letter that illuminates the trial process and the concept of self-defense in California. In a passage discussing the difficulties between the two men that occurred two years before the killing, McNealy wrote that Barton "commenced the affair and shot at Tannahill (twice I think), but didn't hit him, but Tannahill being the cooler man did better work."[75] The sheriff arrested Barton, and McNealy ordered him "to keep the peace in regard to this same land difficulty." Receiving Barton's assurance, Judge McNealy granted a bail reduction but warned him not "to settle his difficulties with shotguns," that he must resolve the issue by law.[76] The Los Angeles land office had decided the dispute in Tannahill's favor just two months before the shooting.

During the trial, Barton's attorney tried to admit testimony about Tannahill shooting Barton during the previous fight. After discussion with the prosecution and defense counsel, Judge McNealy ruled that "it must all come or none." Defense counsel withdrew any testimony about the previous fight, fearing that the jury might read too much into the evidence that Barton had fired two rounds from a double-barreled shotgun at Tannahill. The judge also noted that despite testimony of Barton's workers, the evidence clearly proved that "the blows took effect in the back part of the head," indicating that Tannahill was lying facedown when struck with the gun barrel held by Barton. McNealy further stated that Barton had fired at Tannahill and then had run toward his house. "Tannahill had no arms whatever. . . . I have no doubt but that Barton was afraid of Tannahill and very much so that *he is really a coward.*"[77] The judge (a Southerner) suggested that if Barton was so afraid of Tannahill he should have "avoided all difficulty with him." McNealy suggested that to have shot Tannahill in self-defense because he was carrying a pistol would have been reasonable, but "after failing in an attempt to kill to make his great cowardice a ground for killing when the other party is not using any dangerous weapon" was clearly a violation of the concept of self-defense. McNealy thought that Tannahill was wrong to go "after Barton in the way he did" but that his actions did not justify the killing. He further informed the governor that the first jury had deadlocked eight to four for acquittal. The second jury "was unanimous of course in their verdict and I believe none of them were for acquittal and some of them I have been told were for first degree."[78] Some in the courtroom, including jury members, thought that the sentence of ten years was too light.

The killing of Tannahill should never have happened. If Tannahill had not chased Barton or if Barton had left his gun at home there would have been no killing. In retrospect, it seems so simple, but apparently it was not simple for the participants. Barton had threatened Tannahill with guns twice, and Tannahill, being a young male with his honor at stake and believing that he could best Barton in a hand-to-hand fight, chased him down. No doubt Barton was scared of Tannahill, and when he fell turned and hit him three times with the rifle barrel. The surprising thing is that the governor gave a full pardon after only three years served in prison. There is no indication how the townspeople reacted to the release of Barton. No doubt the community was divided over the killing, some agreeing with Barton and others feeling that he should have been more severely punished for the crime. However, some other homicides committed by whites display an even greater disregard for life, and yet they ended in complete ac-quittals. These cases illustrate another variable at work—race.

Prosecutors rarely charged white defendants who killed Indians; however, two exceptions illuminate the changing attitudes toward California Indians. In Sacramento County the James Hilan murder case provides a rare glimpse of the criminal justice system trying to overcome racial prejudice. On July 1, 1859, the bodies of two Indians were discovered two or three feet apart, one in a sit-ting position along the streambed of the Cosumnes River, near Michigan Bar close to the eastern border of the county. Evidence strongly suggests that Hilan shot and killed Elleck and Poolto, two California Indians, and then beat them in the head with a blunt instrument, probably a rifle barrel.[79] The victims' heads had been severely bashed in, and their brains were protruding from their skulls. Joshua Crouch, the constable who arrested Hilan, testified that he followed the killer's trail for seven miles and, after arriving at Hilan's cabin, matched the foot-prints with Hilan's boots. While the constable was bringing the alleged killer to Michigan Bar, Hilan told him, "[T]here [is] nothing but Indian testimony against [me] and that could not be used" in court.[80] Surprisingly, testimony given by an Indian woman who lived with Hilan corroborated the murder and was accepted in court.[81] The woman told the constable that the rifle had been hidden under a mattress. Crouch retrieved the weapon. George Kingsley examined the rifle care-fully and noticed that "it had the appearance of having been used in striking. There was fresh blood on the inside of the barrel," and it appeared that some-one had "washed off the barrel."[82]

The prosecutor who handled the Hilan case tried hard to gain a conviction but failed. Several whites testified that they had known the two Indian men for several years and attested to their quiet, peaceful demeanor and noted that they had worked at odd jobs for them from time to time. After the trial ended in a hung jury, the judge ordered a new trial. Sometime between the two trials a deputy sheriff took the rifle that was being held as evidence to a gunsmith and asked him to replace the broken stock. The gunsmith threw away an important piece of evidence. Sheriff John McCloy admitted that the gun had been left in his custody, but said he'd forgotten "what he did with the gun." After the first trial, the jailer became suspicious of Hilan's behavior. He entered the prisoner's cell and ordered him off of his bunk. Under the mattress the jailer discovered a big knife, and he noticed that a "bar across the window was partly sawed off." Hilan did not escape from the jail, but the second trial also ended with a hung jury.[83]

It should come as no surprise that two all-white juries in Sacramento could not convict a white man for killing two Indians. These killings occurred in 1859, when whites exhibited a great deal of racial animosity against Native Americans.

Even though several white witnesses had expressed a favorable opinion of the victims, most whites perceived Indians as "barbarians" who had few, if any, redeeming qualities. Some whites probably considered Hilan's actions to be good riddance of undesirables in Sacramento County.

William McLaughlin, of Calaveras County, achieved the unusual distinction of being the only white man in this seven-county study convicted of killing a California Indian.[84] On Sunday, September 29, 1889, around three hundred Miwok Indians from Murphys' Ranchería were attending the final day of a powwow celebration on the outskirts of Murphys. Typically this Miwok powwow fair included dances, cookouts, and entertainment. The festivities were well attended by a good many white citizens from Murphys, West Point, and San Andreas. During the afternoon, Indian Jeff was busily preparing meat over an open fire, while his son John Jeff supplied firewood. Late in the afternoon, William McLaughlin, a fifty-five-year-old white man who worked as a woodchopper, arrived and began to drink from a bottle of liquor. Early in the evening he started to bother several Indian women who were sitting around the fire where Indian Jeff was cooking. Frank Jack testified that "McLaughlin was fooling around with the women two or three hours, Johnny Jeff told him to stay away." An angry McLaughlin jumped up, pulled out a pistol, and shouted, "You son-of-a-bitch!" Standing only a few feet away, Indian Jeff stepped forward two steps and said, "Put the pistol away." McLaughlin instantly fired one shot, which entered Indian Jeff's chest, pierced the lung, glanced off a rib, and lodged in his liver. After lingering for about ninety days, Indian Jeff died from the gunshot wound.[85]

In January 1890, Justice of the Peace J. R. Smith held an inquest into the cause of death. After hearing testimony from witnesses as well as a dying declaration, the coroner's jury found that the deceased came to his death from a gunshot wound inflicted by William McLaughlin. Less than a month later the district attorney dismissed charges of assault to murder and filed an information for murder. On February 4, 1890, Paul C. Morf, counsel for the defendant, entered a plea of not guilty. The three-day superior court trial in San Andreas, presided over by Judge C. V. Gottschalk, was fairly typical for murder trials during the nineteenth century, with District Attorney F. J. Solinsky receiving assistance from J. B. Reddick, a well-known local attorney with experience in homicide cases.

With many witnesses to the killing, the evidence against McLaughlin was strong. First, the prosecution called Dr. Frank Burleigh to describe the wound and state the cause of death. Burleigh testified that when he first examined Indian Jeff he discovered he "was suffering from a [bullet] wound on the right breast." He attended to him several times and stated that "death was the result of the gun shot wound."[86] Prosecution then called Dr. W. M. Murphy, who concurred that the bullet wound was the cause of death. George McCullum, a witness to the crime, testified that he had known the defendant for about fifteen years and saw both him and Indian Jeff by the fire. McCullum said he heard a voice say "son of a bitch" and believed it to be the voice of the defendant. The witness, standing thirty feet away, saw the flash of McLaughlin's pistol when he fired. He also testified that he had seen the defendant drinking before the shooting and declared that "McLaughlin was somewhat under the influence of liquor." George Hahn, another witness, claimed that after the shooting McLaughlin passed him and growled, "I will learn the sons of bitches how they fool with me." Potter Hodge testified that the only thing John Jeff said to McLaughlin was "[H]ow can they [Indian women] set down when you are bothering them."[87] It was at that point that McLaughlin jumped up and pulled out his pistol. Oscar Brittinham also testified that McLaughlin said "he would have no Indians dictate to him." Each prosecution witness identified the defendant as the person doing the shooting and the one who used abusive language. Equally important, they all declared that the victim did not have a weapon in his hand.[88]

In the face of such damaging testimony, defense attorney Morf tried to claim self-defense for his client, suggesting that Indian Jeff had had a knife or club in his hand and was advancing toward the defendant. Further, counsel suggested that the victim died because he did not receive good medical care after the shooting. Defense counsel first called Fenton Davis, who claimed that he heard an Indian say, "God damn you, I will make you shut up." He admitted, however, that he did not remember seeing anything in the victim's hand before the shooting. In a desperate gamble, the defense counsel called the defendant to testify on his own behalf. McLaughlin denied that he had been bothering the Indian women or that he had been under the influence of liquor. He testified that Indian Jeff jumped up and said, "God damn him, I will stop his talk." McLaughlin also claimed that Indian Jeff "had a knife in his hand." Asked why he left the scene, McLaughlin stated: "I was afraid I would be killed, that they [the Indians] would kill me, not that I thought I had done anything wrong."[89] McLaughlin was an unconvincing witness, and the jury found defense counsel's theories unbelievable.

After final arguments, the case was submitted to the jury at about 4:00 P.M., Wednesday afternoon. By 10:00 P.M. the jury still had not reached a verdict, so the court locked them up with instructions to bring in a sealed verdict, if one was reached. Around 2:00 A.M. they handed an envelope to the sheriff. The next morning the judge convened the court and the clerk read the verdict: guilty of murder in the first degree with punishment of life in prison. A newspaper reporter noted that the "announcement was a shock to the prisoner, and though he had appeared unmoved through the trial, his emotions on receiving the verdict were plainly noticeable."[90]

Considering the evidence, the circumstance of the killing, and the changing attitudes of white citizens in Calaveras County, the verdict is not surprising. By 1890 most Miwoks had become an integrated part of the local community and were working for ranchers and businessmen. Equally revealing, many white citizens were attending and participating in Indian powwows held each year. The local Miwok Indians, greatly reduced in numbers, were no longer viewed as threatening, and, of course, the evidence was overwhelming and the circumstances of the killing left little doubt in the minds of the jurors that McLaughlin was guilty. Such an outcome, the conviction of a white man for killing an Indian, could not have happened a decade or two before. This case suggests that sometimes, although rarely, Indian victims gained some satisfaction that justice was served. At least it was in this one case in Calaveras County.

The outcome of this trial suggests that by 1890 the two divergent worlds—white and Miwok—in Calaveras County were beginning to come together. Many white citizens were now attending the big annual Miwok powwow to watch the dances and to partake of Indian-style cooking. Some of the Miwoks lived in Indian *rancherías,* but others resided in Murphys and other white communities in Calaveras County. Equally important, McLaughlin was a marginalized white who lacked social standing in the community. As an indigent, he received a court-appointed attorney, which put him at a disadvantage. In essence, McLaughlin, the "deviant," was being "put away" for the good of the community. Life sentence for a marginal white, perceived by some as a scoundrel, seemed to be logical to members of the community. It was an act of protecting society from an undesirable. In 1908, at age seventy-four, McLaughlin received a pardon after serving eighteen years in prison.

Sacramento County led all counties, with 167 white defendants being indicted. Tuolumne, Calaveras, and San Joaquin Counties also had significant numbers of whites indicted—96, 93, and 81, respectively. White defendants accounted for a high of 80 percent of those indicted in San Joaquin County and a low of 22 percent in Santa Barbara. The conviction rates for white defendants averaged 43 percent for the seven California counties (Fig. 4.1). San Luis Obispo County, with 54.5 percent, had the highest rate, while San Diego County had the lowest, with 32.6 percent. White defendants were found not guilty 34 percent of the time, and 23 percent had charges dismissed.

An examination of white defendants' conviction rates based upon the race of the victim is illuminating. Whites who killed Indians, Hispanics, or Chinese received different treatment from criminal justice officials than did nonwhite defendants accused of killing whites. Whites were accused of killing thirty-five Indians, but just four whites (11.4 percent) were indicted and only one was convicted. It was very difficult to convict a white man for killing an Indian. The

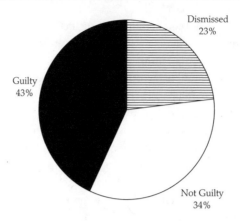

Fig. 4.1. Verdicts: White Defendants, Seven California Counties, 1850–1900

McLaughlin case illustrates that, at least on occasion, the criminal system tried to convict whites accused of that crime. This case also indicates that it required the coming together of both the white and the Indian communities to effect this one instance of justice for a white killing an Indian.

Prosecutors brought charges against nine whites (twenty-four cases) accused of killing Chinese. Thomas Powell and Henry Kramer (white suspects) were tried and found not guilty, and Simon Raten was found not guilty by reason of insanity. The six other white defendants had charges against them dismissed. Four cases in San Joaquin County involved Chinese victims and white perpetrators. Charges were brought against Thomas Bangs, Jacob Tillman, and H. J. Pies, and all were found not guilty. Nevertheless, Sacramento County, because of its sizable Chinese population, had a significant number of cases (seventeen) that involved whites killing Chinese. Although some of the whites were indicted, not a single one was convicted of killing a Chinese victim (Table 4.2). Juries simply would not convict whites accused of killing Chinese.

Whites were also accused of killing 101 Hispanics, but only twenty-eight whites were indicted. Authorities convicted nine of the defendants (32 percent) for killing Hispanics, found eleven not guilty (39 percent), and dismissed eight defendants (25 percent). Conviction rates for white defendants accused of killing nonwhite victims are considerably lower than those for white victims.

This case study reveals a significant level of "honor" among many white defendants accused of homicide, yet it seems clear that the Code of the West was neither generally accepted nor practiced in California. However, whites often refused to back away from a confrontation and were willing to escalate the dispute by using guns to resolve their grievances, real or imagined. A few, like David S.

TABLE 4.2

White Defendants' Conviction Percentages by Victim's Race, 1850–1900

Victim's Race	Number Accused	Number Indicted	Percent Indicted	Percent Convicted
White	627	367	58.8	47
Hispanic	101	28	27.7	32
Indian	35	4	11.4	25
Chinese	24	9	37.5	0
Black	4	1	25.0	0
Totals	791	409		

Sources: Coroners' Inquests and Registers of Criminal Action, San Diego, Santa Barbara, San Luis Obispo, San Joaquin, Sacramento, Calaveras, and Tuolumne Counties, 1850–1900.

Terry, Cave Couts, and Benjamin Morris, were from the South, where they had been indoctrinated with the concept of "chivalry"—you never back down from a fight.[91] If you did you would be branded a coward. Terry probably best exemplifies the Code of the West, but he was the exception. He would not back down from a fight, and his aberrant behavior got him killed. Nevertheless, the Couts brothers and others provide dramatic evidence that most Californians ignored the Code of the West. The gunfights in San Luis Obispo follow a similar pattern, with "honor" as a major ingredient, along with handguns and shotguns. It was hard to convict white defendants accused of such crimes even if they killed white victims. And if the jury did convict them, they stood a good chance of gaining commutation or early release from prison.

The killing of nonwhite victims by whites adds another dimension. Although whites were accused of killing thirty-five Indians, authorities convicted only one white defendant. San Diego County, which had the most cases (seventeen) involving whites killing Indians, did not have a single conviction and seldom even charged whites with such crimes. White and Indian communities in San Diego County had not yet established a common ground upon which they could build a good relationship. Whites also killed twenty-four Chinese, with thirteen indictments of white defendants, but no convictions.

The phrase "white justice," of course, suggests that white defendants had an advantage when they entered the criminal justice system. The evidence supports that hypothesis, and several factors help to explain why. First, white defendants entered a judicial system controlled largely by white sheriffs, police officers, prosecutors, judges, and jurors. This structure gave white defendants the advantage of being tried by juries of their peers. All things being equal, they would have a better chance for acquittal by such a jury. If prejudice appeared, it would most likely be related to social status. Second, white defendants, especially prominent members of the local community, were able to afford good legal counsel. This proved critical in many cases. A good local lawyer knew how to "work the system" to his client's advantage to gain reduced charges or even dismissal. Third, the status of white defendants played an important role in how they would be treated by the courts. Low-status whites were more likely to be prosecuted and given long prison terms than were white defendants of high rank. This explains the conviction of McLaughlin for killing an Indian. The Couts brothers, Royal Barton, and other prominent white citizens received "more" justice. Finally, the race of the victim played an important role in the treatment of white defendants. The murder of whites brought a higher penalty within the criminal justice systems in California. Even white defendants were more likely to be convicted for killing other whites, and if the victim happened to be a white woman of high status the penalty could be severe. However, the killing of Indians, Chinese, and Hispanics by whites was less likely to be deemed a crime. The evidence is convincing that the dominant white society and its law really meant white man, white justice.

Epilogue

Prison, Homicide Rates, and Justice

To Lincoln the most important idea that the law represented was the idea of fairness.
Justice carries a pair of scales that are evenly balanced.
—Arthur L. Goodhart

A basic legal dictum states that the punishment should fit the crime. The data presented indicate that this was not necessarily true, at least for nonwhite defendants. Penal control, of course, is considered to be the strongest form of social sanction used to correct "deviant" behavior.[1] The enforcement of norms tends to divide society between those who are "respectable" and those who fail to meet the behavioral standards set by the majority. Those perceived as deviant are more likely to be disciplined. Discipline takes the form of incarceration for short periods of time at the very minimum, life sentences for more serious offenses, and execution for the most extreme crimes. Incarceration, of course, proved to be the most common method of punishment.[2] The four case studies discussed above have provided some measure of how the criminal justice system treated defendants, but what were the consequences of incarceration in San Quentin and Folsom prisons?

During the nineteenth century, California's criminal justice systems imprisoned 1,901 individuals for murder and manslaughter (Table 5.1). Authorities sentenced only 15 women to prison for such crimes; as noted earlier, homicide in California had been mostly a male endeavor. White inmates accounted for 68.5 percent of the total, followed by Hispanics, Chinese, Indians, and blacks, with 13.8, 9.1, 7.0, and 1.6 percent, respectively. San Francisco, with 313 inmates, sent the most prisoners convicted of murder and manslaughter, while Los Angeles contributed 136. With 295 inmates, the seven California counties studied represented about 15.5 percent of the prison population.[3] Sacramento, with 80, contributed the highest number of inmates, followed by Calaveras, Tuolumne, San Diego, San Joaquin, Santa Barbara, and San Luis Obispo, with 48, 45, 40, 40, 24, and 18, respectively.

Chinese inmates had the highest life sentence rates of any group among the aggregate prison population, with 46 percent of all Chinese inmates receiving life sentences. Among Indian inmates, this figure was 27 percent; among whites,

TABLE 5.1
Prison Population by Race, 1850–1900

Race	Number	Percentage
White	1,303	68.5
Hispanic	263	13.8
Indian	132	7.0
Chinese	173	9.1
Black	30	1.6
Totals	1,901	100.0

Sources: San Quentin and Folsom prison registers, 1850–1900.

26 percent; and among Hispanics, 19 percent. Of the fifty-two Chinese inmates sentenced from San Francisco, 60 percent received life sentences (thirty-one cases). Other counties with high life sentence rates for Chinese included Calaveras, Fresno, Sacramento, Santa Clara, and San Joaquin, with 100, 86, 58, 60, and 50 percent, respectively (twenty-three cases). These figures are quite remarkable, especially since Chinese defendants usually had lawyers at the beginning of the legal process. What explains such dramatic figures? The most logical explanation would be racial prejudice. For example, life sentence rates for white inmates were 20 percent lower, and most of these cases involved white victims. The same applies to Indians, for whom the rate was 19 percent lower, though many of the victims were white. In cases involving Chinese accused of homicide the victims were almost always Chinese as well. It seems odd that judges and juries would sentence Chinese defendants to life for killing other Chinese. It appears, especially in San Francisco, Sacramento, Fresno, and Calaveras Counties, that the prosecutors may have used life sentences as a way to get these Chinese "deviants" off the streets.

In the counties studied, seven Indian defendants received life sentences for killing three white and four Indian victims. Judges sentenced twenty-eight white defendants to life for killing one Indian and twenty-seven whites. Nine Hispanics received life sentences for killing one Indian, four whites, and four Hispanics. Sacramento County officials sentenced one black defendant to life in prison for killing a black male victim. Fourteen Chinese received life sentences; all victims were Chinese.[4]

Sixteen defendants were sentenced to death for killing victims from another race. Eight Indians received the death penalty for killing whites, and six of them ended up on the gallows. A judge declared Gabriel Cuayo insane, and José de Jesus had

TABLE 5.2

Prison Mortality Rates, San Quentin and Folsom Prisons, 1850–1900

Race	Average Age	Percentage Died	Years	Number Died in Prison	Total Number
White	32.2	11.9	7.6	155	1,303
Hispanic	32.4	25.8	6.3	68	263
Indian	26.9	44.0	3.7	58	132
Chinese	36.8	16.2	7.0	28	173
Black	40.0	16.6	13.0	5	30
Totals				314	1,901

Sources: San Quentin and Folsom prison registers, 1850–1900.

his sentence commuted to life in prison. Sheriffs executed José del Carme, Filisario Alipas, and José Luís Osuna, Domingo, and Vicente, while prison authorities executed Jose Gabriel in San Quentin.[5] Tuolumne County officials executed Ramón Velásquez (an Indian) for killing an Asian. Indians were more likely to be given life sentences or condemned to death, particularly if they murdered whites.[6] All seven Hispanics sentenced to death had killed whites in three different counties—four in Calaveras, one in Tuolumne, and two in Santa Barbara. Authorities in Tuolumne County also executed Ah Bun for killing a white victim. Joseph Ebanks, the one African American defendant sentenced to death, had been convicted of killing two white victims in San Diego County. Authorities sentenced to death forty-six whites, all for killing white victims (including four females). Nine white defendants had their death sentences commuted to life.[7] No white defendant suffered the death penalty for killing a minority. In the seven counties surveyed, authorities executed a total of sixty-one men for murder. Whites led with 59 percent (all for killing white victims), followed by Hispanics, Indians, Chinese, and blacks with 18, 10, 10, and 3 percent, respectively.

Pardon rates provide further documentation on the treatment of nonwhites within California's prison system. Fifty-three percent of the white inmates received pardons compared to the Hispanics' 26 percent, with Chinese and Indians following with 25 and 10 percent, respectively. White defendants, with stronger community support and greater access to legal representation, were more likely to receive pardons. Indians, with the weakest ties to their communities, were the least likely to receive pardons and remained in prison considerably longer.

Finally, incarceration in prison affected California Indians more severely than other racial groups. Fifty-eight of 132 Indians sentenced to prison for murder or manslaughter died in San Quentin and Folsom (Table 5.2). Once in prison, Indians survived for short periods of time; 16 expired within one year, 8 within two years, 8 more within three years, and 8 others within four years. Forty-four percent of the Indian inmates died in prison, surviving an average of 3.7 years per inmate.[8] Of a total of 1,303 white inmates in the California penal system, 155, or 12 percent, died in prison. Hispanic, Chinese, and black inmate death rate percentages were approximately 26, 16, and 17, respectively. Those Indian, Chinese, Hispanic, white, and black inmates who died in prison survived an average of 3.7, 7, 6.3, 7.6, and 13 years, respectively, before expiring.[9] For a variety of reasons, Indians could neither mentally nor physically handle imprisonment. Being confined in close quarters with other inmates caused many Indians to become ill with a variety of infectious diseases, such as tuberculosis and other lung infections.[10] Especially for Indians, prison really meant doing "hard time."

The accused/indicted ratio adds another dimension to measuring the treatment of defendants; it refers to the percentage of those individuals actually indicted from those who were identified and accused of murder. These data, collected from coroners' inquests, newspapers, and court records, reveal a bias against nonwhite defendants. For example, the accused/indicted ratios were 82, 70, and 46 percent, respectively, for Indians, Hispanics, and whites in the seven counties.[11] In other words, Indians who were identified and accused were almost twice as likely to be indicted as whites. As already noted, a significant number of whites had killed nonwhite victims, and the data confirm that they had little to fear from the criminal justice system.

Significant differences of opinion as to whether the American West was violent or not can be identified. In fact, exactly how does one determine whether high levels of violence actually existed? One way, of course, is to measure homicide levels, but even this can be difficult. On the surface it seems relatively simple: just adopt the method used by social scientists that measures the number of homicides per 100,000 population and then compare the data by region over time. Some say, however, that it is impossible to apply this method to the nineteenth-century West; in their view, the method is basically flawed because of population differences. For example, what if the population in the area of study is less than 100,000? Would that invalidate the methodology? It is a perplexing question that needs to be addressed.

Recently Robert R. Dykstra suggested that using "the FBI's Uniform Crime Reporting Program, which calculates a ratio for murders per every 100,000 of population," such as Roger McGrath had employed in his study on Bodie and Aurora, is like "comparing apples and oranges—or more appropriately, an early pea and a prize-winning watermelon."[12] Further, Dykstra claimed that my recent essay on homicide in the American West included "the same terminally flawed methodology."[13] After assessing a variety of studies that relied heavily upon an-ecdotal rather than statistical evidence of homicide, he concluded that "violent fatalities in the Old West tended to be rare rather than common."[14] And he is not alone in suggesting that the American West was not especially violent.[15]

Other historians and social scientists, however, have produced studies that show that the United States was violent, not only in the West but in the South as well. For example, Horace V. Redfield, in his 1880 study of violence in the North and South, discovered that between 1870 and 1880, homicide rates in Texas, Mississippi, and Louisiana averaged 32, 32, and 24 per 100,000, respec-tively. And, of course, it is significant that Redfield used the homicides-per-100,000-population method, proving the method predated the FBI's system by many decades.[16] In another example, in 1932, H. C. Brearley, using a similar method, revealed high homicide rates in many regions of the United States in the early twentieth century.[17] William Montell, in his 1986 study of homicide on the Kentucky-Tennessee border (four counties), discovered rates averaging 24 per 100,000 from 1850 to 1900.[18] More recently, Gilles Vandal also found homicide rates as high as 60 per 100,000 in some Louisiana parishes and averaging more than 25 for almost two decades (1866–1884).[19] Finally, John Boessenecker has pro-vided the most recent and meaningful discussion on violence levels in Califor-nia. He discovered nineteenth-century homicide rates that dwarf current rates in Los Angeles and San Francisco and similar violent trends throughout the other counties that he surveyed. For example, he uncovered 44 murders in Los Ange-les County during 1850–1851. Boessenecker concluded: "This is an extraordinarily high number for a county of only about 8,500 people." Using the FBI formula, he calculated "an annual rate of 414 homicides per 100,000." Similarly high ho-micide rates were identified in Nevada, Monterey, and San Francisco Counties, and Boessenecker cites comparable data from previous research in Colorado, Kansas, and Texas.[20] Other scholars support the view that the American West was violent,[21] and in the past, I have joined them in this debate.[22] Could all of these studies be wrong, or is it the method of measuring and assessing homi-cide rates that is the problem?

Recently an anonymous historian reviewing a revised essay on violence in Cali-fornia criticized my argument and astutely observed: "The great frontier violence debate is, in essence, a conversation among blind men grasping different parts of the elephant." After reassessing my own position on the violence debate, I have come to the conclusion that the reviewer is correct; both sides have be-come blinded either by their data or by its absence. I believe that there is a third position in this debate that makes more sense. After a reevaluation of my previ-ous research, it seems clear that the data reveal "enclaves of violence" in Ne-braska, Colorado, Arizona, Kansas, and in some of these seven California coun-ties. A well-defined pattern of interaction exists among minor disputes, alcohol, and heavily armed men; this pattern, coupled with the boomtown effect and the critical convergence of an ethnically diverse, young, and transient male population into these small regional enclaves of violence, explains the high homicide levels. One method of evaluating these enclaves of violence would be to compare the FBI formula with the actual yearly number of homicides that occurred in California and view them from the historical perspective.

Tuolumne County best represents the excess of killings during the first two decades under study because of the critical convergence effect that occurred in towns like Sonora and Columbia. On the other hand, San Luis Obispo County displays a low number of actual homicides. What explains so many homicides in Tuolumne County? Events in Sonora, the county seat and the most populous town, may provide an answer. The dramatic change that occurred there during the gold rush suggests a boomtown effect. One sociological study defined a typical boomtown as a small community, less than 10,000 population, and "situated well over a hundred miles from the nearest metropolitan area."[23] Sonora is located approximately two hundred miles southeast of San Francisco, the largest city in California, and is relatively isolated. Studies of modern-day boomtowns reveal that criminal activities increase at a more rapid rate than population does.[24] Although useful, the boomtown effect by itself does not adequately explain the high levels of violence in Sonora. Critical convergence, a concept defined in my earlier research, offers a better paradigm for examining homicide in the California gold camps.[25]

The critical convergence of several factors—rapid population growth, ethnic diversity, young single men, alcohol, and a gun culture—plus the boomtown effect best explains the social instability that created enclaves of violence in the gold camps of Tuolumne County.[26] For example, Tuolumne County's population doubled from 8,351 in 1850 to 17,657 in 1852—that is critical convergence with a vengeance! In 1850 Sonora became an "instant" city, with a population of 4,000, while Columbia, Chinese Camp, and Big Oak Flat experienced similar growth. These gold camps filled up quickly, mostly with young men from Chile, Peru, Mexico, Australia, France, China, and throughout the United States.

Attempts by American miners to control foreign competition, such as the foreign miners' tax, quickly developed into the persecution of ethnic groups, including the Chinese, French, and Hispanics. This behavior, which was characterized by mob activity and lynchings, along with the dramatic population increase in Tuolumne, helps to explain the high number of homicides, especially in the 1850s and 1860s. Among the other factors at work were the absence of uniform social norms to control the new emigrants; instant statehood that failed to provide an adequate criminal justice system; the increase in saloons, gambling halls, and brothels; and the congregating of thousands of young men who enjoyed themselves by drinking, gambling, dancing, and sometimes fighting. Add to this mix

TABLE 5.3

Homicides and Homicide Rates per 100,000 by Decade, Tuolumne and San Luis Obispo Counties, 1850–1900

	Tuolumne		San Luis Obispo	
Decade	N	Homicide Rate	N	Homicide Rate
1850s	156	95	19	107
1860s	96	88	16	62
1870s	33	42	21	33
1880s	13	19	23	20
1890s	23	29	19	12

Source: Coroners' Inquests, Tuolumne and San Luis Obispo Counties, 1850–1900

alcohol abuse, miners carrying guns and knives both openly and concealed, confrontations over fifty-cent bets, and women, and you have a situation with a high potential for violence.

Coroners' inquests reveal that guns were the weapon of choice in Tuolumne. The actual percentages of handgun use increased from 38 percent in the 1850s to 56 percent in the 1890s. As previously noted, these statistics indicate the availability of cheap handguns that began to arrive in California by 1880. By the 1890s, 87 percent of those who committed homicides in Tuolumne County used firearms.

During the gold rush, Tuolumne County suffered from a rash of killings, with a remarkable 156 homicides (homicide rate of 95 per 100,000) in the 1850s alone (Table 5.3). The following decade saw a decline to 96 homicides. The other counties in the sample exhibit lower numbers, ranging from 16 to 43. Overall, the 1850s statistics suggest that a deadly atmosphere existed in Sonora, Columbia, Jamestown, and other gold camps in Tuolumne County, especially from 1850 to 1870.

San Luis Obispo, the comparative county, experienced a much lower level of homicide during the 1850s and 1860s, with 19 and 16 murders, respectively; however, the homicide rates were 107 and 62 per 100,000. The dramatic rates for the 1850s reflect multiple lynchings by vigilantes. Of course, population growth there proved to be much slower, with 356 in 1850 and 1,782 by 1860. These data suggest that San Luis Obispo enjoyed a more stable society; however, when actual numbers of homicides are related to population figures, we find that one was more likely to be killed in San Luis Obispo than in Tuolumne.

A comparison with the state of Vermont provides an added dimension to the

TABLE 5.4

Homicides and Homicide Rates per 100,000, Tuolumne and San Luis Obispo Counties and Vermont, 1865–1874

	Tuolumne			San Luis Obispo			Vermont		
Years	N	Rate	Pop.	N	Rate	Pop.	N	Rate	Pop.
1865–1869	38	47	16,229	5	56	1,782	2	0.13	315,098
1870–1874	21	57.5	8,150	10	42	4,772	3	0.18	330,551

Sources: Coroners' Inquests, Tuolumne and San Luis Obispo Counties, 1865–1874; H. V. Redfield, *Homicide, North and South;* and U.S. Census.

examination of lethal violence in nineteenth-century California. During 1865–1869, only 2 homicides were reported in Vermont, while 38 and 5, respectively, occurred in Tuolumne and San Luis Obispo Counties (Table 5.4). The half-decade 1870–1874 provided similar numbers. The most remarkable fact is the small population in Tuolumne County (8,150) compared to that of Vermont (330,551). During the entire decade 1865–1874, Tuolumne recorded 59 homicides (approximately 6 per year), while Vermont counted 5.[27] During that same period, San Luis Obispo County, with a population as high as 4,722, had 15 homicides. The high homicide rates for Tuolumne and San Luis Obispo Counties are remarkable when compared with those of Vermont. One of the difficulties in such an exercise, however, is the lack of data for extended periods, and another, of course, is pitting staid, tranquil Vermont against a raucous, wild, rip-roaring gold camp county like Tuolumne. Nevertheless, it is not, to quote Robert Dykstra, like comparing "apples and oranges," and it can be instructive. Gold camp regions in the West tended to be violent for reasons already discussed. They were relatively unsettled, shifting regions that were full of young men on the make, armed to the teeth and willing to use their weapons to resolve disputes. The Tuolumne County homicide data, 156 (1850s) and 96 (1860s) killings, respectively, verify this view. Given this information, would one feel safer living in nineteenth-century Vermont or in Tuolumne County?

Data collected from U.S. mortality statistics for the year ending June 1, 1860, provide another useful comparison.[28] During that one year, fifteen and three homicides were recorded in Tuolumne and San Luis Obispo Counties, respectively, while Vermont had none and other states experienced from two to six (Table 5.5). Considering the population figures for these states compared with those of Tuolumne and San Luis Obispo Counties, the statistics are quite remark-

TABLE 5.5

Homicides and Homicide Rates per 100,000, Year Ending June 1, 1860

Location	Homicides	Rate	Population
Tuolumne County	15	92.40	16,229
San Luis Obispo County	3.00	168.00	1,782
Vermont	0	0.00	315,098
Maine	5	0.79	628,279
New Hampshire	2	0.61	326,073
Connecticut	6	1.30	460,147

Source: Table 3, Deaths in the Year Ending June 1, 1860, *Statistics of the United States, 1860*, vol. 4 (Washington, D.C.: Government Printing Office, 1866); Coroners' Inquests, Tuolumne and San Luis Obispo Counties, 1860.

able. In Tuolumne County the kill ratio was about one per 1,000 population, while in Maine it averaged a little less than one per 100,000 and only Connecticut recorded homicide rates higher than one per 100,000. In 1858, an even deadlier year, twenty-six killings took place in Tuolumne County.

Some may be concerned that a comparison of quiet New England states with California gold camp counties is unfair. Perhaps a look at other regions will provide a more meaningful view of homicides across time and reveal the violent nature of the South and the West as well. As noted earlier, in 1880 Horace V. Redfield discovered high homicide levels in the South and contrasted them with the low levels in the North. In 2000, Gilles Vandal uncovered 4,986 homicides in Louisiana over the course of two decades (1865–1884), adding to our knowledge of Southern violence.[29] That would be about 249 homicides per year in a state with a population of 939,946. Vandal suggests that the racial, social, and economic environment that followed the Civil War created an atmosphere in Louisiana that fostered violence. In his study of violence in California, John Boessenecker found 90 homicides in Los Angeles County (10,000 population) for the period 1855–1859, an average of 18 per year. Nevada County, with a population of around 20,000, recorded 98 homicides from 1851 through 1856, or about 16 per year.[30] Such high numbers suggest that Los Angeles and Nevada Counties also fit within the concept of enclaves of violence. These studies reveal similar high homicide levels in the nineteenth-century South and California that parallel those found in Tuolumne and the other six counties.

During the 1850s the coastal counties experienced high numbers of killings despite having low population figures. For example, Santa Barbara counted twenty-seven (1,185 population), while San Diego experienced sixteen (798 population), and San Luis Obispo had nineteen (356 population) (see Table 0.1). The extremely high ratios of murder to population for the first decade in all seven counties reflect the influences of an unstable society, racial tension, and a gun culture. However, the number of killings in San Diego County jumped dramatically during the 1870s (sixty-two murders with 4,951 population) with many interracial killings involving Indian assailants. Meanwhile, Sacramento also recorded significant increases, doubling the number of homicides to eighty-two killings (24,142 population) in the 1860s. Rural San Joaquin County enumerated thirty-seven killings in the 1850s (population 3,647). All seven counties exhibited higher annual numbers of homicides in relation to much lower population levels and high homicide rates than those found in the Eastern part of the country during the nineteenth century. The data from these various sources confirm that enclaves of violence existed in these seven California counties and elsewhere, such as in Coffeyville, Topeka, and Fort Leavenworth, Kansas.[31]

Finally, what explains the disparities in the treatment of whites and nonwhites within California's criminal justice systems during the nineteenth century? In a 1980 dissenting opinion at the Court of Appeals hearing into the Elmer "Geronimo" Pratt murder conviction, Justice George William Dunn wrote: "A trial which is not fundamentally fair is no trial at all. It is a non sequitur to argue that a defendant is obviously guilty if it is an established fact that the defendant was not afforded a fair trial."[32] Many Indian and Hispanic defendants did not know their legal rights; consequently they were at risk in the white-dominated criminal justice systems. If law enforcement officers, judges, and prosecutors fail to protect all of a defendant's legal rights, it is impossible for that person to receive a fair trial. The issue here is not whether the defendants committed murders but whether the criminal justice systems treated them fairly. The data demonstrate that they did not.

A number of factors illustrate the unfairness of the system that created such a legal imbalance. First, these criminal justice systems tended to favor the white majority who basically controlled them. Sheriffs, jury members, attorneys, and judges came mainly from the white society. White defendants had a built-in advantage in the court system, while minority defendants were at a decided disadvantage throughout the legal process. Second, if defendants could afford legal counsel their chances of acquittal were high. If they were indigent, however, the results could be disastrous. Many Indian and Hispanic defendants received poor legal advice from court-appointed attorneys who were basically "going through the motions," some possibly unaware that they were distorting or subverting the assumed fairness of the judicial system. This unjust process of legal representation also affected some white defendants who lived on the margins of society. Third, nonwhite defendants, by their very nature, confronted a formidable barrier that prevented many of them from being treated fairly. The dominant society perceived many Indian, Chinese, and Hispanic defendants to be deviants, outsiders, loners, or marginal people. They not only looked and dressed differently, they spoke languages other than English, which sharply separated them from white society. Unfortunately, people have the tendency to judge others by their "looks"; one can only imagine how some white observers evaluated José Gabriel on his first personal appearance in the San Diego courtroom. The prison photographs of Gabriel, Augustin Castro, Ah Keong, and other inmates provide further food for thought about the potential first impressions of the jurors, prosecutors, and judges upon seeing some of these defendants for the first time.[33] Fourth, the criminal justice systems punished minorities who killed white people more severely. The murder of a prominent white member of society by a nonwhite struck at the very core of the right to be secure in one's home in a civilized society. Such killings created fear in the hearts of members of that community, and law enforcement officers had to address those concerns. They quickly arrested and prosecuted the offenders. It is clear that during the legal process the race of the victim was important to juries and judges, as well as to the public. By their actions, juries and judges were sending a strong message that nonwhites would be harshly punished, especially if they had killed white people.[34]

During the last half of the nineteenth century, abnormally high levels of violence in California resulted in high homicide rates. A variety of factors offer an explanation. First, the California gold rush stimulated rapid population growth, which in turn created considerable social turmoil. The influx of white miners and settlers disrupted California Indian land patterns, destroyed food supplies, and caused a breakdown in traditional California Indian societal controls.[35] This had dramatic consequences, particularly in Calaveras, Tuolumne, and San Diego Counties, where the collapse of Indian communities was most noticeable. Second, the appearance of large numbers of young single males and the transient nature of the population resulted in instability. The critical convergence of ethnically diverse young men in the gold mining camps created enclaves of violence, especially in Sonora, Mokelumne Hills, Columbia, and other small mining towns in Calaveras and Tuolumne Counties. A similar situation occurred in the Sacramento and Stockton Chinatowns, where young Chinese men fought over economic turf. Equally important, the intermixing of racial groups created tensions that were reflected in a significant number of interracial killings. Third, the economic uncertainty of the 1870s and 1880s contributed to the decline in California Indian societies. Young California Indian men congregating on the margins of established society drifted between ranches and *rancherías* in San Luis Obispo County, Santa Barbara County, and especially San Diego County, where they found seasonal work. Fourth, Californios, who controlled millions of acres in large rancho estates, felt increasing pressure from white settlers and lost title to their land in numerous lawsuits in white-dominated courts. This situation caused dislocation within Hispanic communities. Many young Hispanics, both dispossessed Californios and recent immigrants, tried to survive by working as vaqueros, as sheepherders, and in other low-paying jobs. Fifth, the influx of large numbers of Chinese males created increased hostility against them by whites, who perceived them as outsiders. Ironically, although they were attacked by whites, the Chinese seldom committed murders outside their cultural group. Finally, the availability of cheap handguns in the 1880s contributed to the high homicide rates. Guns by their very nature are more lethal than other weapons, and the very existence of a strong gun culture increased the likelihood that disputes might turn lethal. Handguns were an invitation to violence.

The data clearly demonstrate that in these nineteenth-century California counties, two standards of justice operated—one for whites and another for minorities. The high accused/indicted ratios, conviction rates, and plea bargains along with life imprisonment and death sentences show that California Indians and Hispanics received a different justice than whites did. The criminal justice system severely punished California Indian and Hispanic defendants convicted of interracial killings. The data reveal patterns of direct and indirect prejudice on the part of white law enforcement officers, prosecutors, juries, and judges against California's minorities that tended to legitimate their social and legal oppression. The actions of the California criminal justice systems were disparate and discriminatory, following a nineteenth-century brand of American racism.[36] The educated elite upheld a biased system that had only recently been established to provide safeguards for California Indians, Hispanics, Chinese, and blacks as well as for whites. This system, distorted by racial prejudice, ensured that minorities would pay a much heavier price than whites. In nineteenth-century California the scales of justice were unbalanced.

Notes

PROLOGUE: RACE AND HOMICIDE

1. Confession of José Luís Osuna, 2, July 31, 1878, Justice Court, San Bernardo Township, San Diego County, San Diego Historical Society Research Archives, hereinafter SDHSRA.

2. Ibid., 1.

3. *San Diego Union*, December 28, 1878.

4. Testimony of Samuel Temple, 2, *People v. Samuel Temple*, Justice Court, San Jacinto Township, San Diego County, SDHSRA.

5. As quoted in Phil Brigandi and John W. Robinson, "The Killing of Juan Diego: From Murder to Mythology," *Journal of San Diego History* 40 (Winter/Spring 1994): 4.

6. George Wharton James, *Through Ramona's Country* (Boston: Little, Brown, 1909), 134.

7. Ibid., 135.

8. Decision of Justice of the Peace S. V. Tripp, March 31, 1883, 8, *People v. Samuel Temple*, Justice Court, San Jacinto Township, San Diego County, SDHSRA; Brigandi and Robinson, "The Killing of Juan Diego," 1–24; James, *Through Ramona's Country*, 78–82, 132–39, 142–44, and 153–66.

9. In November 1878, Temple was questioned by a coroner's jury about the circumstances of Refugio Baca, an Indian, hanged in San Jacinto township. Temple claimed that "we found him hanging to a cotton wood tree." Two years after the Juan Diego shooting, Temple was arrested for shooting Gus Purty. Although accused of assault with a deadly weapon, he was not charged. See the Testimony of Samuel Temple, body of Refugio Baca, November 1878, Coroner's inquests, San Diego County; *People v. Samuel Temple*, 1885, Justice Court, San Jacinto Township, San Diego County; and Peace Bond, *People v. Samuel Temple*, February 12, 1886, Justice Court, San Jacinto Township, San Diego County, SDHSRA.

10. Clare V. McKanna Jr., *Homicide, Race, and Justice in the American West, 1880–1920* (Tucson: University of Arizona Press, 1997), 4–5. Statistical data from both Calaveras and Tuolumne Counties support this earlier study.

11. Donald Black, *The Behavior of Law* (New York: Academic Press, 1976), 21.

12. Ibid., 51.

13. Roger Lane, *Violent Death in the City: Suicide, Accident, and Murder in Nineteenth-Century Philadelphia* (Cambridge: Harvard University Press, 1979), 58. See also Lane, "Urban Homicide in the Nineteenth Century: Some Lessons for the Twenti-

eth," in James A. Inciardi and Charles E. Faupel, eds., *History and Crime: Implications for Criminal Justice Policy* (Beverly Hills: Sage, 1980), 91–109; Robert H. Tillman, "The Prosecution of Homicide in Sacramento County, 1853–1900," *Southern California Quarterly* 68 (Summer 1986): 167–81; and Lawrence M. Friedman and Robert V. Percival, *The Roots of Justice: Crime and Punishment in Alameda County, California, 1870–1910* (Chapel Hill: University of North Carolina Press, 1981), 17 and 166–69.

14. For a critique of San Francisco vigilantism, see the appendix in Robert M. Senkewicz, *Vigilantes in Gold Rush San Francisco* (Stanford: Stanford University Press, 1985). For the most authoritative assessment of California vigilante action, see David A. Johnson, "Vigilance and the Law: The Moral Authority of Popular Justice in the Far West," *American Quarterly* 33 (Winter 1981): 558–86. See also Richard Maxwell Brown, *Strain of Violence: Studies of American Violence and Vigilantism* (New York: Oxford University Press, 1975); and Robert W. Blew, "Vigilantism in Los Angeles, 1835–1874," *Southern California Quarterly* 44 (January 1972): 11–30.

15. The practice of carrying concealed weapons in California virtually assured high homicide rates. Prosecutors, judges, and juries accepted this behavior and in many cases refused to prosecute or convict local citizens accused of murder. Consequently, there are a significant number of cases with no indictments. See Philip D. Jordan's essay "The Wearing of Weapons in the Western Country," in *Frontier Law and Order* (Lincoln: University of Nebraska Press, 1970), 1–22; and Richard Maxwell Brown, *No Duty to Retreat: Violence and Values in American History and Society* (New York: Oxford University Press, 1991). For a general discussion on frontier violence, see James Shields and Leonard Weinberg, "Reactive Violence and the American Frontier: A Contemporary Evaluation," *Western Political Science Quarterly* (January 1974): 86–101; Joe B. Franz, "The Frontier Tradition: An Invitation to Violence," in Hugh David Graham and Ted Robert Gurr, eds., *The History of Violence in America: Historical and Comparative Perspectives* (New York: Praeger, 1969); and Gary L. Roberts, "Violence and the Frontier Tradition," in Forrest R. Blackburn, ed., *Kansas and the West* (Topeka: Kansas Historical Society, 1976), 97–111.

16. A comparison of the final data indicated that legal authorities indicted in 59 percent of the cases. In other words, a reliance on indictments would have overlooked 41 percent of the homicides. This is not to suggest that coroners' reports are always complete or accurate, but they are an invaluable tool for historians. For another view, arguing against the use of coroners' inquests, see Margaret A. Zahn, "Homicide in the Twentieth Century United States," in Inciardi and Faupel, *History and Crime,* 114–15.

17. See Richard Crawford and Clare V. McKanna Jr., "Crime in California: Using State and Local Archives for Crime Research," *Pacific Historical Review* 55 (May 1986): 284–95.

18. See Owen C. Coy, *Guide to the County Archives of California* (Sacramento: California Printing Company, 1919); and W. N. Davis Jr., "Research Uses of County Court Records, 1850–1879: An Incidental Intimate Glimpse of California Life and Society," *California Historical Quarterly* 52 (Fall 1973): 241–66 and (Winter 1973): 338–65.

19. Clare V. McKanna Jr., "Ethnics and San Quentin Prison Registers: A Comment

on Methodology,"*Journal of Social History* 18 (March 1985): 477–82; and"The Nameless Ones: The Ethnic Experience in San Quentin, 1851–1880," *Pacific Historian* 31 (Spring 1987): 2133.

20. See David L. Snyder, *Records of the Governor's Office,* California State Archives Inventory No. 4 (Sacramento: California State Archives, 1974).

21. For example, see Clare V. McKanna Jr., "The San Quentin Pardon Papers: A Look at File No. 1808, the Case of Francisco Javier Bonilla," *Southern California Quarterly* 68 (Summer 1985): 187–96.

22. The Calhom, Calindic, and Calpris files are available from the Inter-University Consortium for Political and Social Research at the University of Michigan, Ann Arbor.

23. *Homicide* is defined as a killing of any human being by another that cannot be clearly identified as accidental. In this case "accidental" means a killing during a hunting accident, cleaning a weapon, or some similar type of activity. It does not include being shot by a stray bullet in a saloon brawl, a type of killing that is always treated as homicide.

24. See McKanna, *Homicide, Race, and Justice;* and Jordan, "The Wearing of Weapons in the Western Country."

25. *A History of Tuolumne County, California* (San Francisco: B. F. Alley, 1882), 1–247; Joseph Henry Jackson, *Anybody's Gold: The Story of California's Mining Towns* (San Francisco: Chronicle Books, 1970), 107–40.

26. U.S. Bureau of Census, *Statistical View of the United States: Seventh Census* (Washington, D.C.: Senate Printer, 1854), 200; *California State Census of 1852* (Sacramento, 1852), 982; U.S. Bureau of the Census, *The Eighth Census, 1860* (Washington, D.C.: Government Printing Office, 1864), 28; U.S. Bureau of the Census, *The Tenth Census, 1880* (Washington, D.C.: Government Printing Office, 1883), 1:557; and U.S. Bureau of the Census, *The Twelfth Census, 1900* (Washington, D.C.: Government Printing Office, 1901), 1:575.

27. Lane, *Violent Death in the City,* 62 and 79. Margaret A. Zahn found that in Washington, D.C., handgun use in homicides increased from 36 to 83 percent between 1957 and 1974. Margaret A. Zahn,"Homicide in the Twentieth Century United States," in Inciardi and Faupel, *History and Crime,* 122–23; and Marvin Wolfgang, *Patterns in Criminal Homicide* (Philadelphia: University of Pennsylvania Press, 1958), 84–85.

28. Lane, *Violent Death in the City,* 79.

29. McKanna, *Homicide, Race, and Justice,* 23–26 and 155–63; Clare V. McKanna Jr.,"Seeds of Destruction: Homicide, Race, and Justice in Omaha, 1880–1920," *Journal of American Ethnic History* 14 (Fall 1994): 65–90; and Clare V. McKanna Jr.,"Alcohol, Handguns, and Homicide in the American West: A Tale of Three Counties, 1880–1920," *Western Historical Quarterly* 26 (Winter 1995): 455–82.

30. As quoted in Bill O'Neal, *Encyclopedia of Western Gunfighters* (Norman: University of Oklahoma Press, 1979), vii. For a discussion of American gun culture, see Eric Mottram,"'The Persuasive Lips': Men and Guns in America, the West," *Journal of American Studies* 10 (April 1976): 53–84; and Richard Hofstadter, "America as a Gun Culture," *American Heritage* 21 (October 1970): 4–11 and 82–85.

31. Louis A. Garavaglia and Charles G. Worman, *Firearms of the American West, 1803–1865* (Albuquerque: University of New Mexico Press, 1984), 280–96.

32. For a discussion of Webley British Bull Dog revolvers and cheap copies, see Geoffrey Boothroyd, *The Handgun* (London: Cassell, 1970), 222–24 and 345–46; and A. W. F. Taylerson, *Revolving Arms* (New York: Walker, 1967), 16–43.

33. Sears, Roebuck, and Company, *The Sears, Roebuck Catalog* (Chicago: Sears, Roebuck, and Company, 1902), 316–21.

CHAPTER ONE. RED MAN: WHITE JUSTICE

1. H. C. Brearley, *Homicide in the United States* (Montclair, N.J.: Patterson Smith, 1969); Marvin E. Wolfgang, *Patterns in Criminal Homicide* (Philadelphia: University of Pennsylvania Press, 1958).

2. Gilles Vandal discovered that "blacks were victims of 85% of all homicides that occurred in Caddo [Parish] between 1865 and 1876, while whites were the presumed perpetrators of at least 84% of the blacks murdered." Gilles Vandal, "'Bloody Caddo': White Violence against Blacks in a Louisiana Parish, 1865–1976," *Journal of Social History* 25 (Winter 1991): 376.

3. There were multiple victims in several cases. See Coroner's inquests, *1850–1900*, San Diego County, SDHSRA.

4. Richard L. Carrico, "San Diego Indians and the Federal Government: Years of Neglect, 1850–1865," *Journal of San Diego History* 26 (Summer 1980): 165–84.

5. Ronet Bachman, "An Analysis of American Indian Homicide: A Test of Social Disorganization and Economic Deprivation at the Reservation County Level," *Journal of Research in Crime and Delinquency* 28 (November 1991): 456–71; Henry Zentner, "Reservation Social Structure and Anomie: A Case Study," in Henry Zentner, ed., *The Indian Identity Crisis* (Calgary, Alberta: Strayer Publications, 1973), 1–19.

6. The term "digger" may have been used first by Washington Irving in *Captain Bonneville,* 2:209 (1837). *The Oxford English Dictionary* (Oxford: Clarendon Press, 1989), 4:651.

7. James J. Rawls, *Indians of California: The Changing Image* (Norman: University of Oklahoma Press, 1984), 49; *Oxford English Dictionary,* 4:651.

8. Gerónimo Boscana, *Chinigchinich,* 335–36, in Alfred Robinson, *Life in California* (New York: Da Capo Press, 1969).

9. Francis F. Guest, *Fermín Francisco de Lausén: A Biography* (Washington, D.C.: Academy of American Franciscan History, 1973), 278.

10. Zephyrin Engelhardt, *The Missions and Missionaries of California* (San Francisco: James H. Barry Company, 1912), 2:224 and 236–37.

11. J. Ross Browne, *The Indians of California* (New York: Colt Press, 1864), 7 and 69.

12. Ruth Frey Axe, Edwin H. Carpenten, and Norman Neuerburg, *A Visit to the Missions of Southern California in February and March 1874 by Henry L. Oak* (Highland Park, Calif.: Southwest Museum, 1981), 27.

13. Report of Special Agent John G. Ames on the Condition of the Mission Indi-

ans, October 28, 1873, in Robert F. Heizer, ed., *Federal Concern about Conditions of California Indians, 1853 to 1913* (Socorro, N.M.: Ballena Press, 1979), 56.

14. D. N. Cooley, Tule River Farm, August 17, 1866, *Annual Report of the Commissioner of Indian Affairs* (Washington, D.C.: Office of Indian Affairs, 1867), 98, document 19.

15. As quoted in Robert Heizer and Alan F. Almquist, *The Other Californians: Prejudice and Discrimination under Spain, Mexico, and the United States to 1920* (Berkeley: University of California Press, 1971), 24.

16. Sherburne F. Cook, *The Conflict between the California Indian and White Civilization* (Berkeley: University of California Press, 1976), 4.

17. Dale L. Morgan and James R. Scobie, eds., *Three Years in California: William Perkins' Journal of Life at Sonora, 1849–1850* (Berkeley: University of California Press, 1964), 122 and 124.

18. Ibid., 310.

19. See James Gary Maniery, *Six Mile and Murphys Rancherias: An Ethnohistorical and Archaeological Study of Two Central Sierra Miwok Village Sites,* San Diego Museum Papers No. 22 (San Diego: San Diego Museum of Man, 1987), 5–9; and Eugene L. Conrotto, *"Miwok" Means "People": The Life and Fate of the Native Inhabitants of the California Gold Rush Country* (Fresno: Valley Publishers, 1973), 1–12.

20. Robert J. Chandler and Ronald J. Quinn, "Emma Is a Good Girl," *The Californians* (January–February 1991): 34–37; and Heizer and Almquist, *Other Californians,* 51–58.

21. Heizer and Almquist, *Other Californians,* 27–28. See also Robert F. Heizer, ed., *The Destruction of California Indians* (Santa Barbara: Peregrine Smith, 1974).

22. As quoted in Heizer and Almquist, *Other Californians,* 26.

23. B. D. Wilson, *The Indians of Southern California in 1852,* edited by John Walton Caughey (Lincoln: University of Nebraska Press, 1995), 25 and 28.

24. Browne, *Indians of California,* 22.

25. *San Diego Union,* April 8, May 12, and November 11, 1881; February 1, 1885.

26. Ibid., August 23, 1881; June 25, 1884.

27. Joy Leland, *Firewater Myths: North American Indian Drinking and Alcohol Addiction* (New Brunswick, N.J.: Rutgers Center for Alcohol Studies, 1976), 1–9; Craig MacAndrew and Robert B. Edgerton, *Drunken Comportment: A Social Explanation* (Chicago: Aldine, 1969), 101–63. The literature is voluminous; for an appraisal of other recent alcohol studies, see "A Note on Sources" in Peter C. Mancall, *Deadly Medicine: Indians and Alcohol in Early America* (Ithaca: Cornell University Press, 1995), 245–59.

28. See Nancy O. Lurie, "The World's Oldest On-Going Protest Demonstration: North American Indian Drinking Patterns," *Pacific Historical Review* 40 (August 1971): 311–32.

29. Leland, *Firewater Myths,* 1–9.

30. George H. Phillips, *Chiefs and Challengers: Indian Resistance and Cooperation in Southern California* (Berkeley: University of California Press, 1975), 57 and 65.

31. Ibid., 7.

32. Ibid., 8; Richard L. Carrico, *Strangers in a Stolen Land: American Indians in San*

Diego, 1850–1880 (Newcastle, Calif.: Sierra Oaks Publishing Company, 1987), 1–12.

33. Robert H. Jackson, *Indian Population Decline: The Missions of Northwestern New Spain, 1687–1840* (Albuquerque: University of New Mexico Press, 1994), 173–75.

34. Philip R. Pryde, *San Diego: An Introduction to the Region* (Dubuque: Kendall/Hunt Publishing, 1976), 68.

35. Report on the condition and need of the Mission Indians of California, made by Special Agent Helen Jackson and Abbot Kinney, to the Commissioner of Indian Affairs, July 13, 1883, in Helen Jackson, *A Century of Dishonor* (New York: Indian Head Books, 1994), 459 and 463–64. See also Carrico, "San Diego Indians and the Federal Government: Years of Neglect, 1850–1865," *Journal of San Diego History* 26 (Summer 1980): 165–84.

36. Jackson, *Century of Dishonor,* 489; and body of Francisco, August 4, 1877, Coroner's inquests, San Diego County, SDHSRA.

37. Jackson, *Century of Dishonor,* 491; and *San Diego Union,* August 18, 1877. After this fight three Indians were arrested and taken to jail for burning Helm's house.

38. Jackson, *Century of Dishonor,* 496.

39. Ibid., 479–515; and *San Diego Union,* September 7, 1873; January 24, 1874; September 24 and 25, October 3 and 8, and November 5, 1875; and June 29, 1879.

40. See Calpris (1,901 cases), Inter-University Consortium for Political and Social Research, University of Michigan, Ann Arbor.

41. This kind of medical testimony about the significance of physical evidence was rare until about 1900. Whether suspects José de Jesús, José del Carme, and Clemente Manteca were right-handed is not known. Testimony of Dr. E. D. French before the inquest held over body of John Overend, May 21, 1874, 13, Coroner's inquests, San Diego County, SDHSRA.

42. Testimony of Pío Peña, Captain at Capitán Grande Indian Reservation, statement of Antonio María, statement of José Arcama Peña, and testimony of Dr. E. D. French, ibid.

43. José de Jesús and José del Carme allegedly killed James Johnson on July 10, 1870. José del Carme claimed that José de Jesús had been involved in the killing of the Overend family. See *San Diego Union,* February 10 and September 18, 1875.

44. *San Diego Union,* July 15, 1875. After Manteca fled to Baja California, the sheriff rode south and brought him back.

45. *San Diego Union,* July 15, 17, and 20, 1875.

46. Statements of Filisario Alipas and Gabriel Cuayos to L. J. Crombie, Justice of the Peace, in *People v. Gabriel Cuayos and Filisario Alipas,* Justice Court, San Luis Rey Township; body of William Rogerson, January 29, 1875, Coroner's inquests, San Diego County, SDHSRA; *San Diego Union,* November 9, 1974, and July 9–11, 1875. On September 3, 1875, San Diego County officials executed Alipas.

47. Report of the jury on the Sanity of Gabriel Cuayos, in *People v. Alipas,* San Diego County, District Court, SDHSRA.

48. Ronet Bachman, "The Social Causes of American Indian Homicide as Revealed by the Life Experiences of Thirty Offenders," *American Indian Quarterly* 15 (Fall 1991): 469–92.

49. California Indian population figures are unreliable. Census figures for San Diego County record 3,067 (1860), 28 (1870), 1,702 (1880), 478 (1890), and 2,197 (1900) Indians. Any attempt at analysis would prove illusory.

50. See Robert Glass Cleland, *The Cattle on a Thousand Hills* (San Marino: Huntington Library, 1969), 208–33; and Richard Carrico, "The San Diego County Indian Reservations of 1870: An Unrealized Reality," in Horace L. Dodd, ed., *People of the Southwest and Pacific Coast* (San Diego: San Diego Corral of the Westerners, 1983), 122–24.

51. Carrico, "San Diego County Indian Reservations," 124.

52. Ibid.; Phillips, *Chiefs and Challengers,* 131–59.

53. Letter from Special Indian Agent Augustus P. Greene to E. S. Parker, Commissioner of Indian Affairs, August 30, 1870, in *Report of Secretary of the Interior* (Washington, D.C.: Government Printing Office, 1871), 4:554. Greene noted numerous complaints of squatters on Indian land.

54. Greene to E. S. Parker, February 20, 1871, in *Report of the Secretary of the Interior* (Washington, D.C.: Government Printing Office, 1872), 3:757–60; Greene to Parker, August 30, 1871, ibid., 4:556–57; and Phillips, *Chiefs and Challengers,* 145–54.

55. Sheldon Hackney, "Southern Violence," *American Historical Review* 74 (February 1969): 916. See Anthony Giddens, ed., *Emile Durkheim: Selected Writings* (Cambridge: Harvard University Press, 1972), 1–17 and 173–88; and Dominick LaCapra, *Emile Durkheim: Sociologist and Philosopher* (Ithaca: Cornell University Press, 1972), 156–71.

56. Marvin Wolfgang and Franco Ferracuti, *The Subculture of Violence: Towards the Integrated Theory of Criminology* (London: Tavistock, 1967).

57. Indian agents complained of whiskey peddlers who swarmed into the mountains of San Diego selling liquor to the "mission" Indians. See Greene to Parker, *Report of the Secretary of Interior,* 3:556–57; and Carrico, "San Diego County Indian Reservations," 179–81. For the consequences and misunderstanding of alcohol consumption among American Indians, see MacAndrew and Edgerton, *Drunken Comportment,* 101–63; and Lurie, "The World's Oldest On-Going Protest Demonstration," 311–32.

58. *San Diego Union,* May 13, July 11, and November 8, 1870; January 9–11, 29, 1871; and March 31, May 4, and December 11–14, 1872.

59. Ibid., March 31, 1872. See also January and February 1870.

60. The exact number of Indian killers is difficult to determine because some homicides attributed to "Indians" could not be verified.

61. *San Diego Union,* December 6, 1892.

62. Thomas Smallcomb was a thirty-one-year-old rancher supplementing his income working as a part-time law enforcement officer. Like most constables, he probably had no training in crime scene investigation. See the *Great Register Books, 1892–1894,* San Diego Public Library.

63. Where the tracks began and where they ended was not clear. Either the constable did not know the real meaning of the footprints or most had been destroyed by the farmers walking around the house. See Testimony of Thomas Smallcomb in

Criminal Case #7105, November 29–December 4, 1892, 285–86, *People v. José Gabriel*, Superior Court Department 2, San Diego County, Pardon File #195 in Applications for Pardon, California State Archives, Sacramento, California, hereinafter csa.

64. Ibid.

65. *San Diego Union*, October 23, 1892.

66. *People v. Gabriel*, 314–28.

67. Being under the influence of alcohol might explain his taking his time to ransack the home. But even an inebriate would have known the nature of the terrible crime committed that night and wish to flee quickly for the Mexican border less than two miles away.

68. These purses were never identified as belonging to the Geysers. *People v. Gabriel*, 72–73, and Superior Court Order, December 17, 1892, delivering all money held as evidence to M. L. Rawson, defense attorney, sdhsra.

69. See *People v. Pedro Armento and José Barreras*, Superior Court Case #7160 and #7161; Minutes of the Court, Superior Court Department 2, December 1–2, 1892; and *People v. Pedro Armento and José Barreras*, October 22, 1892, Justice Court, Otay Township, sdhsra.

70. About 50 percent of modern-day homicides are alcohol-related. On the effects of alcohol, see "Wine as Alcohol," in Maynard Amerine and Vernon L. Singleton, *Wine: An Introduction* (Berkeley: University of California Press, 1976), 326–30.

71. See section 987 in *The Penal Code of the State of California* (San Francisco, 1929); *People v. Gabriel*, October 22, 1892, Justice Court, Otay Township; and Minutes of the Court, November 1, 11, 14, 16, 1892, Superior Court Department 2, sdhsra.

72. José Gabriel still had his head bandaged to cover the wounds he received during his capture on Otay Mesa. See photograph, Register #15173, San Quentin Prison, csa.

73. *People v. Gabriel*, 187, 265, 254, 315, and 331. Another passage of testimony from the trial transcript reinforces Gabriel's responses. Defense attorney Rawson asked José Gabriel: "Did you have any talk with Mr. Geyser at that time? *A:* He told me to go down there to work on Monday, or on Sunday—to go there to his house. *Q:* To do what? *A:* To get there and take away the dirt that had been taken from the cistern. *Q:* Did you tell him that you would do so or not? *A:* I told him that I would go." Rawson asked the interpreter for a clarification: "Didn't he reply that Mr. Geyser told him to go there to work and take away the dirt from the cistern? *Interpreter:* He says: He told me to go there to work Monday or Sunday. And you asked me to ask him what for? To take away the dirt that had been taken from the cistern, or dug out from the cistern. I am giving the exact literal translation of his language, as he says it." See R. Valenzuela, interpreter, ibid., 312.

74. This was a short trial; even in Alameda County the average homicide trial lasted seven days. See Friedman and Percival, *The Roots of Justice: Crime and Punishment in Alameda County, 1870–1910* (Chapel Hill: University of North Carolina Press), 185.

75. Since the two issues are distinctly different, the judge should have instructed the jury to separate them before the jury was sequestered. The jury, headed by Jurgen L. Paulsen, included Henrich Braunagel, William A. Crawford, John Dair, Thomas E.

Fultz, Henry Gottesburen, Paul Junker, James D. Kerr, John B. Levet, Denver E. Pardee, Hamilton M. Squires, and William W. Wright. Jury list in *People v. Gabriel,* Case #7105, Superior Court Department 2, SDHSRA, and *Great Register, 1892–1894,* San Diego Public Library.

76. See *San Diego Union,* December 5 and 17, 1892.

77. A series of California Supreme Court decisions did allow the judge to set the penalty if the jury remained silent on that issue. See *People v. Welch,* 49 Cal 174 (1874); *People v. Uzza F. French,* 75 Cal 169–80 (1886); and New Instructions to the Jury, *People v. Gabriel.*

78. Two decades later, in *People v. Floyd Hall,* 199 Cal 451 (1926), the court ruled that if the jury could not agree on the penalty (death or life imprisonment) a mistrial had to be declared. The jury had to be unanimous on the penalty, and a judge could not overrule their choice. See *San Diego Union,* December 5, 1892; *People v. French,* Cal 75 177–78 (1886); and Barry Siegal, "Gideon and Beyond: Achieving an Adequate Defense for the Indigent," *Journal of Criminal Law, Criminology, and Police Science* 59 (March 1968): 73–84.

79. Judge George Puterbaugh's sentence, 364–65, *People v. Gabriel* and *San Diego Union,* December 19, 1892.

80. José Cota, Catholic rector Antonio D. Ubach, assistant priest J. Reynolds, Indian school chaplain J. Barron, Frederick H. Holbrook, Frank Rawson, and a few other local citizens failed to gain a commutation of sentence. See letter from José Cota to Governor H. H. Markham, February 14, 1893; letter from Reverend Antonio D. Ubach et al. to Governor H. H. Markham, February 6, 1893; and letter from Frederick H. Holbrook to Governor H. H. Markham, December 20, 1892, Pardon File #195, Applications for Pardon, CSA.

81. Precise information on the blows might suggest the height of the attacker(s) and whether they were left- or right-handed; however, such information was lacking. See *San Diego Union,* October 18, 1892.

82. See Minutes of the Court, January 24, 1893, Superior Court Department 2, SDHSRA.

83. *San Diego Union,* March 16, 1894.

84. Ibid.

85. *People v. Manuel Amallo,* May 9 and 17, 1894, Case #8175, Superior Court, San Diego County, SDHSRA. In 45 percent of the cases (five) involving Arizona Apache female victims, the Apache defendants (all male) pleaded guilty. See Clare V. McKanna Jr., *Homicide, Race, and Justice in the American West, 1880–1920* (Tucson: University of Arizona Press, 1997), 139–54. See San Quentin Prison Registers, Prison Records, Governor's Papers, CSA.

86. *People v. Juan José Alvarez,* December 15, 1879, Justice Court, San Diego Township, SDHSRA, 10–11.

87. Cook, *Conflict between the California Indian and White Civilization,* 255.

88. Ibid., 256.

89. Ibid., 259 and 351–52.

90. Ibid., 265.

91. Richard L. Carrico and Florence C. Shipek, "Indian Labor in San Diego County, California, 1850–1900," 211–23, in Alice Littlefield and Martha C. Knack, eds., *Native Americans and Wage Labor: Ethnohistorical Perspective* (Norman: University of Oklahoma Press, 1996).

92. *Registers of Criminal Action,* District and Superior Courts, Sonoma and San Luis Obispo Counties, 1850–1900. Clare V. McKanna, Jr., "Life Hangs in the Balance: The U.S. Supreme Court's Review of *Ex Parte Gon-shay-ee,*" *Western Legal History* 3 (Summer/Fall 1990): 197–211.

93. *San Diego Union,* December 6, 1892; July 15, 17, and 20, 1875; October 19 and 23, 1892; and *San Diego Sun,* October 17, 1892; and March 2, 1893.

94. See *People v. Gabriel,* 305–10.

CHAPTER TWO. CHINESE TONGS: GROUP SOLIDARITY

1. John R. Wunder, "The Chinese and the Courts in the Pacific Northwest: Justice Denied?" *Pacific Historical Review* 52 (May 1983): 208. See also Wunder, "Law and Chinese in Frontier Montana," *Montana, the Magazine of Western History* 30 (Spring 1981): 18–31.

2. Alexander Saxton, *The Indispensable Enemy: Labor and the Anti-Chinese Movement in California* (Berkeley: University of California Press, 1971); David V. DuFault, "The Chinese in the Mining Camps," *Southern California Quarterly* 41 (1959): 155–70; Stanford M. Lyman, *Chinese Americans* (New York: Random House, 1974); Elmer C. Sandmeyer, *The Anti-Chinese Movement in California* (Urbana: University of Illinois Press, 1939); and Robert F. Heizer and Alan F. Almquist, *The Other Californians* (Berkeley: University of California Press, 1971).

3. Christian G. Fritz, *Federal Justice in California: The Court of Odgen Hoffman, 1851–1891* (Lincoln: University of Nebraska Press, 1991), 216–23; John R. Wunder, "Chinese in Trouble: Criminal Law and Race on the Trans-Mississippi West Frontier," *Western Historical Quarterly* 17 (January 1986): 25–41; Charles J. McClain Jr., "The Chinese Struggle for Civil Rights in Nineteenth Century America: The First Phase, 1850–1870," *California Law Review* 72 (July 1984): 548–50; Paul Takagi and Tony Platt, "Behind the Gilded Ghetto: An Analysis of Race, Class, and Crime in Chinatown," *Crime and Social Justice* 9 (Spring/Summer 1978): 2–25; and Charles A. Tracy, "Race, Crime, and Social Policy: The Chinese in Oregon, 1871–1885," *Crime and Social Justice* 12 (Winter 1980): 11–25.

4. John R. Wunder, "*Territory of New Mexico v. Yee Shun* (1882): A Turning Point in Chinese Legal Relationships in the Trans-Mississippi West," *New Mexico Historical Review* 65 (July 1990): 305–18; Robert H. Tillman, "The Prosecution of Homicide in Sacramento California, 1853–1900," *Southern California Quarterly* 68 (Summer 1986): 167–81; and Clare V. McKanna Jr. and John R. Wunder, "The Chinese and California: A Torturous Legal Relationship," *California Supreme Court Historical Society Yearbook* 2 (1995): 195–214.

5. *Sacramento Bee,* November 19, 1858.

6. *Criminal Registers of Action, 1850–1900,* Sacramento County, SHSA.

7. Only two Asian female victims and no female murderers appeared within the statistics. See *Sacramento Union,* February 9, 1856.

8. Fifty percent of the Asian assailants used handguns in the commission of their crime, followed by 24 percent who employed knives in their attacks. See Coroner's inquests, *1850–1900,* Sacramento County, SHSA.

9. *Sacramento Bee,* July 17, 1862.

10. Ibid., April 15, 1873.

11. Fred A. Bee, *The Other Side of the Chinese Question* (San Francisco: Woodward and Company Printers, 1886), 29.

12. Ibid., 32.

13. Ibid., 33.

14. Willard B. Farwell, *The Chinese at Home and Abroad* (San Francisco: A. L. Bancroft and Company, 1885), 98.

15. Ibid., 99.

16. Ibid., 101–2.

17. Ibid., 105.

18. Ibid., 114.

19. McClain, "Chinese Struggle," 531. See also Stuart C. Miller, *The Unwelcome Immigrant: The American Image of the Chinese, 1785–1882* (Berkeley: University of California Press, 1959); Saxon, *The Indispensable Enemy;* Stanford M. Lyman, "Strangers in the Cities: The Chinese on the Urban Frontier," in Charles Wollenberg, ed., *Ethnic Conflict in California History* (Los Angeles: Tinnon-Brown, 1970); and Victor G. Nee and Brett de Bary Nee, *Longtime Californ': A Documentary Study of an American Chinatown* (Boston: Houghton Mifflin, 1974).

20. Bee, *The Other Side of the Chinese Question,* 19. The names of the companies vary a great deal in spelling. See also A. W. Loomis, "The Six Chinese Companies," *Overland Monthly* 1 (September 1868): 221–27; Fong Kum Ngon, "The Chinese Six Companies," *Overland Monthly* (May 1894): 518–26; Richard H. Dillon, *The Hatchet Men: The Story of the Tong Wars in San Francisco's Chinatown* (New York: Coward-McCann, 1962); and Stanford M. Lyman, "Conflict and the Web of Group Affiliation in San Francisco's Chinatown, 1850–1910," *Pacific Historical Review* 43 (October 1974): 473–99.

21. Bee, *The Other Side,* 22. See also Shih-shan Henry Tsai, *China and the Overseas Chinese in the United States, 1868–1911* (Fayetteville: University of Arkansas Press, 1983), 31–37.

22. McClain, "Chinese Struggle," 541.

23. Sylvia Sun Minnick, *Samfow: The San Joaquin Chinese Legacy* (Fresno: Panorama West Publishing, 1988), 187–212.

24. Ibid., 191–92.

25. Ibid., 201.

26. Ibid., 202–3.

27. *Lü* means statutes, while *li* refers to substatutes that were developed to further interpret the law as codified within the *Ta Ch'ing Lü Li.* Derk Bodde and Clarence Morris, *Law in Imperial China: Exemplified by 190 Ch'ing Dynasty Cases* (Cambridge: Harvard University Press, 1967), 64–65. There are eight major divisions of the *Ta Ch'ing Lü Li,* but only Section VI, Penal Law, subsection B, Homicide (articles 282–301) is important for our discussion of Chinese law. See Sybille van der Sprenkel, *Legal Institutions in Manchu China: A Sociological Analysis* (London: Athlone Press, 1962), 56–57.

28. Van Der Sprenkel, *Legal Institutions in Manchu China,* 68. See also Bodde and Morris, *Law in Imperial China,* 4–6.

29. From Scaraborough-Allen, *A Collection of Chinese Proverbs,* as cited in Bodde and Morris, *Law in Imperial China,* 135.

30. Ibid., 71–73.

31. Van der Sprenkel, *Legal Institutions in Manchu China,* 77.

32. Bodde and Morris, *Law in Imperial China,* 75.

33. T'ung-tsu Ch'u, *Law and Society in Traditional China* (Paris: Mouton, 1965), 80.

34. Ibid., 82.

35. Ibid., 86.

36. Earlier research revealed similar vendetta or blood feuds among Apache and Italian homicides committed in Gila County, Arizona, and Las Animas County, Colorado, during the nineteenth and early twentieth centuries. McKanna, *Homicide, Race, and Justice,* chapters 4 and 5.

37. See *The Oxford English Dictionary* (Oxford: Clarendon Press, 1989), 7:223.

38. *Sacramento Bee,* June 1, 1892.

39. The day after the first story, the *Bee* once again used bold type to headline the homicide that occurred the previous day: "The Mongolian Mafia. The Insignia of a Highbinder's Headquarters." The story suggested that the police and coroner had discovered records involving the "highbinders." The June 1, 1892, *Sacramento Daily Record-Union* trumpeted: "Shower of Bullets! Chinese Highbinders Fight a Battle in the Streets. About Fifty Shots Fired." See *Sacramento Bee,* November 12–14, 1883.

40. The next day the *Sacramento Bee* headline, "Coats of Mail. Formidable Shields Worn by Chinese Highbinders," documented that police had raided the Bing Ting Hong "secret society" and had captured trophies including "two ponderous coats of mail" weighing twenty pounds each (*Sacramento Bee,* June 3, 1892). The following day the *Bee* changed the story, claiming that it was the Bang Kong Tong that had been raided. Court records indicate that the perpetrator belonged to the Bing Kong Tong. See *People v. Chin Hane and Hoey Yen Sing, Criminal Case Files, 1850–1900,* Superior Court, Sacramento County, Sacramento Historical Society Archives, hereinafter, *Criminal Case Files,* SHSA. Lee Heong, the victim, was alleged to be a member of the Chee Hong Tong. In the daily coverage of the homicide the *Bee* misspelled the assailant Chin Hane's name Ching Hing, Ching Hing Hane, and Chin Hing. The language issue was indeed fuzzy. See also Stanford M. Lyman, "Chinese Secret Societies in the Occident: Notes and Suggestions for Research on the

Sociology of Secrecy," *Canadian Review of Sociology and Anthropology* 1 (May 1964): 79–102.

41. *Sacramento Bee*, October 11, 1881, and *People v. Yee Ah Pong*, Case #240, *Criminal Case Files, 1850–1900*, Superior Court, Sacramento County, SHSA.

42. *Sacramento Bee*, July 9, 1889; *People v. Ah Heong, Criminal Case Files, 1850–1900*, Superior Court, Sacramento County, SHSA; and Inmate Ah Heong, *San Quentin Prison Register, 1850–1900*, Prison Papers, Records of the Governor, Sacramento, California State Archives, hereinafter *San Quentin Prison Register*, CSA.

43. Farwell, *Chinese at Home and Abroad*, 101 and 112–14. Five cases involving Asian victims killed by alleged Asian perpetrators occurred outside of the Chinatown section of Sacramento. Two were committed in Folsom prison by Asian inmates, and the other three occurred in Asian mining camps. See December 14, 1861; September 12, 1881; August 8, 1883; May 6, 1885; and August 9, 1892, Coroner's inquests, Sacramento County, SHSA.

44. Testimony of former San Joaquin prosecutor J. A. Hosmer in Pardon File #341, Applications for Pardon, CSA, and Testimony of Ah Tschin, *People v. Ah Mow*, November 1876, Fifth Judicial District Court, San Joaquin County, County Courthouse, hereinafter, San Joaquin County, SJCC.

45. Testimony of H. L. Farrington, ibid., 75–76 and 25–26.

46. Affidavit of William Gibson, March 16, 1885, in Pardon File #341, Applications for Pardon, CSA. Also see the statement of J J Evans, deputy sheriff, who was the first law enforcement officer to arrive at the scene. He was sure that the witnesses against the defendants perjured themselves. Ibid.

47. Jean Chesneaux, *Secret Societies in China: In the Nineteenth and Twentieth Centuries* (London: Heinemann Educational Books, 1971), 15. See also Mak Lau Fong, *The Sociology of Secret Societies: A Study of Chinese Secret Societies in Singapore and Peninsular Malaysia* (New York: Oxford University Press, 1981); and David Ownby and Mary Somers Heidhues, eds., *"Secret Societies" Reconsidered: Perspectives on the Social History of Modern South China and Southeast Asia* (New York: M. E. Sharpe, 1993).

48. L. Eve Armentrout Ma, "Chinatown Organizations and the Anti-Chinese Movement, 1882–1914," 148–49, in Sucheng Chan, ed., *Entry Denied: Exclusion and the Chinese Community in America, 1882–1943* (Philadelphia: Temple University Press, 1990).

49. Ko-lin Chin, *Chinese Subculture and Criminality: Non-traditional Crime Groups in America* (New York: Greenwood, 1990), 13–14.

50. Ko-lin Chin, *Chinatown Gangs: Extortion, Enterprise, and Ethnicity* (New York: Oxford University Press, 1996), 191.

51. C. N. Reynolds, "The Chinese Tongs," *American Journal of Sociology* 40 (March 1935): 616–21.

52. Stanford M. Lyman, "Conflict and the Web of Group Affiliation in San Francisco's China Town, 1850–1910," 109, in Stanford M. Lyman, *The Asian in North America* (Santa Barbara: ABC-Clio, Inc., 1977); and Armentrout Ma, "Chinatown Organizations," 148–49.

53. Lyman, "Conflict and Group Affiliation," 113 and 110.

54. Ibid., 113.

55. *Oxford English Dictionary,* 18:221. Some writers compared them to modern-day criminal groups: "The famous Tongs were something else, more mysterious—secret societies similar to Mafia families." Ibid.

56. Lyman, "Conflict and Group Affiliation," 103.

57. For a discussion of "tong wars," see C. Y. Lee, *Days of the Tong Wars* (New York: Ballantine, 1974), 31; Gunther Barth, *Bitter Strength: A History of the Chinese in the United States, 1850–1870* (Cambridge: Harvard University Press, 1964); Alexander McLeod, *Pigtails and Gold Dust* (Caldwell, Idaho: Caxton Printers, 1948), 226–37; Richard H. Dillon, *The Hatchetmen: The Story of the Tong Wars in San Francisco's Chinatown* (New York: Coward-McCann, 1962), 167–206 and 241–62; and Joseph Henry Jackson, *Anybody's Gold* (San Francisco: Chronicle Books, 1970), 218.

58. *People v. Ah Fat, Criminal Case Files, 1850–1900,* District Court, Sacramento County, SHSA.

59. *Pardon Application of Ah Fat,* June 13, 1893, Pardon File #5935, Application for Pardon, CSA.

60. Letter from S. Solon Hall to Governor H. H. Markham, December 16, 1892, ibid. Hall had assisted the prosecution in the Ah Fat and Ah Wee trials. Tongs, companies, and benevolent associations often retained lawyers to aid the prosecution, and in some cases hired investigators to gather evidence for either the defense or the prosecution. Michele Shover, "Fighting Back: The Chinese Influence on Chico Law and Politics, 1880–1886," *California History* 74 (Winter 1995/96): 408–33 and 449–50.

61. *Sacramento Bee,* November 13, 1883.

62. Ibid., November 15, 1883.

63. Letter from R. T. Devlin, November 16, 1894, in Pardon File #5866, Application for Pardon, CSA. Devlin claimed that two rival societies, Tong Duck Tong and Hong Duck Tong, participated in the fight.

64. Letter from R. M. Clarken to Governor R. W. Waterman, November 11, 1890, ibid.

65. *Sacramento Bee,* June 1, 1892. The next day they became the "Mongolian Mafia."

66. *People v. Chin Hane and Hoey Yen Sing,* 1–7 and 386–87, *Criminal Case Files, 1850–1900,* Superior Court, Sacramento County, SHSA.

67. Ibid., 388–95.

68. *People v. Chin Hane,* 108 Cal 597-608 (1895). See *Sacramento Union,* December 14, 1895.

69. Motion to Dismiss, 2–3, *People v. Ling Ying Toy (Alias Quong Sing) and Ching Gow Duey (Alias Chin Ah Gow Nuey),* Case #1710, August, 1897, *Criminal Case Files, 1850–1900,* Superior Court, Sacramento County, SHSA.

70. Ibid., 5.

71. Ibid., 5–6.

72. In his opening statement in a murder case against Lee Dick Lung, prosecutor C. T. Jones in referring to Chinese homicide cases claimed: "They are divided into

two sides; it is usually one 'Tong' or company, against another Tong or company." Defense counsel objected to the statement but was overruled. See *People v. Lee Dick Lung,* Pardon File #290, Applications for Pardon, CSA.

73. *The People v. Ah Ton,* Pardon File #652, Applications for Pardon, CSA. The deceased's name has been spelled in a variety of ways in the court documents (Conely, Conley, Conoly, and Coneley). For consistency I have chosen Connoly.

74. Testimony of Toby Flam, *People v. Ah Ton,* 2–4, District Court, Calaveras County, ibid.

75. Petition to Honorable William Gwin, Governor of the State of California, from twenty citizens of San Andreas, Calaveras County, California, November 26, 1879, ibid. Petitioners included businessmen, the sheriff, county treasurer, deputy county clerk, superintendent of schools, and the editor of the *Calaveras Advertiser.*

76. Affidavit of J. Salcido, ibid. Judge Reed said he passed Connoly's bridge and noticed that "Connoly was intoxicated." Ms. Salcido also said Connoly "was very much intoxicated." See Report of Detective James Galbraith, 10–12, ibid.

77. Affidavit from William Lewis, attorney, San Andreas, California, April 6, 1879, to F. A. Bee, Consul General, San Francisco, ibid.

78. Testimony of Toby Flam, 2–4, *People v. Ah Ton,* District Court, Calaveras County, ibid.

79. Testimony of J. B. Machavilli, in Report of Detective James Galbraith, to Colonel F. A. Bee, Consul for Chinese, n.d., ibid.

80. Machavilli suggested that Ah Ton "was not near the bridge at the time that fool boy says he was." Testimony of Sheriff B. F. Haines, 7, ibid. Research on eyewitness identification suggests that white witnesses were able to recognize white faces 68 percent of the time and Asian faces 45 percent of time. Alvin G. Goldstein, "The Fallibility of the Eyewitness: Psychological Evidence," 230, in Bruce Dennis Sales, ed., *Psychology in the Legal Process* (New York: Spectrum Publications, 1977).

81. Testimony of Dr. Robinson, 9, ibid. Detective Galbraith claimed that "the idea was also general that the boy Toby Flam who was with him [victim] all the time had put the thing up for Connoly." Letter from J. B. Reddick, San Andreas, California, to William Irwin, Governor of California, November 26, 1879, ibid. Emphasis in the original.

82. Testimony of Toby Flam, *People v. Ah Ton,* Pardon File #652, Applications for Pardon, CSA.

83. Affidavit of August Flam, November 26, 1879, San Andreas, California, signed by August and Frances Flam, ibid.

84. Letter from J. F. Washburn, San Andreas, January 21, 1880, to George F. Wood, in ibid. J. B. Machavilli supported this view, stating that "the lawyer [for defense] had too much whiskey in him to try any case." See the Report of Detective James Galbraith, to Colonel F. A. Bee, Consul for Chinese, n.d., ibid.

85. Letter from E. C. Marshals, Attorney General, State of California, n.d., to George Stoneman, Governor of California, ibid.

86. Letter from William T. Wallace, E. W. McKinstry, and Addison C. Niles, Judicial Department, Supreme Court, State of California, November 20, 1879, to

William Irwin, Governor of California, ibid. See also *People v. Ah Ton* 53 Cal 741–42 (1879).

87. Affidavit from William T. Lewis, attorney, San Andreas, April 6, 1879, to F. A. Bee, Consul General, San Francisco, ibid.

88. Letter from William T. Lewis, attorney, San Andreas, November 26, 1879, to William Irwin, Governor of California, ibid.

89. Affidavit of Chung Fun taken by F. A. Bee, Chinese Consul, San Francisco, June 9, 1880, ibid.

90. Letter from E. C. Marshals, Attorney General, State of California, n.d., to George Stoneman, Governor of California, ibid.

91. Report of Detective Galbraith, 11–12, ibid.

92. Ibid.

93. *San Luis Obispo Tribune,* August 28, 1875.

94. Transcript of *People v. Ah Sing, et al.* on Appeal to the California Supreme Court, 11, Pardon File #8742, Applications for Pardon, CSA.

95. Defendant's Bill of Exceptions, 24–25, ibid.

96. *People v. Ah Sing* 51 Cal 373 (1876). Emphasis in the original.

97. Ibid., 374.

98. For a similar improper instruction on reasonable doubt a decade later in San Luis Obispo County, see *People v. William Bushton* 80 Cal 162 (1889).

99. Testimony of John LaCosta, *People v. Chung Litt, et al.,* District Court, Tuolumne County, Pardon File #1286, Applications for Pardon, CSA.

100. Testimony of E. M. Archer, ibid.

101. Testimony of Constable Thomas Corcoran, ibid.

102. Testimony of Chu Sow, ibid.

103. Ibid.

104. See *People v. Chung Lit, et al.* 17 Cal 320–22 (1861).

105. *Alta California,* March 27, 1861.

106. *Registers of Criminal Action, 1850–1900,* Sacramento County, SHSA.

107. With good legal counsel, Chinese defendants seldom plea-bargained the way Indians and blacks did. See McKanna, "Seeds of Destruction," "Life Hangs in the Balance"; Mark H. Haller, "Plea Bargaining: The Nineteenth Century Context," *Law and Society Review* 13 (Winter 1979): 273–80; and Lawrence M. Friedman, "Plea Bargaining in Historical Perspective," *Law and Society Review* 13 (Winter 1979): 247–60.

108. See Mary Roberts Coolidge, *Chinese Immigration* (New York: Henry Holt, 1909), 402–7; Shih-shan Henry Tsi, *China and the Overseas Chinese in the United States, 1868–1911* (Fayetteville: University of Arkansas Press, 1983), 124–29; and Chinese Consolidated Benevolent Association, California, *Memorial: Six Chinese Companies, an Address to the Senate and House of Representatives of the United States, December 8, 1877* (Reprint, San Francisco: R and E Research Associates, 1970).

109. The absence of plea bargaining among Chinese defendants explains the strength of having good legal representation. See Fritz, *Federal Justice in California,* 210–49.

CHAPTER THREE. HISPANICS: JUSTICE IN A CONQUERED LAND

1. Richard H. Peterson, "Anti-Mexican Nativism in California, 1848–1853: A Study of Cultural Conflict," *Southern California Quarterly* 62 (Winter 1980): 309–27; Sister Colette Standart, "The Sonora Migration to California, 1848–1856: A Study in Prejudice," *Southern California Quarterly* 58 (Fall 1976): 346; and James M. Guinn, "The Sonoran Migration," *Historical Society of Southern California* 8 (1909): 35–36.

2. Leonard Pitt, *The Decline of the Californios: A Social History of the Spanish-Speaking Californians, 1846–1890* (Los Angeles: University of California Press, 1966); Robert Glass Cleland, *Cattle on a Thousand Hills: Southern California, 1850–80* (San Marino: Huntington Library, 1969).

3. Albert Camarillo, *Chicanos in a Changing Society: From Mexican Pueblos to American Barrios in Santa Barbara and Southern California, 1848–1930* (Cambridge: Harvard University Press, 1979); Richard Griswold del Castillo, *The Los Angeles Barrio, 1850–1890: A Social History* (Berkeley: University of California Press, 1979).

4. *Sacramento Union,* August 6, 1855.

5. Deposition by María Antonio Ortega before Justice of the Peace Charles Haraszthy, January 8, 1851, San Diego County, San Diego Historical Society Research Archives, hereinafter SDHSRA.

6. There were other cases of hungry American Indians being killed for slaughtering cattle, but ranchers were seldom charged. *People v. María Antonio Ortega,* January 1851, Justice Court, San Diego County, SDHSRA. See also Greene to Parker, *Report of the Secretary of the Interior,* 556–57; and George H. Phillips, *Chiefs and Challengers: Indian Resistance and Cooperation in Southern California* (Berkeley: University of California Press, 1975), 151–59.

7. Samuel Parsons Scott, *Las Siete Partidas* (New York: Commerce Clearing House, 1931).

8. Charles Sumner Lobingier, "Introduction," ibid., xlix–liv.

9. "The Alcalde System of California," in Appendix, *Reports of Cases Determined in the California Supreme Court of the State of California* I (San Francisco: Bancroft-Whitney, 1906): 559–82.

10. Charles R. Cutter, *The Legal Culture of Northern New Spain, 1700–1810* (Albuquerque: University of New Mexico Press, 1995), 114–17.

11. Ibid., 122–23.

12. Ibid., 125–28.

13. Ibid., 131–33.

14. William B. Taylor, *Drinking, Homicide, and Rebellion in Colonial Mexican Villages* (Stanford: Stanford University Press, 1979), 98. Taylor found that the colonial government preferred to put "criminals—who were legal slaves under the Spanish system of justice—to useful work" rather than execute them. Ibid., 100.

15. Charles R. Cutter, "Judicial Punishment in Colonial New Mexico," *Western Legal History* 8 (Winter/Spring 1995): 126. In a similar historical study of criminal prosecution in colonial Mexico City, Michael C. Scardaville noted that "not one case resulted in the death penalty." Michael C. Scardaville, "(Hapsburg) Law and (Bourbon) Or-

der: State Authority, Popular Unrest, and the Criminal Justice System in Bourbon Mexico City," *Americas* 50 (April 1994): 519; Charles R. Cutter, "Community and the Law in Northern New Spain," *Americas* 50 (April 1994): 467–80; and Colin MacLachlan, *Criminal Justice in Eighteenth-Century Mexico: A Study of the Tribunal of the Acordada* (Berkeley: University of California Press, 1974), 50–52 and 114–15.

16. David J. Langum, *Law and Community on the Mexican California Frontier: Anglo-American Expatriates and the Clash of Legal Traditions, 1821–1846* (Norman: University of Oklahoma Press, 1987), 80–81. See also Langum, "The Legal System of Spanish California: A Preliminary Study," *Western Legal History* 7 (Winter/Spring 1994): 15.

17. Jill Mocho, *Murder and Justice in Frontier New Mexico, 1821–1846* (Albuquerque: University of New Mexico Press, 1997), 17–18. Mocho examined only eleven homicide cases.

18. Richard L. Carrico, "Spanish Crime and Punishment: The Native American Experience in Colonial San Diego, 1769–1830," *Western Legal History* 3 (Winter/Spring 1990): 32–33.

19. Langum, *Law and Community on the Mexican California Frontier,* 69.

20. Ibid., 90. Langum concluded that in some smuggling cases white defendants were "given preferential treatment."

21. Ibid., 94.

22. The term "machismo" is used to identify a male way of thinking in Hispanic culture. Octavio Paz provides the best general discussion of machismo and its impact on Mexico. See Octavio Paz, *The Labyrinth of Solitude: Life and Thought in Mexico* (New York: Grove Press, 1961), 65–88. For critics of this concept, see Elizabeth E. Brusco, *The Reformation of Machismo: Evangelical Conversion and Gender in Colombia* (Austin: University of Texas Press, 1995), 1–12. See also Alfredo Mirandé, *Hombres y Machos: Masculinity and Latino Culture* (Boulder: Westview, 1997); Aniceto Aramoni, "Machismo," *Psychology Today* (January 1972): 69–72; Marvin Goldwert, "Mexican Machismo: The Flight from Femininity," *Psychoanalytic Review* 72 (Spring 1985): 161–69; Matthew C. Gutmann, *The Meaning of Macho: Being a Man in Mexico City* (Berkeley: University of California Press, 1996); Evelyn P. Stevens, "Machismo and Marianismo," *Society* 10 (September/October 1973): 57–63; A. Rolando Andrade, "Machismo: A Universal Malady," *Journal of American Culture* 15 (Winter 1992): 33–42; and José B. Torres, "Masculinity and Gender Roles among Puerto Rican Men: Machismo on the U.S. Mainland," *American Journal of Orthopsychiatry* 68 (January 1998): 16–26.

23. The original *chingada* was La Malinche or Marina, the Aztec mistress sexually violated by Hernán Cortés during the Spanish conquest of Mexico. She represents everything bad that has happened to the Mexicans. Paz, *Labyrinth of Solitude,* 76–81.

24. Ilán Stavans, "The Latin Phallus," in Ray González, ed., *Muy Macho: Latino Men Confront Their Manhood* (New York: Doubleday, 1996), 143–64.

25. Rudolfo Anaya, "'I'm the King': The Macho Image," in González, *Muy Macho,* 57–74.

26. Luis Alberto Urrea, "Whores," in González, *Muy Macho,* 99–110.

27. Richard W. Slatta, "Comparative Frontier Social Life: Western Saloons and Ar-

gentine Pulperias," *Great Plains Quarterly* 7 (Summer 1987): 155–65; John Charles Chasteen, "Violence for Show: Knife Dueling on a Nineteenth-Century Cattle Frontier," in Lyman L. Johnson, ed., *The Problems of Order in Changing Societies: Essays on Crime and Policing in Argentina and Uruguay*, 47–64 (Albuquerque: University of New Mexico Press, 1990); Robert J. Glynn, Joseph S. LoCastro, John A. Hermos, and Raymond Bossé. "Social Contexts and Motives for Drinking in Men," *Journal of Studies on Alcohol* 44 (November 1983): 1021–22; and William C. Sayres, "Ritual Drinking, Ethnic Status, and Inebriety in Rural Colombia," *Quarterly Journal of Studies on Alcohol* 17 (March 1956): 53–62.

28. Paz, *Labyrinth of Solitude*, 80.

29. Taylor, *Drinking, Homicide, and Rebellion*, 81–83.

30. Mocho, *Murder and Justice*, xii.

31. Petition for Executive Clemency for Joseph Hurtado, n.d., 1–3, Pardon File #206, Applications for Pardon, CSA.

32. Ibid., 4.

33. Ibid.

34. Ibid., 7.

35. Ibid., 8.

36. Ibid.

37. Brief for Appellant, *The People v. Joseph Hurtado*, California Supreme Court, criminal case #1565, CSA.

38. Letter of John Aunstory, Superior Court Judge, to Governor George Stoneman, July 26, 1883, Pardon File #206, Applications for Pardon, CSA.

39. *Vidette*, n.d. (1883), ibid.

40. Petition for clemency on behalf of Joseph Hurtado to Governor George Stoneman, n.d., Pardon File #206, Applications for Pardon, CSA. The petition was signed by six attorneys, a steamboat owner, two railroad engineers, several other railroad employees, and the president of California Transportation company, all whites.

41. Letter from R. F. Del Valle to Governor George Stoneman, August 15, 1883, ibid.

42. Brief for Appellant, 9, *The People v. Joseph Hurtado*, California Supreme Court, criminal case #11565, CSA. Emphasis in original.

43. Ibid., 10–11.

44. Ibid., 15.

45. Ibid., 17.

46. Ibid., 18.

47. *People v. Hurtado* 63 Cal 292 (1883).

48. Appellant Brief, 20, *People v. Hurtado*, California Supreme Court, criminal case #11565, CSA.

49. *People v. Hurtado* 63 Cal 293 (1883).

50. Hurtado's lawyers appealed the death penalty sentence to the U.S. Supreme Court, which affirmed the sentence in an opinion handed down on March 3, 1884. See *Hurtado v. People of the State of California* 110 U.S. 516–37 (1884).

51. See the discussion of homicides committed over infidelity in Mexico in Taylor, *Drinking, Homicide, and Rebellion*, 85–88 and 91–94. Hispanic officials were more le-

nient in the punishment of men accused of killing their spouses over adultery.

52. For other examples involving machismo and love triangles, see Coroners' inquests, female victims of Luis Meléndez, Luis Melinda, and Manuel Chávez (San Diego County); José Alípaz and Pedro Gallego (San Luis Obispo County); Ramón López (Santa Barbara County); Alejandro Berkio (Sacramento County); and León Lebrun (Tuolumne County).

53. Testimony of W. B. Carleton, body of Matthew Alderson, April 6, 1872, 1, Coroner's inquests, San Diego County, San Diego Historical Society Research Archives, hereinafter sdhsra.

54. Ibid., 2.

55. Testimony of Dr. R. J. Gregg, ibid., 1.

56. Testimony of Carleton and J. Mathias, ibid., 3–4.

57. Testimony of Ben Mannasse, ibid., 8.

58. Testimony of H. Baslow, ibid., 9.

59. Testimony of Constable A. M. Young, ibid., 10–11.

60. Testimony of Sheriff S. W. Craigue, July 11, 1872, 3–5, *People v. Augustin Castro,* District Court, San Diego County, sdhsra.

61. *San Diego Union,* April 26, 1872.

62. Years later in a letter requesting a pardon, Castro claimed that he was advised by Sheriff S. W. Craigue and Chalmers Scott to plead guilty. Letter from Augustin Castro to Governor Henry T. Gage, January 18, 1899, in Pardon File #6601, Applications for Pardon, csa.

63. Testimony of Augustin Castro, 1, July 11, 1872, *People v. Castro,* District Court, San Diego County, sdhsra.

64. Testimony of Constable Young, body of Matthew Alderson, 11, Coroner's inquests, San Diego County, sdhsra.

65. *San Diego Union,* April 4 and July 15, 1872.

66. Ibid., April 6, 1872.

67. Obituary on Chalmers Scott in the *San Diego Union,* November 17, 1898, and May 7, 1872.

68. Letter from W. T. McNealy to H. C. Rolfe, May 19, 1890, ibid.

69. Letter from H. C. Rolfe to Governor Henry T. Gage, January 9, 1899, ibid.

70. Camarillo, *Chicanos in a Changing Society,* 31 and 41.

71. Patricio Bonilla became *mayordomo* of Rancho Laguna on May 14, 1868, and was removed on July 24, 1868, the day of the killing. See Transcript of *People v. Francisco Javier Bonilla,* District Court, Santa Barbara County, Pardon File #1808, Applications for Pardon, csa.

72. *Los Angeles Porcupine,* May 22, 1886.

73. Testimony in *People v. Bonilla.*

74. Judge Pablo de la Guerra claimed that Patricio Bonilla brought his son to José de la Guerra y Noriega's home and turned him over to the sheriff. The Bonilla family lived in Santa Barbara with Antonio María de la Guerra, younger brother of Pablo de la Guerra, for five years. Pablo de la Guerra to Governor Henry H. Haight, November 13, 1868, and Antonio María de la Guerra to Governor Haight, December 25,

1868, Pardon File #1808, Applications for Pardon, CSA; Charles Enoch Huse, *The Huse Journal: Santa Barbara in the 1850s,* ed. Edith B. Conkey (Santa Barbara: Santa Barbara Historical Society, 1977), 257; and *Santa Barbara Post,* August 28, 1868.

75. Minutes of District Court 1, 255, 270–73, District Court, Santa Barbara County, County Courthouse, hereinafter SBCC.

76. Letter from Charles E. Huse to Governor Haight, November 12, 1868, Pardon File #1808, Applications for Pardon, CSA.

77. Walker A. Tompkins, *Santa Barbara History Makers* (Santa Barbara: McNally and Loftin, 1983), 115.

78. Letter from Charles E. Huse to Governor Haight, November 12, 1868, Pardon File #1808, Applications for Pardon, CSA. A trial transcript was forwarded to the governor; however, it was not "complete." It provided some testimony, but lacked instructions to the jury and cross-examination. See *People v. Bonilla,* ibid.

79. See Tompkins, *Santa Barbara History Makers,* 117. Newspaper accounts, petitions to the governor on Bonilla's behalf, and reminiscences are unrevealing. See also Clare V. McKanna Jr., "The San Quentin Prison Pardon Papers: A Look at File No. 1808, the Case of Francisco Javier Bonilla," *Southern California Quarterly* 57 (Summer 1985): 187–96.

80. Letter from Pablo de la Guerra to N[icholas] Hubert, Santa Barbara, August 22, 1860, as quoted in Robert Willis Blew, "Californios and American Institutions: A Study of Reactions to Social and Political Institutions" (Ph.D. diss., University of Southern California, 1972), 144–45. For a cinematic discussion of this language barrier and its consequences, see *The Ballad of Gregorio Cortez.*

81. *People v. Bonilla,* Pardon File #1808, Applications for Pardon, CSA.

82. *Los Angeles Porcupine,* March 22, 1886.

83. Letter from Horace Bell to Reverend William H. Hill, San Quentin Prison, January 19, 1882, Pardon File #1808, Applications for Pardon, CSA.

84. *Ventura Free Press,* June 19, 1882; letter from J. H. Kinkaid to Governor Perkins, November 21, 1882, ibid.

85. Kenneth Grubb, "False Fears," *Insurance Counsel Journal* 26 (October 1959): 480. Mark Twain has an even harder assessment, suggesting that "the jury system put a ban upon intelligence and honesty, and a premium upon ignorance, stupidity and perjury." See Mark Twain, *Roughing It* (New York: P. F. Collier and Son, 1913), 57.

86. Oliver Wendell Holmes, "Law in Science—Science in Law," *Collected Legal Papers* (New York: Harcourt, Brace, 1921), 237–38.

87. Saul M. Kassin and Lawrence S. Wrightsman, *The American Jury on Trial: Psychological Perspectives* (New York: Hemisphere Publishing, 1988), 6.

88. See Daniel H. Swett, "Cultural Bias in the American Legal System," *Law and Society Review* 4 (August 1969): 96–97.

89. Valerie P. Hans and Neil Vidmar, *Judging the Jury* (New York: Plenum, 1986), 50–51.

90. *People v. Bonilla,* File #175, n.d., *Criminal Case Files, 1850–1900,* District Court, Santa Barbara County, SBCC.

91. *People v. Francisco Xavier Bonilla* 38 Cal 699–700 (1869). Emphasis in original.

92. Decision of Justice Silas W. Sanderson, ibid.

93. Ibid., 700–701.

94. Letter from José A. Godoy, Mexican Consul, San Francisco, to Governor H. H. Haight, September 30, 1868, Pardon File #1808, Applications for Pardon, CSA.

95. Letter from Pablo de la Guerra, Judge of the First District Court, to Governor H. H. Haight, ibid.

96. Petition to Governor H. H. Haight, n.d., ibid. Although most of the petitioners were Hispanic, it included whites such as F. A. Thompson, County Clerk, and Sheriff Ezra Porter.

97. *Santa Barbara Post,* January 20, 1869. Bonilla served twenty years before being pardoned on March 28, 1888.

98. *Calaveras Chronicle,* June 22, 1872.

99. Ibid.

100. Testimony of R. K. Thorn, Sheriff of Calaveras County, 30, in *People v. Coyado,* California Supreme Court, File #11959, CSA.

101. Testimony of R. K. Thorn, Sheriff of Calaveras County, 32, in *People v. Coyado,* California Supreme Court, File #11959, CSA.

102. Ibid., 33.

103. Challenge by W. L. Hopkins, 8, *People v. Coyado,* District Court, Calaveras County, California Supreme Court, File #11959, CSA.

104. Ibid., 10.

105. Judgment of the court, ibid., 13.

106. Walter L. Hopkins, Argument for Appellant, *People v. Coyado* 40 Cal 586–88 (1871).

107. Jo Hamilton, Attorney General, Argument for Respondent, ibid., 591.

108. Opinion of Justice Jack Temple, ibid., 592. Concurred in by Justices Augustus L. Rhodes, Joseph B. Crockett, and William T. Wallace.

109. Ibid., 593.

110. See *People v. Coyado,* Pardon File #1810, Applications for Pardon, CSA.

111. *Calaveras Chronicle,* June 22, 1872.

112. Ibid.

113. Ibid.

114. Griswold del Castillo, *The Los Angeles Barrio,* 116–17.

115. *Minutes of the First District Court,* 255, September 1868 Term, Santa Barbara County.

116. *San Quentin Prison Register, 1850–1900,* Prison Papers, Records of Governor, CSA.

117. Henry Miller, *On the Fringe: The Dispossessed in America* (Lexington, Mass.: Lexington Books, 1991), xi–xxii.

CHAPTER FOUR. WHITE MAN: WHITE JUSTICE

1. *High Noon* (1952), starring Gary Cooper, became the stereotypical Hollywood portrayal of Western shoot-outs.

2. Rufus K. Porter, letters to the *San Francisco Bulletin,* October 1866.

3. *San Diego Union,* January 20, 1871.

4. *San Luis Obispo Tribune,* March 16, 1878.

5. See, for example, Hubert Howe Bancroft, *Popular Tribunals* (San Francisco: History Company Publishers, 1887), 1; and Thomas J. Dimsdale, *The Vigilantes of Montana* (Norman: University of Oklahoma Press, 1953).

6. *Sacramento Bee,* November 16, 1861, and body of unknown Chinese male, November 11, 1861, Coroner's inquests, Sacramento County, SHSA; and body of Fru Dow, Coroner's inquests, Calaveras County, CCM.

7. Lewis Atherton, *The Cattle Kings* (Bloomington: Indiana University Press, 1961), 39–40; C. L. Sonnichsen, *Cowboys and Cattle Kings: Life on the Range Today* (Norman: University of Oklahoma Press, 1950), 44; Robert Utley, *High Noon in Lincoln: Violence on the Western Frontier* (Albuquerque: University of New Mexico Press, 1987), 20; Richard Maxwell Brown, "Western Violence: Structure, Value, Myth," *Western Historical Quarterly* 24 (February 1993): 15; C. L. Sonnichsen, *Tularosa: Last of the Frontier West* (New York: Devin-Adair, 1963), 21; and Joseph G. Rosa, *Wild Bill Hickock: The Man and His Myth* (Lawrence: University Press of Kansas, 1996), 105.

8. Brown, "Western Violence," 15; Sonnichsen, *Tularosa,* 21–23; and Utley, *High Noon in Lincoln,* 20–21.

9. Atherton, *The Cattle Kings,* 39–40.

10. Ibid., 41 and 43.

11. Sonnichsen, *Cowboys and Cattle Kings,* 44.

12. Utley, *High Noon in Lincoln,* 20.

13. Rosa, *Wild Bill Hickock,* 105.

14. Richard Maxwell Brown, *No Duty to Retreat: Violence and Values in American History and Society* (New York: Oxford University Press, 1991), 5. See also Thomas J. Kernan, "The Jurisprudence of Lawlessness," *Reports of American Bar Association* 39 (1906): 450–67; J. H. Ehrlich, *Ehrlich's Blackstone Part Two: Private Wrongs, Public Wrongs* (New York: Capricorn Books, 1959), 384–401; and Joseph H. Beale Jr., "Retreat from a Murderous Assault," *Harvard Law Review* 16 (May 1903): 567–82.

15. David A. Williams, *David C. Broderick: A Political Portrait* (San Marino: Huntington Library, 1969), 232.

16. Dueling had been illegal in California for several years, but many who followed the concept of chivalry accepted it as a right to challenge anyone who made disparaging remarks. See *Statutes of California, 1855* (Sacramento: B. B. Redding, State Printer, 1855), 152–53. On dueling, see Jack K. Williams, *Dueling in the Old South: Vignettes of Social History* (College Station: Texas A&M University Press, 1980).

17. *An Illustrated History of San Joaquin County, California* (Chicago: Lewis Publishing, 1890), 90–94.

18. Stephen J. Field, *Personal Reminiscences of Early Days in California* (New York: Da Capo Press, 1968), 70–71 and 242–44. Richard Maxwell Brown suggests that "the killing of Terry by Neagle was indirectly related to the Mussel Slough conflict." In other words, Brown views it as a pro–Southern Pacific Railroad faction (Field) versus the anti–Southern Pacific group (Terry) squabble that began in the 1880s. See Brown, *No Duty to Retreat,* 108.

19. A. E. Wagstaff, compiler, *Life of David S. Terry* (San Francisco: Continental Publishing, 1892), 519–20.

20. Field, *Personal Reminiscences,* 308.

21. Testimony of T. W. Stackpole, body of David S. Terry, August 14, 1889, 21, Coroner's inquests, San Joaquin County, Stockton, County Courthouse, hereinafter SJCC.

22. Field, *Personal Reminiscences,* 314.

23. Testimony of Stackpole, body of David S. Terry, 21, Coroner's inquests, San Joaquin County, SJCC.

24. Field, *Personal Reminiscences,* 318.

25. George C. Gorham, "Attempted Assassination of Justice Field by a Former Associate on the State Supreme Bench," in Field, *Personal Reminiscences,* 314 and 313.

26. Testimony of John Barrett, body of David S. Terry, 18–19, Coroner's inquests, San Joaquin County, SJCC.

27. Field, *Personal Reminiscences,* 319.

28. *Sacramento Record-Union,* August 15, 1889; and *Alta California,* August 15, 1889.

29. *Sacramento Record-Union,* September 17 and 18, 1889.

30. *Thomas Cunningham, Sheriff of the County of San Joaquin, v. David Neagle,* 135 U.S. 661–62 (1889).

31. Ibid., 662.

32. Ibid., 664.

33. Ibid., 672.

34. Benjamin Hayes, *Pioneer Notes from the Diaries of Judge Benjamin Hayes, 1849–1875* (Los Angeles: privately printed, 1929), 282–83.

35. Richard W. Crawford, *Stranger Than Fiction: Vignettes of San Diego History* (San Diego: San Diego Historical Society, 1995), 52.

36. *San Diego Herald,* April 25, 1857; May 2, 1857; July 18, 1857; and August 8, 1857. The correct spelling of William Couts's middle name is unclear. It has been variously spelled Blount, Blunt, and Blounts. For consistency, Blunt has been chosen.

37. Testimony of Tomás Alvarado in Preliminary Hearing, May 18, 1863, *People v. William B. Couts,* County Court, San Diego County, San Diego Historical Society Research Archives, hereinafter SDHSRA.

38. Testimony of Tomás Alvarado, Ramón Castro, and Syriaco Estrada, ibid.

39. Testimony of Ramón Castro, Syriaco Estrada, Tomás Alvarado, and José Alvarado, ibid.

40. Testimony of Syriaco Estrada, ibid.

41. Letter from Cave J. Couts to Judge Hayes, January 14, 1863, in Hayes, *Pioneer Notes,* 283. Emphasis in original.

42. Motion to set aside indictment, April 22, 1865, *People v. William B. Couts,* District Court, San Diego County, SDHSRA.

43. Richard F. Pourade, *The Silver Dons* (San Diego: Union-Tribune Publishing, 1963), 251. Lyle C. Annable also suggests that Vásquez "jumped the fence and charged Blunt with a spade and a knife." See Lyle C. Annable, "The Life and Times of Cave Johnson Couts, San Diego County Pioneer" (master's thesis, San Diego State University, 1965), 124. Both historians apparently accepted Cave Couts's version of the shooting, taken

from his letter to Judge Hayes. See Hayes, *Pioneer Notes,* 283.

44. Annable suggests that Blunt Couts was "acting as sheriff on orders from the Justice of the Peace, Cave." It is doubtful that Cave Couts had any authority to "deputize" his brother. Annable, "Life and Times of Cave Couts," 124.

45. Hayes, *Pioneer Notes,* 282–83.

46. *San Diego Herald,* September 9, 1854; June 23, 1855; August 5 and 25, 1855; and September 22, 1869. See also Annable, "Life and Times of Cave Couts," 5.

47. There is no record of an indictment on this charge. See *San Diego Herald,* July 14, 1855.

48. Annable, "Life and Times of Cave Couts," 184 and 180; and *San Diego Union,* May 19, 1870.

49. Paul Bryan Gray, *Forster vs. Pico: The Struggle for the Rancho Santa Margarita* (Spokane: Arthur H. Clark, 1998), 111.

50. Testimony of G. P. Tebbetts and Louis Rose, body of Juan Mendoza, February 6, 1865, Coroner's inquests, San Diego County, SDHSRA; and Pourade, *The Silver Dons,* 256.

51. Pourade, *The Silver Dons,* 255–56.

52. Annable, "Life and Times of Cave Couts," 183–84.

53. Most of their facts in the Couts shooting came from Rufus K. Porter, *Letters to the San Francisco Bulletin,* 1866. In fairness to both authors, Pourade's *Silver Dons* is a popular history for local consumption, and Annable's work is a master's thesis in history. It is possible that neither writer was aware that the coroner's inquests and court records were available.

54. Testimony of G. P. Tebbetts, body of Juan Mendoza, Coroner's inquests, San Diego County, SDHSRA.

55. Testimony of Louis Rose, ibid.

56. See Porter's letter of October 9, 1866, to the *San Francisco Bulletin.*

57. Deposition of Eugenio Morillo, October 11, 1866, *People v. Cave J. Couts,* District Court, San Diego County, SDHSRA.

58. See Letter from Our Correspondent, October 15, 1866, in Porter, *Letters to the San Francisco Bulletin,* 1866. There is no proof that such murders occurred in Baja California. Forster, who acted as interpreter for the court, also testified for the defense and helped to post a bond for the release of Cave J. Couts before his trial.

59. Ibid. Andrew Cassidy, a member of the jury, also had helped to post a bond for Couts's release on bail.

60. *San Luis Obispo Tribune,* March 7, 1884.

61. See C. L. Sonnichsen, *I'll Die Before I'll Run: The Story of the Great Feuds of Texas* (New York: Devin-Adair, 1962).

62. *San Luis Obispo Tribune,* March 7, 1884.

63. Affidavit of Henry Huston in Melvin Congdon Pardon File #3821, Applications for Pardon, Historical Case Files, Governor's Papers, California State Archives, hereinafter CSA.

64. *San Luis Obispo Tribune,* July 20, 1885. The men ranged from nineteen to twenty-eight years of age; all were carrying guns.

65. Ibid.

66. Ibid., July 17, 1885.

67. See body of A. M. Sherwood, November 11, 1891, Coroner's inquests, San Luis Obispo County, County Records Center; *San Luis Obispo Tribune,* November 12, 1891; and *San Luis Obispo Tribune,* July 16, 1886; and September 1, 1892; and *Sacramento Bee,* February 7, 1894.

68. *San Diego Union,* May 13, 1875.

69. Testimony of A. P. Tyler and C. B. Robinson, June 23, 1877, body of John Tannahill, Coroner's inquests, San Diego County, SDHSRA.

70. Ibid.

71. *San Diego Union,* June 24, 1877.

72. Testimony of José Delores, body of John Tannahill, Coroner's inquests, San Diego County, SDHSRA.

73. Statement by Royal M. Barton, December 6, 1877, *San Diego Union,* April 12, 1878.

74. Letter from Royal Barton to Bell Barton, March 20, 1879, in Royal Barton, Pardon File #2555, Governor's Office, Prison Papers, CSA.

75. Letter from W. J. McNealy to Governor William Irwin, March 15, 1879, 2, ibid.

76. Ibid., 2–3.

77. Ibid., 3–5. Emphasis added.

78. Ibid., 5 and 8.

79. See testimony of Dr. J. A. Barber, *People v. James Hilan,* Case #286 and 287, 5, *Criminal Case Files, 1850–1900,* Sacramento County, SHSA.

80. Testimony of Constable Joshua Crouch, ibid., 22, and testimony of Sylvester Sloan, ibid., 28. Sloan had been deputized to help arrest Hilan.

81. In 1850, the California legislature passed a law stipulating: "No black or mulatto person, or Indian, shall be permitted to give evidence in favor of, or against any white person." Chapter 99, title 14, in *Statutes of California, 1850* (San Jose: J. Winchester, State Printer, 1850), 230. In *People v. Hall* a murder conviction against defendant George W. Hall was overturned because the testimony of a Chinese witness had been accepted by the court. The supreme court justices argued that "the Legislature . . . adopted the most comprehensive terms to embrace every known class or shade of color, as the apparent design was to protect the White person from the influence of all testimony other than that of persons of the same race." *People v. Hall* 4 Cal 403 (1854).

82. Testimony of George Kingsley, 30, *People v. Hilan,* District Court, Sacramento County, SHSA.

83. See *People v. James Hilan,* Case #286 and 287, District Court, Sacramento County, SHSA.

84. See *People v. William McLaughlin,* March 10, 1890, Superior Court, Calaveras County, Calaveras County Museum, hereinafter CCM.

85. Testimony of Frank Jack, Dr. Frank L. Burleigh, and John Jeff, body of Indian Jeff, January 7, 1890, Coroner's inquests, Calaveras County, CCM.

86. *Calaveras Prospect,* March 1, 1890.

87. Ibid.

88. Ibid. Prosecution also called Frank (an Indian), John Jeff, Fenton Davis, D. Pillsbury, and W. H. Oxendine.

89. Ibid.

90. Ibid. See verdict, February 27, 1890, *People v. McLaughlin,* Superior Court, Calaveras County, CCM.

91. See Edward L. Ayers, *Vengeance and Justice: Crime and Punishment in the Nineteenth-Century American South* (New York: Oxford University Press, 1984); Sheldon Hackney, "Southern Violence," *American Historical Review* 74 (February 1969): 908; Wilbur J. Cash, *Mind of the South* (New York: Vintage Books, 1940); and Bertram Wyatt-Brown, *Southern Honor: Ethnics and Behavior in the Old South* (New York: Oxford University Press, 1982), 95.

EPILOGUE: PRISON, HOMICIDE RATES, AND JUSTICE

1. Donald Black, *The Behavior of Law* (New York: Academic Press, 1976), 105–6. For a discussion of lynching as a form of social control, see Roberta Senechal de la Roche, "The Sociogenesis of Lynching," in W. Fitzhugh Brundage, ed., *Under Sentence of Death: Lynching in the South* (Chapel Hill: University of North Carolina Press, 1997), 48–76

2. Black, *Behavior of Law,* 111–18.

3. This number does not include defendants sentenced to death who were executed within the jurisdiction of the seven counties. State authorities did not begin executing prisoners sentenced to death within the prison system until 1893, when José Gabriel became the first inmate to be hanged in San Quentin.

4. *Criminal Registers of Actions, 1850–1900,* San Diego, Santa Barbara, San Luis Obispo, Sacramento, San Joaquin, Calaveras, and Tuolumne Counties.

5. *San Diego Union,* September 18, 1875; December 28, 1878; and March 4, 1893; and entry #1, José Gabriel, *Execution Books, 1893–1967,* San Quentin Prison, CSA.

6. Apache defendants in Arizona Territory, 1880–1912, also experienced high death penalty rates. See Clare V. McKanna Jr., "Life Hangs in the Balance: The U.S. Supreme Court's Review of *Ex Parte Gon-shay-ee," Western Legal History* 3 (Summer/ Fall 1990): 209.

7. *Criminal Registers of Actions, 1850–1900,* San Diego, Santa Barbara, San Luis Obispo, Sacramento, San Joaquin, Calaveras, and Tuolumne Counties.

8. Apache inmates experienced a similar fate in the Arizona Territorial Prison in Yuma, with 37 percent of them dying, most within four years. Hah-skin-gay-gah-lah and Ilth-kah died from a lung infection after a few months of incarceration in the Ohio State Penitentiary while awaiting an appeal before the U.S. Supreme Court. See Clare V. McKanna Jr., "Murderers All: The Treatment of Indian Defendants in Arizona Territory, 1880–1912," *American Indian Quarterly* 17 (Summer 1993): 359–69; and McKanna, "Life Hangs in the Balance," 206.

9. The ages of Indian, Chinese, Hispanic, white, and black inmates upon incarceration averaged 21, 32, 37, 41, and 21, respectively. *San Quentin Prison Registers, 1850–1900* and *Folsom Prison Registers, 1880–1900*, CSA.

10. The prison records provide little information on the cause of death. Occasionally the prison authorities would list "died of consumption" or "died of fever" in the *Daily Logs*. These brief notations were rare, and nineteenth-century prison medical records are nonexistent. *San Quentin Prison Daily Logs, 1856–1900, San Quentin Prison Registers, 1850–1900*, Prison Records, Governor's Papers, CSA; and Sherburne F. Cook, *The Population of the California Indians, 1769–1870* (Berkeley: University of California Press, 1976), 104–42.

11. Coroner's inquests, *1850–1900*, seven California counties.

12. Robert R. Dykstra, "Field Notes: Overdosing on Dodge City," *Western Historical Quarterly* 27 (Winter 1996): 505–14; and Roger McGrath, *Gunfighters, Highwaymen, and Vigilantes: Violence on the Frontier* (Berkeley: University of California Press, 1984).

13. Dykstra, "Field Notes," 510. He was criticizing my essay "Alcohol, Handguns, and Homicide in the American West: A Tale of Three Counties, 1880–1920," *Western Historical Quarterly* 26 (Winter 1995): 455–82. See also Dykstra's critical review of my book *Homicide, Race, and Justice in the American West, 1880–1920* (Tucson: University of Arizona Press, 1997), which appeared in *Reviews in American History* 27 (March 1999): 79–86.

14. Dykstra, "Field Notes," 515, especially his source citations for homicides on pp. 512–14. See also Dykstra, "To Live and Die in Dodge City: Body Counts, Law and Order, and the Case of *Kansas v. Gill*," in Michael A. Bellesiles, ed., *Lethal Imagination: Violence and Brutality in American History* (New York: New York University Press, 1999).

15. Other scholars who claim that the American West was not violent include Frank Richard Prassel, *The Western Peace Officer: A Legacy of Law and Order* (Norman: University of Oklahoma Press, 1972); W. Eugene Hollon, *Frontier Violence: Another Look* (New York: Oxford University Press, 1974); Lawrence M. Friedman and Robert V. Percival, *The Roots of Justice: Crime and Punishment in Alameda County, California, 1870–1910* (Chapel Hill: University of North Carolina Press, 1981); Lynn I. Perrigo, "Law and Order in Early Colorado Mining Camps," *Mississippi Valley Historical Review* 28 (June 1941): 41–62; and Harry N. Anderson, "Deadwood, South Dakota: An Effort at Stability," *Montana: The Magazine of Western History* 20 (January 1970): 62–74.

16. H. V. Redfield, *Homicide, North and South* (Philadelphia: Lippincott, 1880); and B. J. Ramage, "Homicide in the Southern States," *Sewanee Review* 4 (February 1896): 212–32.

17. H. C. Brearley, *Homicide in the United States* (Chapel Hill: University of North Carolina Press, 1932). Brearley provides data by state and city from 1906 to about 1930. His statistical analysis reveals high homicide rates especially in the South and West. While homicide rates were high in California cities such as Sacramento, San Bernardino, and Santa Cruz, in certain Southern cities they were incredibly high. See pp. 209–19. Also see Kenneth E. Barnhart, "A Study of Homicide in the United States," *Social Science* 7 (April 1932): 141–59.

18. William Montell, *Killings: Folk Justice in the Upper South* (Lexington: University

Press of Kentucky, 1986); and Robert M. Ireland, "Homicide in Nineteenth Century Kentucky," *Register of the Kentucky Historical Society* 81 (Spring 1983): 134–53.

19. Gilles Vandal, *Rethinking Southern Violence: Homicides in Post–Civil War Louisiana, 1866–1884* (Columbus: Ohio State University Press, 2000), 48 and 137.

20. John Boessenecker, *Gold Dust and Gunsmoke: Tales of Gold Rush Outlaws, Gunfighters, Lawmen, and Vigilantes* (New York: John Wiley, 1999), 323–24.

21. Some of the scholars who have suggested that the American West was violent include Joe B. Frantz, "The Frontier Tradition: An Invitation to Violence," in Hugh Davis Graham and Ted Robert Gurr, eds., *The History of Violence in America: Historical and Comparative Perspectives* (New York: Praeger, 1969), 127–54; Joseph G. Rosa, *The Gunfighter: Man or Myth?* (Norman: University of Oklahoma Press, 1969); Harry Sinclair Drago, *The Great Range Wars: Violence on the Grasslands* (Lincoln: University of Nebraska Press, 1970); Richard Maxwell Brown, *Strain of Violence: Historical Studies of American Violence and Vigilantism* (New York: Oxford University Press, 1975); David A. Johnson, "Vigilance and the Law: The Moral Authority of Popular Justice in the Far West," *American Quarterly* 33 (Winter 1981): 558–86; Richard Maxwell Brown, *No Duty to Retreat: Violence and Values in American History and Society* (New York: Oxford University Press, 1991); James Truslow Adams, "Our Lawless Heritage," *Atlantic Monthly* 142 (July–December 1928): 732–40; Stanley Vestal, *Queen of Cowtowns: Dodge City* (Dutton, 1928); R. W. Mondy, "Analysis of Frontier Social Instability," *Southwestern Social Sciences Quarterly* 24 (September 1943): 167–77; Mabel A. Elliott, "Crime and the Frontier Mores," *American Sociological Review* 9 (April 1944): 185–92; W. C. Holden, "Law and Lawlessness on the Texas Frontier, 1875–1890," *Southwestern Historical Quarterly* (October 1940): 188–203; C. L. Sonnichsen, *I'll Die Before I'll Run: The Story of the Great Feuds of Texas* (New York: Devin-Adair, 1962); Nyle H. Miller and Joseph W. Snell, *Why the West Was Wild: A Contemporary Look at the Antics of Some Highly Publicized Kansas Cowtown Personalities* (Topeka: Kansas State Historical Society, 1963); Gary L. Roberts, "Violence and the Frontier Tradition," in Forrest R. Blackburn, *Kansas and the West* (Topeka: Kansas State Historical Society, 1976), 96–111; and "The West's Gunmen," parts 1 and 2, *American West* 8 (January 1971): 10–15, 64; (March 1971): 18–23, 61–62.

22. My examination of 977 homicide cases in three counties in the American West revealed high homicide rates. See McKanna, *Homicide, Race, and Justice.*

23. William R. Freudenburg and Robert Emmett Jones, "Criminal Behavior and Rapid Community Growth: Examining the Evidence," *Rural Sociology* 56 (Winter 1991): 620.

24. Ibid., 638. Although they are studying modern boomtowns, Freudenburg and Jones's research revealed dramatic crime rate increases from 26 to 112 percent per year. Areas studied included rural counties in Arizona, Colorado, Utah, Wyoming, and Washington.

25. McKanna, *Homicide, Race, and Justice,* 4–5.

26. For a discussion of the impact of young men on levels of violence, see David T. Courtwright, *Violent Land: Single Men and Social Disorder from the Frontier to the Inner City* (Cambridge: Harvard University Press, 1996).

27. The Vermont homicide data provided by Redfield may not be complete. However, it is believed that they reflect close approximations to the actual number of killings. See Redfield, *Homicide, North and South,* 144–47.

28. These statistics gathered by the U.S. Census Bureau may not be complete, but they do mirror the observations of Redfield and other researchers who have investigated homicide in New England. See ibid., 9–20 and 144–47; and U.S. Bureau of the Census, *Statistics of the U.S. in 1860* (Washington, D.C., 1866), 4:1–45.

29. Vandal, *Rethinking Southern Violence,* 21.

30. Boessenecker, *Gold Dust and Gunsmoke,* 323–24.

31. See Clare V. McKanna Jr., "The Coffeyville-Omaha Connection: Enclaves of Violence in Kansas and Nebraska, 1890–1920" (manuscript under review, *Kansas History*).

32. As quoted in an editorial essay by Charles L. Lindner, "A Study of Diverging Careers in the Geronimo Pratt Case," *Los Angeles Times,* February 28, 1999.

33. See mug shots of José Gabriel, Augustin Castro, and Ah Keong, in *San Quentin Photo Album,* CSA; and after p. 72 of the present study.

34. Donald Black, *Sociological Justice* (New York: Oxford University Press, 1989), 58–61.

35. For a discussion of food destruction and white conflict with Indians in Tuolumne County, see William Perkins, *Three Years in California: William Perkins' Journal of Life at Sonora, 1849–1852* (Berkeley: University of California Press, 1964), 122–23, 261, and 309–11.

36. For an overview, see Frederick E. Hoxie, *A Final Promise: The Campaign to Assimilate the Indians, 1880–1920* (Lincoln: University of Nebraska Press, 1984). For contemporary assessments of American Indians, see Lyman Abbott, "Our Indian Problem," *North American Review* 167 (December 1898): 719–29; William Graham Sumner, "The Indians in 1887," *Forum* 3 (May 1887): 254–62; and J. Evarts Greene, "Our Dealings with the Indians," *Lend a Hand* 17 (July–December 1896): 128–35. See also Thomas F. Gossett, *Race: The History of an Idea in America* (Dallas: Southern Methodist University Press, 1963).

Selected Bibliography

PRIMARY SOURCES

Applications for Pardon. Historical Case Files, Executive Pardons, and Letter Books, 1851–1900. Governor's Office Record Series. Sacramento, California State Archives.

Case Files, California District Courts, 1850–1880. County Records Centers.

Case Files, California Superior Courts, 1880–1900. County Records Centers.

Coroners' Inquests, 1850–1900. County Record Centers.

Minutes of the Court, California District Courts, 1850–1880. County Records Centers.

Minutes of the Court, California Superior Courts, 1880–1900. County Records Centers.

Register of Actions, California Superior Courts, 1880–1900. County Records Centers.

San Quentin and Folsom Prison Registers, 1851–1900. Sacramento, California State Archives.

SECONDARY SOURCES

Ayers, Edward L. *Vengeance and Justice: Crime and Punishment in the Nineteenth-Century American South.* New York: Oxford University Press, 1984.

Bankston, William H., and H. David Allen."Rural Social Areas and Patterns of Homicide: An Analysis of Lethal Violence in Louisiana." *Rural Sociology* 45 (Summer 1980): 223–37.

Brearley, H. C. *Homicide in the United States.* Chapel Hill: University of North Carolina Press, 1932.

Brown, Richard Maxwell. *No Duty to Retreat: Violence and Values in American History and Society.* New York: Oxford University Press, 1991.

Ferdinand, Theodore N."The Criminal Patterns of Boston since 1849." *American Journal of Sociology* 73 (July 1967): 84–99.

Fong, Walter N."The Chinese Six Companies." *Overland Monthly* (May 1894): 525.

Frantz, Joe B."The Frontier Tradition: An Invitation to Violence." In *The History of Violence in America: Historical and Comparative Perspectives,* edited by Hugh Davis Graham and Ted Robert Gurr, 127–54. New York: Praeger, 1969.

Friedman, Lawrence M., and Robert Percival. *The Roots of Justice: Crime and Punishment in Alameda County, California, 1870–1910.* Chapel Hill: University of North Carolina Press, 1981.

Fritz, Christian G. *Federal Justice in California: The Court of Odgen Hoffman, 1851–1891.* Lincoln: University of Nebraska Press, 1991.

Gastil, Raymond P. "Homicides and a Regional Culture of Violence." *American Sociological Review* 36 (June 1971): 412–27.

Goodhart, Arthur L. "Lincoln and the Law." *American Bar Association Journal* 50 (May 1964): 441.

Graff, Harvey J. "Crime and Punishment in the Nineteenth Century: A New Look at the Criminal." *Journal of Interdisciplinary History* 7 (Winter 1977): 477–91.

Hackney, Sheldon. "Southern Violence." *American Historical Review* 74 (February 1969): 906–25.

Inciardi, James A., and Charles E. Faupel. *History and Crime: Implications for Criminal Justice Policy.* Beverly Hills, Calif.: Sage, 1980.

Johnson, David A. "Vigilance and the Law: The Moral Authority of Popular Justice in the Far West." *American Quarterly* 33 (Winter 1981): 558–86.

Kleck, Gary, and Karen McElrath. "The Effects of Weaponry on Human Violence." *Social Forces* 69 (March 1991): 669–92.

Lane, Roger. *Violent Death in the City: Suicide, Accident, and Murder in Nineteenth-Century Philadelphia.* Cambridge: Harvard University Press, 1979.

McClain, Charles J., Jr. "The Chinese Struggle for Civil Rights in Nineteenth-Century America: The First Phase, 1850–1870." *California Law Review* 72 (July 1984): 529–68.

McDowall, David. "Firearm Availability and Homicide Rates in Detroit, 1951–1986." *Social Forces* 69 (June 1991): 1085–1101.

McGrath, Roger. *Gunfighters, Highwaymen, and Vigilantes: Violence on the Frontier.* Berkeley: University of California Press, 1984.

McKanna, Clare V., Jr. "Alcohol, Handguns, and Homicide in the American West: A Tale of Three Counties, 1880–1920." *Western Historical Quarterly* 26 (Winter 1995): 455–82.

———. *Homicide, Race, and Justice in the American West, 1880–1920.* Tucson: University of Arizona Press, 1997.

———. "A Special Kind of Justice: The Treatment of Hispanic Murderers in California, 1850–1900." In *Chicano Social and Political History in the Nineteenth Century,* edited by Richard Griswold del Castillo and Manuel Hidalgo, 95–115. Encino: Floricanto Press, 1992.

McKanna, Clare V., Jr., and John Wunder. "The Chinese and California: A Torturous Legal Relationship." *California Supreme Court Historical Society Yearbook* 2 (1995): 195–214.

Monkkonen, Eric H. *The Dangerous Class: Crime and Poverty in Columbus, Ohio, 1860–1885.* Cambridge: Harvard University Press, 1975.

Montell, William. *Killings: Folk Justice in the Upper South.* Lexington: University Press of Kentucky, 1986.

O'Brien, Patricia."Crime and Punishment as Historical Problem." *Journal of Social History* 11 (Summer 1978): 508–20.

Pourade, Richard F. *The Silver Dons.* San Diego: Union-Tribune Publishing Company, 1963.

Redfield, Horace V. *Homicide, North and South.* Philadelphia: Lippincott, 1880.

Takagi, Paul, and Tony Platt."Behind the Gilded Ghetto: An Analysis of Race, Class, and Crime in Chinatown." *Crime and Social Justice* 9 (Spring–Summer 1978): 2–25.

Tillman, Robert H."The Prosecution of Homicide in Sacramento, California, 1853–1900." *Southern California Quarterly* 68 (Summer 1986): 167–81.

Tracy, Charles A."Race, Crime, and Social Policy: The Chinese in Oregon, 1871–1885." *Crime and Social Justice* 11 (Winter 1980): 11–25.

Vandal, Gilles."'Bloody Caddo': White Violence against Blacks in a Louisiana Parish, 1865–1876." *Journal of Social History* 25 (December 1991): 373–88.

———. *Rethinking Southern Violence: Homicides in Post–Civil War Louisana, 1866–1884.* Columbus: Ohio State University Press, 2000.

Wolfgang, Marvin E. *Patterns in Criminal Homicide.* Philadelphia: University of Pennsylvania Press, 1958.

———."Victim Precipitated Criminal Homicide." *Journal of Criminal Law, Criminology, and Police Science* 48 (March 1957): 1–11.

Wunder, John R."The Chinese and the Courts in the Pacific Northwest: Justice Denied?" *Pacific Historical Review* 52 (May 1983): 191–211.

———."*Territory of New Mexico v. Yee Shun* (1882): A Turning Point in Chinese Legal Relationships in the Trans-Mississippi West." *New Mexico Historical Review* 65 (July 1990): 305–18.

Index

wine, 23, 25, 60. *See also* alcohol, liquor,
    and saloon
Wunder, John R., 32

Yee Ah Gee, 38
Yee Ah Pong, 38
Yee Chim, 43
Yee Kie, 43
Yen Wo, 35
Yong Wo, 35
Yorba, Isabel, 63
Young, Constable A. M., 61–62
Yount, George C., 16
Yong Wo Company, 39–40